A Theater Divided

A Theater Divided
The Postwar American Stage

by Martin Gottfried

LITTLE, BROWN AND COMPANY · BOSTON · TORONTO

We are grateful for permission to reprint the following copy-
righted material:

Lines from "Rose's Turn" from *Gypsy*. Copyright © 1960
by Norbeth Productions, Inc. and Stephen Sondheim. Used by
permission of Chappell & Co., Inc.

Lines from "That's Entertainment." Copyright © 1953 by
Chappell & Co., Inc. Used by permission.

Selections from *The Knack* by Ann Jellicoe. Copyright ©
1958, 1962 by Ann Jellicoe and used by permission of Dell
Publishing Co., Inc. and of Faber and Faber Ltd., London.

Selection from *George Washington Crossing the Delaware*
from *Bertha and Other Plays* by Kenneth Koch, published by
Grove Press in 1966. Used by permission of the author and his
agent Marvin Josephson Associates, Inc.

Selection from *A Streetcar Named Desire* by Tennessee Williams. Copyright 1947 by Tennessee Williams. Reprinted by
permission of New Directions Publishing Corporation.

Lines from "Tonight" from *West Side Story*. Copyright ©
1957 by Leonard Bernstein and Stephen Sondheim. Used by
permission of G. Schirmer Inc.

Contents

A Theater Divided

CHAPTER ONE

The Premise

THE American theater, since the Second World War, has been split by two natural forces. These forces — one tugging toward change, the other pulling toward tradition — have become so polarized that they have ceased to work as countervaling powers. The theater that they should shape has been divided. Instead of the whole properly thriving on the influence of each, the theater's two halves are flying apart.

Of these forces, or wings, the left is liberal, moving toward change and involved with the new; the right is conservative, moving toward tradition and involved with the old. Because of the separation, neither wing is relating to the other except in extraordinary circumstances, and the result is a stultification of stage development. In one way or another, all of the complaints about modern American theater (that it is too erratic, that it is not experimental enough; that it is too commercial, that it is not artistic enough; that Broadway is too slick, that resident theater is too amateur; that there are too many musicals, that the dramas are outmoded; that it is dead, that it should be) are really based on this isolation of influences.

Of these wings, the right remains within its boundaries, consolidating and reconsolidating past gains, letting old habits grow entrenched, with no pressure from the left to explore. The left wing, alienated, develops increasingly radical changes, untempered by the practical influences of the right. It is as if a prosecutor and a defending attorney argued in different courtrooms. Without the advocate system, the truth could never be found.

Like such a lost truth, the theater is floating between the disaffected left and the superdominant right wings, while the creative theater people and the audiences have no central body they really want to join. They are faced with the unwanted choice of going with either the professional and commonplace or the amateur and original. And as these choices are made, the wings grow more isolated, the division aggravated by its very existence.

"Left wing" and "right wing" are terms with political connotations. I am using them in an ordinary but definitely nonpolitical sense. Yet the fact that one or the other term is pejorative in everyday political conversation is very applicable to the theater, where those in the left wing consider all rightists reactionaries and those in the right wing consider all leftists radicals. Theater people are as reasonable as everybody else — they reject anyone who disagrees with them. Neither theater wing is "bad" in any application, and certainly not in this. They are merely points of view — ideological forces.

The right wing in the American theater is the establishment. That is, the theater that represents The Theater to the uninformed public — the successful, expensive, professional and essentially Broadway theater. It is where all but a handful of our new plays are produced. It is what appears to the public to be the American theater. For all its mediocrity, it is, in fact, what will appear to history as the American theater.

What I mean by history is the past of this country as landmarked, as significant, rather than history as charted by the historian or academician. The literal history of a country's theater would have to include every stage production, whether on the university, experimental or community level. Realistically speaking, the contemporary American theater will be recalled by history as that of Broadway. Virtually every new professional play, comedy or musical is produced *there*.

But while Broadway is the mainstream of our theater, today's right wing is more than Shubert Alley. It runs vertically through the big repertory theaters, institutional theaters, cultural centers, festivals, touring companies, summer stock, music tents — any theater that is accepted by the public, the government, the powers that be. It runs horizontally across all "safe" productions and conservative *kinds* of plays: dramas restricted to Ibsenist-Chekhovian realism, conventional in style, in intellectual-moral attitude and in staging concept; comedies set in overdecorated apartments on Manhattan's East Side, filled with verbal humor in the radio-wisecrack style; musical comedies and neo-operettas.

There are also right-wing styles of producing and directing, right-wing styles of design and performance. These will be discussed in later chapters.

Away from Broadway, major resident theater and festival right wing is, financially speaking, the healthiest theater in midcentury America. It is big-time culture in a big-time right-wing way, selecting plays from the blue chip classical literature. Here, Shakespeare is King of the Wing, so long as one is talking about the Big Four tragedies (and, of them, *Lear* is the King of Kings). Some of the histories (*Henry V, Richard III*) and comedies (*Comedy of Errors, Midsummer Night's Dream, Taming of the Shrew*) are comfortably on the right, too. These plays are ultimately acceptable to the most hidebound of producers, boards of education and audiences.

In Shakespeare's court are a number of other classical playwrights of triple-A rating, but in their cases too only the Very Well-known plays are done. (For example, Chekhov's *The Cherry Orchard* and *The Three Sisters* are almost as right wing as *Hamlet,* while *The Sea Gull, Ivanov* and *Platonov* are left wing. Now you might say that *The Cherry Orchard* and *The Three Sisters* are Chekhov's greatest plays, but that is irrelevant. The mere fact that they are in theatrical currency makes them right wing.) In big-time repertory and festival theater, the works in good general grace are constantly performed and reperformed, every theater checking to see what the others are doing. Directing styles there, too, remain in established modes and whatever originality is attempted is what has been called original for many years: the period play in modern dress, the Shakespeare comedy with touches of slapstick or musical dance interpolation and so on.

The summer circuit's right-wingedness is much more extreme, with stock companies relying on inexpensive, one-set, small-cast Broadway comedy successes (and failures); and the tents doing guaranteed-commercial musical revivals with over-the-hill Broadway stars. These musicals and comedies make the tent and stock circuits after all post-Broadway national and bus-and-truck companies have drained the dwindling tour business.

All of this describes the right wing in something less than adulatory terms. It does not indicate the tremendous accomplishments that have come of it. Most essentially, the right wing provides nearly all of the theater in America in the simple sense of audience size and entirely irrelevant of artistic quality (which, there, is usually irrelevant). But it should be made quite clear that this theater is the "legitimate" theater in the very best sense. It includes almost everybody who has training, experience, technique, craft.

To be sure, it is because the right wing is the established theater that the most talented people gravitate toward it (despite their brief hesitations regarding its seriousness). But whatever the explanation, they are there and their work is extraordinarily polished. In terms of the suavity that experience allows, the right wing is full-scale theater. It is, really, the very meaning and the justification of experience. It is professional.

The *left* wing includes most of the newer resident theaters that have developed in the United States. These theaters are concerned with producing theater art — the classical literature in particular. They are not nearly so adventurous as they think and their work is concentrated in war-horse classics (Chekhov, Shaw, O'Neill and Shakespeare), but their object is serious, and their directors are usually bright and talented young men who became disenchanted with Broadway (to a degree because they couldn't get any work there) and left for art's sake.

Most of these theaters have wing divisions within themselves. Many are not nearly as left wing as they like to think. Their choices of plays, directing styles and aesthetic bases tend to be conservative. A company like the Association of Producing Artists, for example, considers itself an idealistic theater, fighting the so-called commercial condescension of Broadway. It is, in fact, a very conventional company that chooses very conventional plays.

Too, the resident theaters are institution prone and in their own way become as establishmentarian as the Broadway they so detest. In many cases, they are without the vigor that characterizes the make-or-break theater that depends entirely on box office receipts rather than subsidization.

But broadly speaking, resident theaters have been staging the left-wing classical literature as well as modern, unconventional plays and in advanced styles of production. Perhaps some of the more established ones such as Houston's Alley Theater and the Arena Stage in Washington, D.C., have become institutional, settling into war-horse production. But, nearly all gravitate toward the left wing.

The left wing also includes off-Broadway, or at least some of it, now that middle age, high production costs, excessive union demands and the profit motive have reduced most of its participants to junior Broadwayites. Whatever part of off-Broadway still looks for the artistic, the noncommercial, the offbeat is left wing.

The left wing *must* be antagonistic to the norm. It pushes for change. By nature it resists *popularity*. If its ideas were accepted it would become part of the right wing and then there would be *new* leftists.

The *artistic* changes that the left wing propagates are in style, for example naturalism as against the artificial or expressionism as against the naturalistic. The present left-wing-style revolution is that of surrealism (usually mislabeled "theater of the absurd").

The *intellectual* changes are in content — attacks against reigning customs, values, beliefs. An example would be antiwhite racism (Genet's *The Blacks* or LeRoi Jones's *The Slave*). Another, and perhaps more interesting, example is the "content of nil." This is the content of theatricality — the excitement or interest or stage vitality of a play being its central purpose and in a real sense its *subject* (another way of putting this is the idea of style as content).

One of the most difficult ideas for the right-winger to understand is the existence of theater for its own sake. He demands content, meaning, significance, and at the bare minimum a coherent story — one that is, if nothing else, *believable*. He refuses to sit still and soak in a dramatic experience, despite the example set by music, which (except for the few cases of programmed music) simply exists as an artful joy that is most pleasurable in the complete, open submission. Nonrepresentational art, which often intends to have no meaning outside its colors, shapes, designs and visual impressions, long fought this battle and still fights it. The theater's left wing has yet to make the possibility of such visceral stage experiences acceptable to the traditionalists.

Harold Pinter developed the content of nil in a left- right-wing situation of his own, influenced on the left by Ionesco and Beckett and on the right by the traditional English right-wing realism of Pinero and Rattigan. Pinter combined outer realism with bizarre plotting for the purposes of mood, audience manipulation and theater magic as contents.

This doesn't mean that Pinter writes about *nothing*. Quite the reverse, he regularly deals with emotional pressures, but these (like Chekhov's) are *subjective* contents: confidence, in *The Birthday Party;* mutual responsibility, in *The Caretaker;* the nature of truth, in *The Collection;* the nature of love, in *The Lover;* the nature of family relationships and sex, in *The Homecoming.*

Still, Pinter's theater milieu is the theater itself, and the excitement that can be made there — strangeness, fear, comedy. Theatricality is his primary concern. Just as the painter's main objective is his picture, Pinter's is his play and how it operates on a stage.

But Pinter, at least in the American production of his plays, is disallowed this objective. Right-wing audiences and critics demand guaranteed "meanings," insisting that unless such meanings can be neatly put down in a Harvard outline the play must be "bad." Although, in his case, there *are* intellectual significances, the main purpose of his playwrighting is dramatic life. Neither he, nor any playwright, could possibly create viable drama while following a predetermined, point-making scheme. The writing of a play demands so much concentration on strictly stage matters — dialogue, plot, climax, humor, whatever — that there is simply no space for pattern-awareness. Even when analysts find justifiable "meanings" in the final work, they are usually meanings that the playwright never considered. This does not mean that they are "wrong." In many ways, a play exists apart from a playwright. If the ideas are there, they are there whether he saw them or not and this is true of all art. But the greatest thrill a theater can provide is the magical one, and now that left-wing playwrights are working for just that they are running headlong into a theater too long dominated by formulated intellectualism.

Edward Albee tries to be the leader of the content of nil movement in the United States. But beginning with *Who's Afraid of Virginia Woolf?* his plays were subjected to the deepest, most pretzeled analyses. Unfortunately, although Albee had wanted his plays to exist primarily as theater pieces, he accepted the philosophical and intellectual dissections as if they were valid, and then proceeded to try to write intellectual-philosophical plays *intentionally* (this was his downfall). As a result, Albee has influenced a number of American playwrights toward theater-as-theater while moving away from it himself. While his followers are developing abstract surrealism over very broad points, he remains hamstrung by an extremely unjustified intellectual conceit and an attraction to where-is-God routines danced to a secret homosexual litany.

Samuel Beckett is responsible for the left wing's other major development in content. If existentialism is the sense of our time (and there is no doubting it), then Beckett is expressing it; and if it seems ironic that a left-wing — or minority-group — artist should be speaking for a general human attitude at a particular time, it is indicative of America's domination by rightists. The incorporation of existentialism into the dramatic literature has been the artistic purpose of other playwrights — Sartre, of course, in particular — but it has been Beckett whose plays *dramatify* the philosophy, rather than dramatize it. Sartre's plays are existentialist message plays. Beckett's are the insides of existentialism.

Beckett, like Pinter, ought not be pinned down too specifically. Both are artists and Beckett is a genius and they are flowing their own ways. For each, the play is the art. But if one is to seek mid-twentieth-century left-wing changes in dramatic content, Pinter can be reasonably described as the developer of the content of nil and Beckett the developer of the content of existentialism.

These major changes are long term. They will inevitably move into the American right wing after the present divisive crisis is past. I say "after it is past" because it *will pass*. Although our present theater inertia is due to the violent separation between the forces of progress and the forces of tradition, the separation is not a permanent one. Rather, it is an overlong and consequently debilitating threshold between stimulus and reaction.

It is in the nature of all things for left-wing innovations to move rightward and add to the sum of progress. Moreover, it is on the right where they are developed and most fruitfully worked. It is from the *right* that masterworks come, and where working, *master playwrights* regularly produce major works for a full-functioning theater. It will be a long time before such an interacting relationship returns to America, but when it does the present left-wing developments in content will be consolidated into right-wing, mature work.

Stylistic changes are much more ephemeral. Generally, they are born and die in the left wing, where they are invented, practiced and discarded. Too superficial or faddish to be necessary to the existing theater body of the right, they frequently run their course before they are even noticed by the public theater. On the other hand, there are stylistic changes that can change the look of theater so much as to substantially add to the development of drama. And, as opposed to changes in content, they are assimilated quite rapidly.

The most significant stylistic change in modern theater is that of surrealism. This came out of the French left wing, developing with Jarry, Cocteau, Artaud and Tardieu. While its originators remained pure, as originators will, acceptance into the right wing brought dilution, and with more generalized practice by such playwrights as Genet, Beckett, Pinter and Ionesco it is settling down into establishment European theater.

It is now influencing English theater to a tremendous degree, and with the heavy West End export business to Broadway, it would have its effect on the American right wing if there was a proper interwing influence. But as for native surreal plays, we have few. What there is ranges from the ridiculous (Tennessee Williams's *The Milk Train Doesn't Stop Here Anymore*) to the collegiate (Arthur Kopit's *Oh Dad, Poor Dad, Momma's Hung You in the Closet and I'm Feelin' So Sad*). The new dimension that the surrealist style provides is bound to influence the American right wing sooner or later.

Most of the European surrealists have been irrevocably classified as "theater of the absurd," a term coined by Martin Esslin, an English critic. Unfortunately, this term has been accepted in a sense different from Esslin's, but that is of little matter since neither

Esslin's definition (a group of playwrights who are anguished by the absurdity of the human condition), nor the public's (nonsense plays in cartoon style) is of much value because these playwrights are highly individual. But since the term has come to communicate the look of the plays there is little point in fighting it. It may even be useful.

The other major left-wing stylistic change is that of total — or absolute — theater. Like theater of the absurd, "total theater" is a simplistic term, making for slogan and careless thinking. It refers to a theater that uses all stage elements: dance, rhythm, lighting, music, ritual, masks, mime, and so on. Not quite spectacle and not quite drama, it is a recognition of the theater as a place for "production" as opposed to "plays"; a recognition that a script is only the beginning of a stage organism and that the things that happen on the stage when the curtain rises are considerably more involved and have considerably more dimensions than the spoken word.

This new production theater is evolving in Poland and England particularly, although some examples of it can be found in the more left-wing of the American resident theaters. Its roots are in the epic theater-production styles of Brecht and Erwin Piscator (a German director who ran experimental theaters in Moscow, New York and West Berlin). Antonin Artaud, the French dramatic theorist, laid some of the foundation for it in his ideas on the "theater of cruelty" and his name has lately been littering the floors of dramatic conference rooms.

Artaud, in formulating the theory of cruelty, was obsessed with gut reactions to nonverbal theatrical stimuli with an emphasis on horror and gore, and much of his thought can be seen in the new, all-out theater.

It took time for production theater to be accepted. But by 1965 (thirty-seven years after its creation!) an electrifying version of the Brecht-Weill opera *The Rise and Fall of the City of Mahagonny* could be staged by the Stratford (Ontario) Shakespearean Festival — a right-wing bastion (incredibly, the opera's North American première), and not much later, Peter Weiss's *The Persecution and Assassination of Marat As Performed by the Inmates of the Asylum of Charenton Under the Direction of the Marquis de Sade* was to be selling out on Broadway. In that same season, still another production using full-theater techniques would be produced on Broadway. If Peter Shaffer's *The Royal Hunt of the Sun* happened to be a spectacular bore, it remained that the right wing of Broadway was quite ready to embrace this left-wing development.

Still, the use of such full-production techniques in America (outside of the musical theater) has been limited to leftist resident companies and far left-wing experimentalists. In addition to *Marat /Sade,* which led the way in America, the most successful of such productions that I have seen were William Ball's flamboyant staging of Albee's *Tiny Alice,* mounted for the American Conservatory Theater; Douglas Seale's circus version of Max Frisch's *The Chinese Wall,* and his violent *Titus Andronicus,* produced at Baltimore's Center Stage; John Hancock's pop art-grotesque *Midsummer Night's Dream,* which he originated with the Actors Workshop in San Francisco and then reproduced at the Pittsburgh Playhouse; and Rochelle Owens's Artaud-oriented *Beclch* as directed by André Gregory at the Theater of the Living Arts.

Joseph Chaikin, drawing upon techniques of Judith Malina and Julian Beck's Living Theater, also employed such methods at his Open Theater, and out of it came such striking productions as Megan Terry's *Viet Rock* and Jean-Claude van Itallie's *America Hurrah.*

The existence of these left-wing plays in polished productions may suggest that there is some wing interaction, but the suggestion is there only because I am discussing *them* rather than the overwhelming majority of conservative productions. None of these full-production examples originated in New York's commercial milieu and only a few appeared there. Compared to the more than a hundred pure right-wing openings in New York each season, and the three hundred or so plays that are presented each year by the resident companies, they are hardly noticeable. Indeed, they appear under extraordinary circumstances.

The left wing, however, is not restricted to inventing styles and contents of plays. In its function as the perpetually disgruntled — as the mover for change — it means to alter *all* parts of the reigning theater. It pushes for special-taste, uncommercial productions; for unproduced classic drama; for overlooked art; for plays that have been forgotten — from Ghelderode to Wedekind, Lorca to

Büchner, Kleist or Gertrude Stein. It pushes radical newcomers. Edward Albee, Jack Gelber and Jack Richardson began there. Rochelle Owens and Jean-Claude van Itallie are emerging from there. Kenneth Koch and Arnold Weinstein are languishing there. It digs up the ignored plays of right-wing, institutionalized playwrights — the "other" plays of Ibsen (*Peer Gynt*), Pirandello (*Enrico IV*), Strindberg (*Dance of Death*).

In its devotion to changing the state of things, the left wing is bound to include many strange, nonessential types: the compulsively far-out, would-be intellectuals, dilettantes, professional nonconformists and upper bohemians. These non-professional people often drag innovation toward extremism.

The left wing is also bound to be amateur, especially in its more experimental phases. In fact, it is this amateurism that is its greatest weakness as well as its strength. So long as the rewards and the opportunity to practice are offered by the right, the people with extraordinary talent will go to it, with the result that a left-wing play generally suffers from enthusiastic but erratic directing, acting and production.

On the other hand, amateurism has inherent virtues. Zelda Fichlandler, the founder of Washington's Arena Stage, once told me that her aim was to develop professionalism, but not at the expense of amateurism. What she meant was that the amateur seeks ideals and attempts greatness. The amateur *dares,* he *experiments;* he is not handicapped by right-wing rationalizations of "good judgment" or "maturity." He is able to become excited and carried away by enthusiasms that the more mature suppress or have forgotten.

As each of the wings has its own identities, theaters, playwrights, performers, audiences and attitudes, so each has its own critics. It would not be fair — indeed, it would not be true — to say that these critics are consciously siding or concerning themselves with one wing as opposed to the other. But left-wing, special-audience publications attract special-taste critics, while right-wing or mass publications attract public-taste critics, and they solemnly refuse to recognize the existence of each other. But it is perfectly normal for rightists to regard leftists as amateurs and leftists to regard rightists as philistines. The critics follow the norm. Left-wing critics spend paragraphs differentiating between "critics" and "reviewers." They demand critical credentials that coincidentally fit themselves. They criticize, or rather insult, right-wing critics in the midst of articles presumably devoted to the criticism of a play. Very often they seem intent on attacking a popular success just for perversity's sake. Many reject Broadway musicals and comedies out of hand and some even refuse to go to them, dismissing productions they have not even seen.

The problem with the left-wing critics in today's theater is their lack of genuine intellectuality and their abundance of unsubstantiated opinions (a fault they share with their right-wing counterparts). The left-wing critic should be either entirely uneducated but committed to the wildest of adventure or be completely educated and committed to pure art. Ours are neither. They pose as erudite but the pose is transparent and there is no true education or background beneath the self-consciously arched eyebrows. Their envy of the right-wing critic's public recognition is palpable, their petulance heavy, their writing usually very bad, sloppy and confused, and the sarcasm third-rate Dorothy Parker. Too, while rejecting the Broadway that is the main theater of their time, few ever bother to visit theaters outside of New York.

The right-wing critics are incapable of understanding modern theater and invariably reject the most exciting plays in any season. Like their left-wing counterparts, they are musically ignorant and know too little about musical theater to criticize it. They have lost touch with contemporary movements, contemporary thinking, and have patience only for the common entertainment and the traditional dramatic style, point and purpose. They are without the writing style that once was expected in theater criticism and, more seriously, are without the background as well. Prone to ridiculous, quotable ecstasies that are irrelevant to criticism, they propagate the wing division through their own taste for the right wing. There are several critics in both wings who are above most of these faults but, as interwing theater, they are only incidental blooms in a vast desert.

Such a situation is natural to a wing division, but it is also causal because the right-wing critic is perhaps the first point of contact with the left wing and vice versa. If the two wings are ever to enjoy a healthy interaction, their critic-spokesmen must spearhead the dialogue that will lead to it. The critic can begin to draw right-wing influences to the left or left-wing influences to the right. Ideally, the right-wing critic would complain about and *affect* left-wing pretension, immaturity, extremity and amateurism, while the left-wing critic would complain about and *affect* right-wing backwardness, slickness, shallowness, commercialism, stuffiness and timidity.

But the critics are as divided as their theater, and have virtually no influence upon the opposition. Left-wing critics, gorged on anti-right-wing prejudices, strut pompously, denying the existence of the only theater the general public knows. Right-wing critics, with few exceptions, work from judgment bases anchored in a thirty-year-old theater, unaware of modern ideas and expressions. The new represents a challenge to their fundamental values and is in a strange language that they do not understand. They have become as aged as their left-wing counterparts have become childish, forced into extremity by the division. While the left-wing critics are defensive about their lack of status and envy the right-wing critic's power, the right-wing critic is defensive about that power and does not use it for the positive force it can and should be.

Each wing has its own house organ, although, to be fair, the two publications are even further apart than the wings themselves. Neither does justice, in any sense, to the kinds of theater they ostensibly represent. The right-wing house organ is *Variety,* whose point of departure lies at the extremity of commercialism and which considers all theater in terms of grosses, road potential, stock possibilities and movie sales. If *Variety* brings the right wing face to face with its harshest reality, it does not reveal the vaguest understanding of the genuine qualities and artistic sensibilities of establishment theater. The publication is all that it is cracked up to be, which is about the worst one can say about it.

The left-wing house organ is *The Drama Review* (long known as *The Tulane Drama Review*), predictably a quarterly, but beyond the nerve of prediction so determinedly antagonistic to the right wing that it all but has a tantrum when one of its ideas is actually shared by somebody in the professional theater. It is a self-conscious jumble of would-be academicians and Bronx bohemians (I refer to its editorial attitude rather than contributors, many of whom are quite serious). Remarkably similar to *Variety* in its closed-minded extremism, the publication is nearly as unintelligible in self-created jargon and obtuseness. But despite their comic exaggeration, both publications represent their wings, the right as backwardly conventional and glossy show; the left as blindly radical and self-consciously serious. Neither publication is especially harmful.

Although nearly all of American theater is now divided between the wings, there is a small but important part of it that falls between them.

Between the wings lies the theater that ought to result from a proper left-right axis: *the theater that should be;* the healthy theater, thriving on new ideas, developing close to the historical mainstream, pitching experience against idealism, finesse against ambition, responsibility against adventure. It is from here that a theater moves forward, develops.

But because of the divisive crisis, it is in this wasted Eden that little theater grows. For a left-wing production to thrive there — to move, say, onto Broadway — it must push itself through the pavement cracks. And when it arrives it will invariably be misunderstood and rejected. The further right — the more orthodox — it is, the better its commercial chances, and although a left-wing production will occasionally take root on Broadway, that usually is because it is either rightish enough or *appears* to be (*Who's Afraid of Virginia Woolf?*, *A Funny Thing Happened on the Way to the Forum*).

Whatever lies between the wings is the best of the American theater. Not only on Broadway but, really, throughout the country. A *The Caucasian Chalk Circle* at the Tyrone Guthrie Theater in Minneapolis, a *Tartuffe* at the Repertory Theater of Lincoln Center, a *Marat/Sade* on Broadway. It is where one will find theater that is at once daring and adept, originally conceived and professionally executed.

This left- right-wing idea is not a grid being placed over the American theater, forcing that theater to conform to a theory for theory's sake. Such attempts are foolish and illogical, bound to distort a subject to prove a point. The theater is no different than, and just as variable as, any other human activity. It will not fit any pat theory.

The left and right wings are, rather, descriptive devices, explaining the present situation in the American theater; and if this explanation is in somewhat particular terms, those terms are merely representative of the conflict between the old and the new, the conservative and the liberal, that runs through history in general and art in particular. American painting today, for example, may be too left inclined for its own good. As soon as a new movement comes out of the left it is swallowed up by the right. This is unstable, just as an overpowerful right makes interaction sluggish. The progress of any art depends upon the working relationship between the wings, each acting against the other in proportionate measure so that innovation and youth are deepened but not retarded by tradition and maturity. An art that is too left oriented will not develop — it will only ricochet from one fad to the other. And while a fad may have the look of a developmental phase, it is only the look. Phases are the stepping-stones to the future. Fads are circular roller coasters.

While the pressures of the left and right may shift and swing from one period to another, varying in effect from one art to the other, they are as ever present as opposing traditional and progressive influences on morality or politics or science, moving in cycles and ever leftward, always toward growth, with the solidity of progress depending on the right's maturing influence.

This ebb and flow, always inching forward, is simple evolution. Stepping-stones in science become axioms, propositions and theorems once they are tested and proved. Those in the arts become classics, remaining as bases for comparison, evaluation and constant truth.

As there are differences in left- right-wing balance in every art, in every time, so there are balance differences among countries. France has traditionally inclined leftward, warm toward the new, and it is there that the most challenging as well as the most ridiculous innovations regularly appear. It is no coincidence that the classic political revolution is France's or that "avant-garde" is a French term. But French innovations have always tended toward the extreme (only France could produce an Artaud, a Genet). In twentieth-century Germany, on the other hand, while the left wing is nearly as active, the right wing has been much more influential. Until Hitler murdered German art, there was no finer example of

left- and right-wing interaction than that in German music, painting, literature and drama.

One can begin with Schiller, who represented the right wing in
the midst of the eighteenth century, and follow the Shakespearean
influence through Kleist, Büchner, Wedekind, Hauptmann and
Brecht. It is this kind of dramatic development that is ideal. Most
of these playwrights reached German right-wing status, and while
their plays are of varying artistic importance they all added and
then developed, added and then developed (with the exception of
the tragic genius Büchner, who didn't live long enough to develop).
In each case and as a collective dramatic entity, they moved against
an entrenched theater that finally gave way, if slightly; and upon
resettlement was different, bigger, better.

It is difficult to see a similar artistic development in America.
Our country is so young and has been artistically primitive for so
long that whatever theater evolved was rooted in the popular: variety shows, operettas, broad comedies, melodramas. Yet, that theater thrived during the first half of this century. Why has it begun to
fall apart?

One explanation is the extreme gap between American industrial
development and American cultural development. Given great natural wealth and fortuitous historical circumstances, the drive of
this young country was able to produce enormous material progress in less than two hundred years. Culture cannot develop with
such speed, but where there are people there is a theater and one
sprung forth — not from a traditional pool (since there was none)
but from the ever-present need for entertainment. As a result,
America's present right wing is our old popular theater, as contrasted with the right wings of older countries, which are rooted in
classic theater. We *have* no rooting — no national classics, no national tradition and only the beginnings of a national identity.

Another factor contributing to the present polarization was the
Second World War. Particularly in the intellectual-artistic sense,
America grew up as its prewar culture grew outmoded in those six
years.

The Second World War was a traumatic event in the adolescence
of American culture. It was the first war we ever really *had to fight,*
a war for a moral reason. It involved us deeply and bloodily with

the rest of the world and with the deaths of millions of people living thousands of miles away. It caused a life loss in the generation that was supposed to have accounted for our immediate future. And we had more than seen the atomic bomb — we had actually invented it, developed it, used it.

The result was inexpressibly complex. Wars of adventure, of imperialism, of morality were over, another major one unquestionably being the last. The international political stature of our country became dominant and we assumed responsibility for the rest of the world (define "responsibility" any way you choose). We were dragged into manhood.

At the same time, the age spread of our population had shifted, with the average American becoming ever younger. Our wealth, burgeoned by war, was used for the education of that youth.

While the young were growing old enough to take over the reins of America, while the education was being absorbed and readied for use, the theater continued into an artistic middle age. In short, the right wing grew fat.

During the ten years immediately following war's end, it appeared that American drama was in good shape — that perhaps even a golden age had begun. Arthur Miller wrote *All My Sons, Death of a Salesman* and *The Crucible* in rapid succession. Tennessee Williams created poetic masterpieces in *The Glass Menagerie* and *A Streetcar Named Desire*. William Inge seemed a genuine stage artist, writing *Come Back, Little Sheba* and *Picnic*. Robert Anderson appeared to be beginning a rich career with *Tea and Sympathy*. It really did seem as if they had slipped into the gap opened by the departure into the right wing of the old order: Sidney Kingsley, Clifford Odets, Lillian Hellman, Maxwell Anderson, Elmer Rice, Sidney Howard, etc.

This was a false start. Not that Miller, Williams and Inge were mistakenly respected (Anderson simply never fulfilled his promise). Miller was — and remains — an important playwright, current critical whimsies notwithstanding. Williams was a true original, working in a kind of theater all his own and entirely apart from old forms. He was indeed a leftist, even if he was later to fall in love with commercial success and allow his public image to become his artistic identity. Inge's talents were quite as real.

But, neither Miller nor Inge were ever true leftists, and the postwar middle-class theatergoers had little trouble adjusting to their plays. The playwrights and their audiences were people whose youth had been usurped by the war and who had returned in intellectual middle age. They had outgrown their rebellious periods without ever having enjoyed them. And so what might have appeared to be a healthy left-right interaction in Broadway drama was really just some very good right-wing drama.

It was much too long without cultural recycling and the postwar generation grew restless. It began a criticism of everything right wing — everything that was reflexively accepted. A fresh, skeptical intelligence was afoot. Suddenly, college students were not satisfied with our international policies. Suddenly, America was not assumed to be the Good Guys. Suddenly, there was anger over social conditions, racial conditions — an idealism coupled with an eagerness to do something about it. The country began to grow up.

This postwar left-wing generation found the theater of the time so powerful and so alien that no thought of changing it was even plausible. In revolting against the overgrown backwardness of Broadway, its fight was only a pathetic shadow-boxing. Its theater taste was entirely apart from the mainstream and its excited discovery of Beckett, Ionesco and Genet was something the existing theater did not share. Even if *Waiting for Godot was* produced on Broadway in 1956, it was never accepted by the theatrical establishment as being a part of its theater. There was never a chance of this great play affecting the course of American dramatic development at that time. That it was produced on Broadway was a bizarre accident. The wings were separated beyond connection. There was no longer any relationship between the left and the right.

Frustrated by its inability to affect the development of the theater, the new generation turned away from it, seeking an art form of its own time. And this it found in the movies. Here, where the right wing was reeling from television's attack, a medium was ready for wholesale left-wing pressure. The postwar revolutionaries leaped in, bringing the form to life with giant doses of innovation. When *Open City, Paisan* and *The Bicycle Thief* brought Italian neorealism to the few art houses in New York, the stifled theater left-wingers found a place to go. Within twenty years, scores of intelligent, well-produced foreign films of considerable artistic value (and some of genius) were pouring into the movie theaters. The wings became international. The results were precisely what a healthy left- right-wing axis propels: a medium satisfying the new, broadly educated, very up-to-date intelligence. New comedy, new drama, new form, new style, new art. And the young theater audiences were shanghaied. All that was left for the right-wing theater was the right-wing audience — the expense account and tourist trade for the musicals or comedies and the intellectually middle-aged for the handful of old-fashioned dramas.

Despite this abandonment by the left-wing audiences, a new theater emerged — the left-wing musical — and this new theater was on Broadway. It was the first example in three decades of a genuine, major right- left-wing fusion. Out of its form will develop the new dramatic and comic theater as well.

The development of the new musical theater, although terribly exciting, is but a pinpoint flash in an overall pattern of retardation. The present theater establishment is out of contact with the taste of the modern American young adult. Still worse, while that adult cannot be satisfied by the backward, professional theater of the right, he is impatient with the raw newness of the left.

So the contemporary inclination to black comedy, all-out theater, quick-changing forms of design and structure is being developed and polished in the films and not on the stage. There are no playwrights for it, few directors and only a handful of actors.

Consequently, with the future of the American theater riding on progress (like the future of anything else), the *implements* of progress — new ideas — are alienated from the theater body. That is the present state of extreme polarization between the left and the right wings of the American theater. And divided as that theater is today, it will collapse unless they are rejoined.

But in a way, the present division has its positive aspects (Let Us Look for the Silver Lining). In the separation of the wings, their identities are more easily observed. Defined as they are, and as they are going to remain for a while, they can perhaps be more easily examined for their values and drawbacks.

The most sweeping value of the right wing is in its representation of the theater today as a result of the theater of the past. No true development is possible unless there is a constant building upon foundations that were tried and proved. So artistic adventures are dared, tested against current values, and when developed, accepted. Those that fail are discarded (sometimes mistakenly, to be retested long afterward against later values). Some are mistakenly accepted and prove ephemeral. In all cases, the right wing provides the challenge for the left wing's proposition and a defeat at its hands usually will prove mortal.

In a way, this is the test of popularity (that is, by the public). It can be argued that theater must be able to reach the public to be valid. That is partly true, but only partly. It depends on what one considers "valid." On the one hand, the audience is an elemental part of the theater and what it accepts or "likes" is the theater of the period — the theater that *is*. On the other hand, what it rejects is the left wing, and that is either valuable or worthless. If the new is valuable (or valid), it will eventually move rightward, no matter how much time it takes.

On the other hand, who the hell is the public to decide what is valid and what is not? To decide what is art and what is not? This largely ignorant, generally uneducated and uncivilized mass. In fact, its greatest enthusiasms are for extreme right-wing theater. Is this mass to be allowed the responsibility of judging the validity of art? Judging it by the wretched test of ticket-buying?

Or is this public simply the sum of man, managing instinctively to weed out the true from the false? Is it only the public that truly knows?

The public-taste argument (if "the people" like it, "it works") is an appealing one because it is a gut argument, seemingly linked with definitions of art as universal. But that linkage is only seeming. Universality does not mean that everyone can be reached by true art, but that true art *applies* to everyone. Still, the public *does* decide what can be moved from left to right — what the theater is ready for at a given moment in time.

So the argument goes both ways. In any case, the proving process is the function of the right wing and the general audience for the established theater of any period is a basic part of that wing. In its role of mere attendance, simple enthusiasm or rejection, the public is essential to the development of the theater.

Yet there is a kind of theater to which the public traditionally flocks despite the fuming exasperation of the left wing. This is not the calculated commercial theater, capitalizing on vulgar instincts. It is the really public theater: the circus, carnivals, burlesque, vaudeville. It is decidedly right wing, oblivious to ideas of art. It is also at the very heart of theater. From time to time, the determinedly esoteric will leap upon such shows with supercilious appreciation, clasping them to the breast and nearly crushing them with analysis. Fortunately, the bear hug is generally well over the head of this low theater, which continues to splash about quite light-headedly at the feet of erudition. Perhaps only Shakespeare and Brecht ever truly appreciated and worked with it.

A secondary value of the right wing is in its function of repetition. Upon the initial acceptance of an innovation, the theater proceeds to reproduce it, to the eternal impatience of the leftists. It is taken apart and reconstructed, applied to varying types of productions, tested and retested in practice. With the minor creative tools at his disposal, the secondary playwright polishes the new style, matures the new content. Perhaps he adds certain structural qualities that were lacking in the original. Perhaps he develops niceties of humor or character construction. This process perhaps dilutes the original excitement of the innovation, but the subsequent theater is clearly one step ahead and one wrinkle fewer. With each reapplication of the new idea — as revolution moves into trend and finally tradition — the step the theater has taken broadens from a foothold to a horizonwide extension. When the right wing has finally digested the advance, it is in general practice, accepted by the working theater and the public.

The patience with which the right wing examines the ideas of the left, the brutality with which it demands proof, and the polishing and acceptance with which it sometimes rewards are its most important contributions to the theater. For the left wing has no time for careful development, no interest in the refining process. It is already onto something new, bored with what is already passé. It has no concern for the lasting strength of maturation. It is looking for new pastures, once the seed has been planted in the old.

So the right wing fertilizes what the left wing has planted and the theater does the reaping. All very nice if you're big on metaphor.

The left wing is more attractive than the right in theory and less attractive in practice. Their importance is no more than exactly the same and the exactitude is essential — an imbalance will cause either general backwardness or general instability. The value of the left is in its grab for tomorrow.

The left wing opposes both the middle class (the pseudo-artistic) and the lower class (the commercial, mass appeal). But it detests the upper class, whose refinement of yesterday's solid introductions is a reminder of its own immaturity, its inability to consummate invention. These antagonisms are the reverse side of an eagerness to be accepted.

But for all that, the left wing is purely altruistic, contemptuous of the slow-witted and sterile, brimming with freshness. Current playwrighting is too old-fashioned for it — the realism is too restricting, the language too dated, the structure too conservative, the humor too broad, the morality too backward, the points too obvious, the climaxes too artificial, the stories too ornate, the restrictions too rigid. Direction is too old-fashioned for it — the script is too revered, the blocking too square, the dynamics too pat, the movement too superficial, the fire too banked. Acting is too old-fashioned for it — the passions are too sterilized, the actors too personality geared, the styles too "realistic."

The left wing has, as its greatest resource, the very age of the right wing. It has the future to itself. Flushed with youth and eager to implement change, it has the confidence of inexperience and is dead certain of what is terribly wrong (much more certain than of how those wrongs can be righted). It is newly educated; its knowledge is at hand, its hopes unspoiled and it cannot comprehend why neither that knowledge nor those hopes are being applied to the theater. It is restless, it is energetic and it is terribly bright.

It is also infinitely more conscious of society as a whole. It has a new awareness, a new seriousness, a new humor. It is hypersensitive to the pompous, the pretentious, the self-serious. It finds ideas everywhere, interests everywhere. It is more involved with the minutiae of daily life, having rejected old moral and religious certainties. With more uncertainties than its predecessors, the left wing today has begun to see *exactly* where it is living and is choosing to face it, apply itself to it, rather than accept a hierarchy of values that its predecessors inflicted upon themselves and then became enslaved to.

It represents the sense of its society's most advanced guard, and the theater of its tomorrow. But because of the extreme wing separation in American theater today, its movement rightward is barely in sight. We have yesterday's plays not only in today's playhouses but in tomorrow's. Our time lag has become crucial.

The continuation of this lag is assured so long as the wings remain apart. Without a dialogue the solid, performing right wing will have no understanding of, and no pressure from, the innovating left and will continue its drift rightward, producing increasingly backward theater. The left, so uninfluenced by craft, will move further toward the childish and dreamy, handicapped by technical underdevelopment.

There is no solution to the division. When a separation of such severity occurs, it cannot be righted — nothing can be "done" about it. We and our theater must suffer, waiting out time and the endless cycles.

Still, exceptions to the right-wing rule are happening; like water that is beginning to boil, a few bubbles are springing to the surface. A resident theater will produce a left-wing play and find an audience coming with interest and leaving with excitement (Genet's *The Balcony* at the Hartford Stage Company). A company will produce an obscure classic and learn that the enthusiasm it evokes is legitimate, vital, even passionate (Brecht's *Caucasian Chalk Circle* at the Minnesota Theater Company). A Broadway producer will try a radical play and see those long-absent theatergoers — the college students and just graduated — chatting headily in the lobby (*Marat/Sade*).

It is no reason for optimism. The division in the American theater remains violent. A collapse would be catastrophic and reconstruction would only come after irrevocably lost years, audiences and theater life. Those few bubbles on the surface of the sickly still waters of today's theater are all we have to rely on.

The cruciality of the division is the premise on which this book is based. So long as the forces of conservatism and liberalism cannot relate to each other, progress is impossible and intelligent theatergoers will be deprived of a theater equal to them. More alarmingly, with the continuation of this situation, the American theater *itself* will suffer.

In the following chapters, the natures of the left and right wings will be explained in greater detail, to be followed by a general study of the divisive crisis in our resident theaters, summer festivals, in the Broadway musical, comedy and drama, and off- and off-off-Broadway. The forces for change and for tradition will be described in terms of writing, directing and acting styles; tastes in plays; commercial, religious and sexual influences; audience attitudes; senses of humor, and the myriad of factors that affect the direction of the theater. Specific examples of course will be given, all from the postwar American stage in and out of New York. Finally, some conclusions will be drawn and some expectations sketched. No course of action will be suggested, because I don't believe that anything can or should be done to alter the natural course of any art form. Finally, there will be no doubting that the American theater will survive. Whatever form it assumes, whatever direction it takes, our theater is rooted in our natures — the idea of theater is as natural to this country as it has been to every country, every civilization, every man, always. If the present unhealthy control of our theater by right-wing forces drives it past reaction and into ruin, there will always be somebody in a basement, in an attic, with wooden crates for his audience and paper bags for masks, trying again.

CHAPTER TWO

The Right Wing

ANY discussion of the theater's right wing must begin on Broadway, if only because in a coldly realistic sense the Broadway theater *is* the American theater and will remain so indefinitely. Whether this is as it should be, whether the Broadway theater really *is* theater, whether the profit motive can ever produce art, is irrelevant. From even the most primitive perspective, it is *this* theater that is acknowledged as *the* theater of America, whether by New Yorkers, Midwesterners, the world or history. It is the home base of our theatrical establishment and the mainstream of our theatrical evolution. As such, it represents the very heart of the right wing and, by extension, the expression of our country's theater.

Because of this, it is altogether logical that the left wing reserves its most damning epithets for Broadway, which is its natural opposite. It finds everything there contemptible, from the commercial rooting to the kind of work produced, the style of production, the actors, directors and designers — the very finesse. All of these aspects of the Broadway theater, right wing in each of their particular areas, are hateful to the left wing. Yet, it was Broadway and Broadway alone that created the American theater.

What are these right-wing aspects of Broadway theater? The natural place to begin is with its commercial nature. On the one hand, the profit motive provides the strictest test for the ability of a dramatic work to reach an audience. On the other, it identifies Broadway theater as an investment enterprise. Backers are convinced that a play (which in marketplace terminology is called a "property") is so good that it will receive marvelous reviews, run three years, tour for three more with three companies, be produced abroad and finally, heaven allowing, be sold to Hollywood. Like the tax-advantage purchase of paintings, it is a business proposition with warming cultural overtones as well as show business glamour.

It might be easily concluded, then, that the criterion for Broadway production is a play's commercial prognosis. Yet, I doubt whether any Broadway producer has ever presented a play in the conviction that the work was bad but the commercial prospects excellent. Whatever script he reads, the producer judges it according to its merit. That is, he will assume that the better the play, the better its financial prospects.

It is tempting to except the artistic play from this rosy description, but such an exception would deny reality to fit a theory of Broadway philistinism. The only artistic play a producer will consciously reject is a revival. And the unpleasant truth is that a revival is a sure bet for a financial loss unless it has an extraneous public attraction (such as the sensational private life of a star) or a big promotional buildup.

There should be no need to stress the importance of revivals. There can be no theater if the dramatic literature is not kept alive. But every aspect of the producing theater has its functions, and as it is neither the function nor within the economic capabilities of a resident theater to produce a big-time musical, it is neither the function nor within the economic capabilities of Broadway to reproduce classics.

Obviously, this is not the way things *should* be. It has been said a hundred times, and perfectly correctly, that it is shameful for the Broadway theater to be representative of American theater. Shameful because a commercial theater is so frequently limited and shallow; shameful because the theater of a nation has no business being concentrated in so small a geographical area; shameful because the theater is art and while art has survived commercial situations it is hardly desirable that no healthier conditions should exist; and shameful, finally, because the vast majority of Broadway productions are beneath discussion. But it is the way things are.

We are now experiencing a boom in resident theaters, and despite their drawbacks (there are many) they will be assuming the responsibility of maintaining classic drama. Whatever their success, and whatever the effect of the indirect governmental subsidies they receive, it will be *Broadway* that the audiences and theater people will look to for contemporary American theater — *Broadway* that time will regard (certainly with greater scorn than praise) as the theater of this period. It is only in the recognition of that reality that a true picture of modern theater in the United States can be realized.

It might be noted, too, that cultural developments have always been concentrated in a country's major city. Artistic ferment depends on artistic concentration—not just for communication between artists but for a sense of total activity. A country's theater ought not be restricted to a single city, but there must be a *center* of theater; a place where the theater is concentrated. The publishing houses concentrate in the cultural capital, the major concert halls concentrate in the cultural capital, the theaters for the new and most important plays should concentrate in the cultural capital. For England it is London, for France it is Paris, and for America — as well as, probably, for the world — it must be New York.

A few paragraphs ago, you may have noticed a kicker in the statement that a Broadway producer will never "consciously" reject an artistic play. It was meant as such. The Broadway producer is a victim of his own tastes and those tastes are right wing. Whether or not he can be blamed for their narrowness is something which could be argued indefinitely. Yes, he is stupid for not recognizing the important when he sees it. Yes, he is wasteful in mistaking the ludicrous for the worthwhile. Yes, it is killing that our senses of humor are being deprived because his is juvenile.

The very nature of the Broadway theater as an art form in a marketplace is necessarily irritating. When the serious work is produced there and languishes without business, finally closing, we become furious. Who should have the right to close this? Why can't the play be subsidized? Can't the people who would appreciate it be given a chance to see it? How can the fate of a nation's theater be placed in the hands of businessmen?

This is howling in the wind. It is not the producer's fault that nobody has come. It is not the producer's fault that "the people who would appreciate it" have not bought balcony seats, have not bought twofers, have not even bought seats placed on sale for one dollar. Perhaps perceptive right-wing critics might have helped with enthusiastic reviews, but the critical wings are too divided for this to happen. It was the producer who believed in the play in the first place. He should be the last blamed.

Yet, people involved in short-lived Broadway productions have castigated their producers for nonsupport, as if the man with the financial stake had purposely turned his back on the possibility of saving his investment. They will say he refused to advertise, refused to ask for royalty waivers and salary reductions. This is absurd. The Broadway producer, at least as far as commerce is concerned, is a very knowledgeable man and if he makes occasional mistakes they are invariably on the side of keeping a play running against his better business judgment. He knows that when audiences are not coming, no amount of advertising is going to help. He knows when the difference between gross and operating cost can be made up and when it cannot. He also knows when a production is bad, although, unfortunately but necessarily, only after it has been mounted.

Most Broadway productions are comedies and musicals. It has been argued that the lack of serious American plays is due to a commercial distrust for them as bad box office bets. That is only partly true. A more striking reason is that right-wing drama has neither audiences nor playwrights. The playwrights, pushed too far rightward by the wing separation, continue to write the kind of plays that the audiences have long since outgrown and they write them badly. These audiences, which once could keep a good Tennessee Williams or Arthur Miller play running for a season or two, can now scarcely support a perfectly respectable right-wing play like *The Subject Was Roses* even when it has the solid commercial support of the Pulitzer Prize Committee and the Drama Critics Circle.

One of the hallmarks of the right wing is its *professionalism,* and that is nowhere more apparent than on Broadway. This word, and what it represents, is a constant source of antagonism to the left wing. It is usually used with bitter mimicry in defensive left-wing attacks upon the right wing, where professionalism is denounced as an end in itself. While it is true that many right-wing productions attempt, in the crisis of last-minute and futile patchwork, to cover bad work with slickness, it is childish to believe that such disguise was ever desired. Ultimately, any attempt to dismiss polished technique as being fundamentally antitheater is absurd.

It is logical for the left wing to be defensive about professionalism, for the lack of it is its greatest weakness. But it is impossible to defend oneself against the charge of amateurism. Difficult as it is to substantiate any artistic value judgments, technical finesse is among the most tangible qualities in the theater. Almost anybody, even (and perhaps especially) the most dedicated leftist, can spot professionalism when he sees it, for when work is characterized by craftsmanship, it shines. It is apparent, before anything else, that the thing — whatever its worth — has been done by somebody who knew how to do it.

Nowhere is this professionalism more clear-cut than in a production's physical qualities: the scenery, the lighting, the costumes. While the designs and their originality, color and dramatic effect are what we usually notice, there are matters of technique and execution that we seldom appreciate because we are so accustomed to them. When they are missing, we are baffled, not being familiar with such technical shortcomings.

For example, a scenic designer must be aware of the size of his stage, the storage area, the time it takes to change sets. If he did not take such matters into account he would produce scenery that might look perfectly beautiful but could not fit the theater. On Broadway, you seldom see badly painted scenery or sets that don't fit where they are supposed to, but think back to an evening when you found yourself sitting too long in a darkened theater, waiting for a set to be changed. In the darkness, you glimpsed and heard stage hands pulling tables and chairs offstage and replacing them with new properties; you heard a turntable rumbling. If any mood had been created, it was effectively destroyed.

Such are the demands for craftsmanship, but if the right-wing designer's technique is awesome, his ideology seems typically conservative. The standard right-wing scenic designer specializes in the reproduction of reality. His sets for drama and comedy are detail-for-detail replicas of living rooms, in no way different from those of thirty years ago. His craft at this is remarkable and the applause of an opening night audience when the curtain rises is, if only partly, appreciative of this realism (the applause is mostly one automatic response of many by any opening night audience).

Consider the mechanical engineering in twisting, shifting sets; the planning for their storage; the mastery of materials in making wallboard look exactly like wood paneling; the knowledge of historical periods; the technique needed to make a brightly lighted stage look, to a spectator, like the most ordinary of rooms; the experience to plot the lighting scheme of a musical.

Consider the pathetic waste of all this impeccability. Play after play has the same picture-box living room set with the same furniture in mildly differing upholstery, the same books in mildly differing bindings, the same bars (without which there would be no Broadway comedy) with mildly differing liquor brands. Imagination is dead.

Right-wing designs for musicals have their standard patterns too. The curtain rises to reveal the brightly lighted scrim, its design one of the endless variations of colored nothings to watch while the overture is being played. As usual, the end of the overture cues the backlighting, which causes the colored nothing to disappear; the scrim rises and the opening scene is revealed behind.

What follows is the formula succession of drops and wagons. The scene-in-one (all the way downstage, in front of the very first curtain) so that bulky scenery can be changed. The chorus marching in front of a traveler curtain. The swirling lights for a nightmare scene. Even the follow spotlight.

It is all predictable, the colors too familiar, the attempts at realism too futile, the meshing sets too well remembered from a hundred other musicals. All comfortably usual for the right-wing audiences and the right-wing creators.

But the work of a designer is often limited by the production itself and the director's conception of it. A designer is not always free to create whatever he desires. In the first place, if the play is straight right wing — a realistic drama or comedy in a realistic living room or house — he must proceed according to *its* design. In the second place, few directors allow designers free rein, having their own ideas about how the production should look. Certainly, the director's right to dictate the total look of his production is indisputable.

But because the directors of right-wing plays are right-wing people themselves, and because they seldom have the scenic imagination of a designer, they are hardly inclined to suggest imaginative sets. Even when they do, their grasp of materials, scenic practicalities and the basics of design is so limited that their suggestions are bound to be vague and impractical.

The result is the hamstringing of designers, most of whom incline to the left and ache to try something new. Of all the people in right-wing theater today, perhaps only the designer and the artistic director of a resident theater are operating with a continuing influence from the left.

For the designers, this can be seen where they *are* given freedom, for example in festival Shakespeare or classic theater, where there is no conservative scenic tradition for a producer to cling to. Unless a producer or director is making backward, restrictive demands on his designer (as at Stratford, Ontario, where there is a permanent set and where, despite an awesome lighting plant, light schemes are barely changed), there is fair freedom to invent. The invention can be formidable, displaying perfectly the proper working combination of rightist technique and leftist creativity.

The right-wing, professional American actor is as easily spotted as (and often could also be called) professional scenery. During the heyday of the Actors Studio, there was a popular anecdote about directors and their problems with Studio actors: a director demands that an actor carry an ashtray cross-stage and when the actor asks the so-called standard Studio question ("What's my motivation?") the director replies, "Your motivation is that I told you to." The root of this story was in the practical demands of professionalism. An actor worth paying is an actor who can do what the director wants done. It does not mean that he is doing it with depth, that he is doing it with art, that he is doing it with understanding of the role or its relationship to the play. It simply means that he is *doing* it — placing a book on a table, fixing a drink, whatever. He is not standing on stage snapping his fingers, looking at the audience or wondering whether his illegally parked car is being towed away.

Most professional American actors are professional ashtray carriers. They are also professional part memorizers, direction follow-

ers and sprint runners (according to the Broadway directing style).
They are not, however, actors. That is, they do not *act*. They never
become anybody. When they, *personally,* are magnetic, they become stars.

Such smooth performing will often pass for acting when the performer is attractive and the audience unaccustomed to the real
thing. The right-wing theater has grown up on this and as a result
the American theater is virtually without actors. This is never more
striking than in various attempts to do classics. When the American
actor is confronted with period theater, or anything outside of contemporary drama or comedy, he flounders. That our actors occasionally manage Shakespeare is only because there are some opportunities to acquire such experience. Even in these cases, they have
little sense of diction, vocal projection, style or discipline.

Curiously, the big splash made by Method people was not the
revolution in realism (or Stanislavskian "inner beingness") that Lee
Strasberg insisted it was. It was only an extension of the American
style of acting — the actor's being himself on stage. The Method's
psychological realism was not disciplined by the day-to-day practicalities of the stage. It was not concerned with impersonating a
character. It was directed to the thoughts of the actor himself. In
associating his role with his own experience, and pampering his
ego, the Method actor merely played himself. As a result, the Studio people often found it difficult to do the simplest things required
by the playwright's character, for these things were alien to their
own experience (an actor is supposed to be playing *someone else*).
At the same time, their devotion to the Method ritual made the
most trivial stage necessities exaggerated projects.

Yet, their inverted concentration intensified their stage presence
and the result was a group of vivid theatrical personalities.

In a small sense, the popularity of Studio actors in the ten years
following the Second World War was an example of movement
from left to right wing by actors. The Method was originally prop-
agated by the Group Theater to rebel against the then right-wing
style of flamboyant, artificial acting. That accomplished, the postwar Method actors could only use it as a mannered kind of acting.
The rightward movement finally gelled when Marlon Brando's
magnificent performance in *A Streetcar Named Desire* catapulted

him and them into faddism and acceptance. Within a few years Geraldine Page, Paul Newman, Ben Gazzara, Kim Stanley, Pat Hingle and the rest were accepted as "great," virtually running Broadway drama. In fact, most of them were simply souped-up personalities. Among them were a number of talented actors who joined the Studio because it was the major acting school in New York, and who would have succeeded in any case. Ironically, with their quick movement rightward, these actors came to be rejected by the left wing that spawned them in the first place. It is the traditional irony.

Strasberg and his Studio are not to be condemned. The group was (and remains) tremendously dedicated to serious theater as art, and such idealism is both admirable and rare in a profession much more concerned with billing and movie contracts. Method actors are often very effective performers.

The Broadway actor is, really, a performer, and when he is given the chance to merely perform he is relaxed and smooth. This is best seen in the musical, where he must be able to sing, dance and work in ensemble. New York's pool of talented musical actors is extraordinary and it is no longer surprising to find the singing chorus of any musical stocked with trained voices. A choreographer can demand the most strenuous and complicated work and get it from dancers who are ballet trained and able, at first rehearsal, to do anything he asks. The only necessary work required for such performers is the final polish.

The Broadway comedy is nearly as fortunate. If the acting requisites are as limited as the genre itself, they are nevertheless there — poise, polish, projection. The comedy benefits from the actor-as-a-personality to a greater degree than the musical or drama. A peculiar ingenue like Sandy Dennis, or a superdry character performer like Walter Matthau or the late Donald Cook, can nearly make a comedy. But because the right-wing comedy is basically a playwright's play, the actor who can do what the writer asks without contributing a depth of his own is precisely the one that is wanted. There is a sizable group of actors who can do just this and with great aplomb (for example, Robert Preston, Tom Ewell, Barry Nelson, Barbara Bel Geddes as leading players; Mildred Natwick, Bernie West, Lou Jacobi, Martin Balsam, John McMartin, George S. Irving as featured players; Sidney Armus, Nathaniel Frey, Herbert Edelman as supporting players).

There is another division of right-wing acting that, happily, is disappearing; a division that might be called the Great Lady School (Katharine Cornell, Peggy Wood, Ina Claire, Margaret Webster, Helen Hayes, etc.). Patriotic and respected, it represents the sedately dusty manner that is associated with heavy sets, heavy costuming and evening gowns being swept along by white-gloved hands.

Such acting, confined to a theater that was artificially regal and plainly phoney, placed great emphasis on matters of elocution, posture and elegance, but in an entirely sterile sense. Restricted to formal realism and stilted theater, it was merely a shallow imitation of classical style. Indeed, such acting still passes for classicism. It is one of the more polished jokes in the American theatrical museum.

The lack of actors in American establishment theater is nowhere more debilitating than in the burgeoning resident theaters. The Minnesota Theater Company in Minneapolis, for example, began by being headed by "names" precisely like any Broadway play. Of the people originally imported by Tyrone Guthrie, only Jessica Tandy was in any sense capable of handling a variety of dramatic styles. The biggest (because he was a movie) name, Hume Cronyn, was accustomed to playing character roles in the American sense, which means playing his own type. As a result, Cronyn was Cronyn, whether the play was *Richard III* or *The Cherry Orchard*. The company followed suit, unable to adapt itself to a style other than contemporary realism. Tandy and Cronyn subsequently left and the Minnesota Theater Company began to develop legitimate, trained actors (only to lose them soon afterward).

In Stratford, Connecticut, where things are worse, the abandonment of the original big-name policy only led to the hiring of lesser-known but equally shallow personality performers. When sheer experience provided classical foundations for Douglas Watson or Patrick Hines or Rex Everhart, Stratford managed to ignore them. It preferred a drawing card like Morris Carnovsky, who could overwhelm the right-wing critics with bombastic and absurd right-wing performances.

It is perfectly true that the development of the resident theaters, *by identity,* was left wing, introducing a new element into an established scheme that had refused it. But as they were introduced, built and supported, they moved quickly into the arms of the right, dependent upon it for finances. The idea of culture will always appeal to establishment interests, and resident theaters were as cultural as symphony concerts — *as long as they were kept in the right place.*

And the major ones have been. The resident theaters are in no way as experimental as their supporters would have us believe. In fact, they are rooted in easy-to-take classics — indisputably valid classics but always the same, *reputable* ones. They are dependent on O'Neill, Shaw and, of course, Shakespeare.

Most of the plays complement these war-horse playwrights — "typical" Restoration comedy in *The Country Wife,* "typical" Molière in *Tartuffe,* and so on.

Most surprising, the modern art playwrights are rarely done. Surprising because these theaters have created the impression that they are serious, artistic and original. In fact, except for producing Brecht, they are not. And Brecht has become very right wing, or perhaps *doing* Brecht has become very right wing. What would resident theaters do without a *Mother Courage* here and a *Galileo* there?

And they are not performing in repertory; that is, the daily change of bill. Nearly all schedule in series, one play running for so many weeks. They are doing virtually no new plays. Their choices are conservative, often in the extreme. And they are ultimately controlled by right-wing elements, so that the leftish inclinations of their artistic directors are always subject to censure. Now this might appear as healthy wing interaction, with the boards' conservatism tempering the directors' progressivism. How lovely if it were true. Financed by establishment interests with establishment tastes, and operating only with their approval and support, these theaters too often incline toward official art, official interpretation, official design, direction and acting.

That notwithstanding, these theaters are managing to produce important plays; they are providing the first *regular,* classic theater for their areas — theater produced on-the-spot, primarily for the local population. They may be rightist powered and even rightist oriented, but they are the first sign of a broadening of the American theater base, and in providing a counterbalance to the violent entrenchment of the right wing in New York they are a development of notable proportions.

So if this theater is beginning as *official* theater — a theater that is forbidden the individual vision necessary for adventurous, idealistic, insistently leftist theater — its financial stability will insure an experience for America with serious theater.

The right-wing actors at these theaters are much more offensive than they are on the Broadway for which they were trained (if training is the word for the background that actors develop in disorganized acting schools, summer stock and hack plays under hack directors).

This is perfectly understandable. They have had no experience in the classical repertory. Yet, while these Broadway techniques are utterly useless in classical theater, the techniques that repertory teaches work marvelously on the commercial stage. For acting — genuine acting — will work in any theater. And once you see a real actor playing even the most trivial role in the most trivial play you realize the difference in *kind* between the performer and the actor.

Because we allowed the wings of our theater to divide, the only theater to which an American actor could aspire was Broadway. If there now are theaters scattered about the country, they are only starting to be artistic enough, attractive enough, high paying enough and publicized enough to lure an actor away from Broadway.

The actor who has a drive to succeed is drawn — naturally — to where all the active, *famous* theater is — where all the action is — and that is Broadway. To ask an actor to step back from this attraction is to deny his energy and psychology. Our tradition is the commercial theater, good and bad. We have created the lowest status for a repertory education — an education that demands years of minor, unrecognized playing. What motive can an actor have for sidestepping the Broadway that will give him a chance for glory? We have given him none, throwing every other country's most traditional kind of acting technique into the rejected corner — our left wing.

Right-wing direction, by definition, is the kind of direction one sees in nearly any theater in this country. It is attached to realistic drama and farcical, ostensibly sophisticated comedy and, in both cases, it is not very much different from the direction of such plays many years ago. The reason is that these are exactly the same kinds of dramas and comedies that were produced years ago.

That may make the directors dated but it does not make them amateur and, to repeat what has already been repeated, they are absolute professionals. When a right-wing director stages a play, it is going to look tight, easy and fully rehearsed, no matter how ridiculous the script. In fact, for all the idiotic dramas and comedies on Broadway, perhaps one percent is sloppy in direction (and consequently in performance). And that one percent is invariably directed by people outside the right-wing coterie.

There indisputably is such a coterie, as any out-of-work director will tell you. It exists because experience breeds employment and because producers feel they minimize their financial risks when they hire known people (the result often being that the conservative elements become more deeply entrenched, drawing the right wing even further to the right). These directors include Harold Clurman, Joseph Anthony, Abe Burrows, Arthur Penn, Herman Shumlin, Arthur Storch, Peter Kass, Herbert Machiz and Albert Marre for the straight plays and comedies. And George Abbott, Bob Fosse, Michael Kidd and the late Vincent J. Donehue for musicals. The work invariably goes to them. Nor can there be any denying their right to much of it. They are masters of their trade.

Right-wing directing in contemporary drama is noncreative in any thematic sense. The director will add to the *look* of things but not to the *scheme* of things. He will take a script and translate it to the stage, crisply and logically. His blocking is straightforward and his awareness of probable audience reactions continuous. There is little concern with ensemble movement or interaction. If things are not going well, either in rehearsal or in tryouts, he will add still more external matters, but not according to a private vision. By and large he will play it as the author wrote it. This kind of direction has been distilled on Broadway to give any play a smooth exterior and it will only fail to do so in cases where the director does not understand the play (that is, when a right-wing director is handling a left-wing play or vice versa).

If there is a single reason why Broadway does the plays it does, it would have to be the producer — a man who is assumed by everybody to be the interloper in a world of art. He is, contrarily, a most necessary element. It is he who makes the theater possible, whatever and wherever it is; he who is responsible for what is seen. For it is the producer who most accurately reflects the tastes and inclinations of the audiences, and it is the producer who selects the plays that will be presented to them.

The right-wing producer is a businessman who is in love with the theater, generally to its detriment. His theater is fundamentally his taste and his taste is middle-class and middle-aged. The effect is the present avalanche of Thirties and Forties musicals and comedies, combining wishful commercial reliability with as much quality as he can comprehend. Nevertheless, the result is the very theater of modern America — the annual influx and continued presentation of works for the stage. No matter how the intellectual community's attitude toward the theater changes, no matter how impossible the producer's taste and the homogeneity of his output, because of him *there is a theater*.

The most frustrating aspect of Broadway theater is that the producers have absolutely no idea what they are doing. If there is a trend in musicals, they will miss it; if something dynamic has happened in the *kinds* of dramas being submitted it will go over their heads; if a comedy suddenly proves that audiences are quite able to enjoy modern humor, they will act as if it never happened. There is not even the primitive attitude of television in attempting to duplicate prior successes. If something new manages to work on Broadway it is only because nobody noticed it was new, and as soon as it is running everybody forgets it has happened. This obliviousness to development is a trait shared by nearly all of the creative people in the right-wing theater and it is bizarre.

Nevertheless, the right wing on Broadway has managed to achieve what will unquestionably prove to be the most significant development in twentieth-century theater. It has done it despite the solid rejection — the complete dismissal — of the development by most of the left-wingers.

This is the musical theater, moving out of the operettas and revues into Twenties flapper musicals, Thirties shipboard musicals and the pseudoserious "music drama" of the Forties. By then, the more aware left-wing theater people realized what was happening and began the serious innovation that is finding in the show business of the musical the stuff of pure theater.

The American musical theater is qualitatively different from any other kind of theater, anywhere, ever. In its combination of musical and dramatic elements it is related to opera, although infinitely more involved with dance, and not so composer dominated. Rather, it gives equal power to the director and choreographer.

Today, the musical is the healthiest theater in New York and its popularity on Broadway is proof of that health. It carries with it the vitality of a thriving form.

As for Broadway comedies, if the scripts ever achieved half the finesse of the actors, directors, scenic designers and lighting men they would not be nearly so offensive. But these plays are usually humorless and stupid, sloppily written, generally patched with last-minute revisions and frequently designed for summer stock audiences, basing a series of heavy-handed and obvious wisecracks on heavy-handed and obvious central situations.

Still, there is an entertainment in the Broadway comedy that cannot be denied, and from time to time this right-wing theater provides a real humor and a legitimate theater that needs no apology. And it does it with the colorful sureness that is the right wing's most valuable asset. A brittle, wisecracking comedy (*Nobody Loves an Albatross,* for example) is a perfectly respectable kind of theater, irresistibly engaging.

It is not the popularity of these right-wing musicals and comedies that has driven the drama from the theater, for there is no limitation on space. It is not the *existence* of this theater that has divided the wings but the *domination* by it.

Off-Broadway has abandoned the drive that made it, between 1959 and 1963, a glimmer of hope for a left- right-wing interaction. It is still substantially more liberal than establishment theater but it is no longer playing the left wing to Broadway's right. Instead, for the greater part, it has joined the right.

Most off-Broadway productions are plays by beginner playwrights, piano-celesta musicals, café-style revues or showcases for precious homosexual ingroups. Although there are not as many vanity productions as there were at the peak of off-Broadway activity, this obnoxious but unavoidable travesty of theater has settled down to provide each season with its share of self-financed, husband-financed or family-financed productions.

The plays off-Broadway are usually based on the same conservative dramatic principles and reflect the same bourgeois points of view as those on Broadway. In fact, some of their producers have devised new styles of right-wing extremism, one of the most cynical being productions of irreproachable cultural quality, specifically geared to theater parties of schoolchildren and subsequent touring of the lucrative college circuits (*In White America, Medea, The Trojan Women,* each bland and institutional).

Today, a few left-wing off-Broadway producers remain — Clinton Wilder, Richard Barr and Albee; Ted Mann, Paul Libin (who now relies on productions imported intact from such places as Yale Drama School, Judson Poets Theater and the New York Shakespeare Festival).

Away from New York, the dominating right wing provides the two kinds of theater that most Americans are familiar with — second-string Broadway (touring companies, summer stock, music tents) and the big-time repertory, resident or festival theater. The conservatism of the first is apparent enough: the Broadway successes are sent across the country to satisfy all the provincials who have read about them in the slick magazines. In reproductions ranging from fair to miserable, they provide fair to miserable theater. That such theater was, until recently, the only theater in these cities is proof enough of the right wing's domination of the United States stage.

The conservatism in the summer festival theaters is more subtle. In the guise of culture, these theaters provide a nice institutional propriety, a modicum of shrubbery and a certain amount of self-congratulation for a city feeling defensive about its artistic desolation. Urged ever onward by restless dilettantes, local bankers, industrialists and merchants (who have visions of tourists filling their cash registers), they get themselves their professional right-wing festival man — Tyrone Guthrie in one guise or another — raise a few million dollars, hire a high-powered advertising-public relations agency, engage a business consultant who specializes in audience potentials for regional theaters and proceed to have some concrete prestressed around a thrust stage. Then, with the leftist director bribed by promises such as artistic freedom, the opportunity to escape Broadway rightism and local prestige, a band of young New York actors is hauled out with precisely the same promises.

Now, with all parts of the culture machine greased and oiled, the first season already oversubscribed, and a handsome grant from a foundation in hand, the program can be arranged: *The Cherry Orchard, Caesar and Cleopatra, The Skin of Our Teeth* and the rest of the right-wing-culture plays. For these are the plays that have become indisputably associated with Art and the right-wing institutional theater thrives on the indisputable. They are chosen because they are the plays to do. And everybody does them.

After a while, the director decides to exercise some of that artistic freedom he was promised. A little tired of the right-wing clichés, he becomes aware of the subtleties of his (and his theater's) imprisonment and, in accordance with his left-wing inclinations, he determines to do something really original that demands artistic autonomy. With this, the truth appears: the right-wing executive board blanches at the appearance of a left-wing idea and the director is relieved of his duties (cf. William Ball and John Hancock at the Pittsburgh Playhouse). Another variation on this theme is the realization by the board that, despite its avowed determination to ignore commercial considerations, the productions are not "hits." Faced with rejection by right-wing audiences and critics, harangued by the society matrons who so influence American culture, the artistic freedom is again forgotten, the director again pressured out (cf. the right-wing Robert Whitehead and Elia Kazan and the left-wing Herbert Blau at Lincoln Center).

Throughout the theater, but particularly in the right wing and especially on Broadway, there is a permeating influence which colors its tone, its selections and its attitudes. Apologizing (to both, I guess) for the coupling, the Jews and the homosexuals are the dominating factors in New York theater, creatively and, especially in the case of Jews, in audiences, financing and production. I have little doubt that without their participation, the Broadway theater would probably collapse.

Both left- and right-wing critics, in a burst of interwing activity prompted by smug courage, have taken to attacking theater homosexuals. It has become an easy route to outspokenness. It is partly justified, although too often it boils down to persecution. And it is particularly ironic coming from right-wing critics, since homosexuals, although sexually left wing, are generally inclined to defend traditional values. They tend to stand for family, God and country. Whatever the explanation, by and large the theater that homosexuals propagate is the right wing of Broadway.

The sub (and sometimes not so sub) rosa homosexual influence in American theater is extremely unhealthy. It is unhealthy because it is dishonest — with the audiences, with the theater and with itself. It is unhealthy because it adversely affects artistic judgment. It is unhealthy because it can result in a put-on attitude toward heterosexual audiences.

This influence can be manifested in many ways. The homosexual playwright will write a drama that is presumably about male-female romance, although he really has male-male in mind. He will inject ingroup asides, campy references, parallel interpretations (I am not discussing unintentional reflections of his emotional makeup; these are impossible to trace and any artist must be assumed to have control over his work even while many of them obviously do not). The homosexual director will cast productions not necessarily for ability but because certain actors are either part of his sexual set or because they represent homosexual jokes — that is, actresses who are unwitting parodies of women or actors who are absurdly "masculine." The homosexual designer will ignore the needs of a play for the sake of his special-group tastes, or he will either consciously or subconsciously make females look awkward.

The female star of a Broadway musical is often at the mercy of homosexual creators and even audiences who, because they incline to hyperenthusiasm, tend to *adore* such a woman (exactly as they do the opera diva). Sometimes this is a kind of delighted contempt,

sometimes true admiration. In either case it promotes the already
existing vanity of the ladies and leads them into excesses of performance and costuming. They begin to camp, sometimes intentionally, sometimes unconsciously, playing for the boys in the balcony or the chorus. In most cases, these women are talented and in
most cases they continue to be, but when they are being conned by
choreographers or directors, they are made fools of, and this produces a truly vulgar kind of theater — vulgar and deceitful since it
purports to be the surface show while undercurrents of mockery and
irrelevance swirl sneakily beneath. Such ladies range from Judy Gar-
land to the late Sophie Tucker; Bette Davis and Tallulah Bankhead
to Ethel Merman and Dolores Gray. Musicals like *Hello, Dolly!*
(with its procession of Carol Channing, Ginger Rogers, Martha
Raye, Betty Grable) and *Mame* (Angela Lansbury) are built for
them. Some of these women are clever enough to know exactly what
has been happening and manage to put even their claques on (Channing in particular, and Bankhead). Others, unfortunately, are used
without their knowing it. In all cases, they are sincere and effective
performers doing their best and often doing it marvelously, either
despite the homosexual aura or even because of the enthusiasm of
the homosexual contribution.

A homosexual lyricist can introduce all sorts of special meanings
to songs and sometimes not so subtly. One major Broadway musical
(*Mame*) that seemed to move entirely from a homosexual point of
view gave its leading lady dubious sexual interests and created an
extremely mannish actress for her "bosom buddy." Their duet lyric
read, "I'll always be Alice Toklas/if you'll be Gertrude Stein."

Choreography for Broadway musicals has proved the most fla-
grant area for homosexual influence. Choreographers will hire
dancers on the basis of personal interest. They will sex up the
chorus boys (who too often welcome the treatment). Girls will be
abysmally treated and given purposely clumsy choreography.

On the other hand, the theater (as well as much of this country's
artistic life) would be decimated by an exclusion of homosexuals.
As a group, they are probably more active in artistic fields than any
other. Their contributions are enormous and in many cases the
"they" of this is unfair. Not all homosexuals are faggots or queens;
that is, not all of them are inescapably effeminate. Many refuse to

allow their personal practices to interfere with their professional lives. They are often unfairly maligned, especially considering the amount, the quality and the importance of the work they do.

There is a real prejudice against them and, as might be expected, it comes from the self-styled liberals who claim to be so terribly upset by racial or religious bias. Prejudice in any area is not only unjust but illogical. It must never be tolerated. When the homosexual is being artistically dishonest, allowing irrelevant interests to affect his judgment, he can be properly criticized. But there is no point in putting him down out of hand. He has as much right to work in the theater as someone addicted to, say, chewing gum.

On the audience side homosexuals comprise a negligible bloc. But on the other hand, *Jewish* people make up so large a segment of the ticket-buying public that without their support Broadway would probably disappear. This applies to theatrical investment as well. And outside of New York, while there are not nearly so many Jews proportionately, their theater influence far outweighs their numbers. A professor at the University of Toronto once attributed the artistic and financial success of the Manitoba Theater Center in Winnipeg to the large Jewish community there.

Is it good for a single group to so decisively influence the theater?

A general question first. While so many theater people — creators, investors, audiences — may be Jewish by birth, does that give them a homogeneous quality? It is a touchy question — a question that is now and will remain argued — and a question without an answer. One Jewish person may have only his native religion in common with another. But this is only the beginning. Depending on the environment in which he developed and the experiences that ensued, he may have an attitude, a set of values, a cultural taste, perhaps even a personality in common with other Jews. That is, he will be "Jewish" as opposed to Jewish to one degree or another.

Because this phenomenon exists in so public a situation as the theater and show business, it draws reactions from the non-Jewish American population. The Gentile watching network television is constantly faced with comedians whose material is studded with Yiddishisms and Jewish references. Jewishness has become nationalized. Does the Gentile feel an outsider? Sometimes. Does he resent it? Perhaps.

Every season brings pure right-wing productions specifically designed for Jewish tastes. The Jewish–New York comedies. The bar mitzvah musicals. But while their producers certainly are mindful of the influence wielded by Jewish theater-party groups, that is not the only reason for such productions. In many cases, it is just a matter of the producers' personal tastes and the styles of Jewish playwrights and composers. Though there will occasionally be a *Fiddler on the Roof* to apply a genuinely artistic treatment to the Jewish cultural tapestry, the general rule is the supercommercial taste-scavenger (*The Zulu and the Zayda, I Can Get It for You Wholesale,* etc.).

These are obvious examples of Jewish influence on the Broadway theater. Digging a little deeper, a more subtle effect can be seen. Jewish playwrights, directors and producers are in superabundance. Often enough to notice, their work and their choice of productions reflects their heritages, their tastes and their values.

For example, the Group Theater may have seemed a minor Broadway influence when it agitated briefly during the Thirties, but it did produce Clifford Odets, setting the tone by which the period's theater will be historically known. More significantly, two of the Group Theater's driving personalities — Harold Clurman and Lee Strasberg — went on to create the identity of postwar Broadway drama. Clurman directed many of the period's plays and Strasberg ran the Actors Studio that provided their casts (as well as the casts for many other important dramas of the time).

Was the Group Theater "Jewish" because its organizers and many of its policy-making members were Jewish? Of course not. It was "Jewish" because of the kinds of people they were and the values they had. The Russian influence was deep, the Yiddish Art Theater influence was deep, the Jewish-intellectual influence was deep.

The work that these people did, the work that today's "Jewish" Jewish theater people do, is work that continues to set the shape of right-wing American theater.

The reception of that work by the Jewish audiences will suggest an acceptance and an understanding of it that is really only paro-

chial. I suppose that as the Gentile audience is increasingly exposed
to these special tastes it understands more and develops an appreciation of them.

But where does that leave the theater? As with the homosexuals,
it leaves it heavily weighted in the direction of a special group. It
robs it of a terribly needed versatility. It alienates nonmembers of
that group. Jewish theater people have little in common in some
senses, but they have a great deal in others. They understand each
other. However talented, intellectual, artistic and knowing, they
will naturally pour their backgrounds into their work.

One can hardly deny them their success. The large New York
Jewish population was bound to exert an influence over the theater
there, and since New York's theater is so representative of America's, that influence would naturally be magnified. If the ambition,
the interest and the capability were there, why shouldn't they have
progressed? They deservedly did.

Too, Jewish people have traditionally been interested in the theater, as in art generally. These interests are a part of their cultural
personality. Wherever there is a Jewish community there is an involvement with books, with music, with education and with the
theater. If there is no theater when they arrive, they will create one.
Their contribution to the American stage is as stimulating, as valuable and as necessary as the homosexual's. As anybody's.

But no art form will benefit by special-group orientation. The
Gentile and the heterosexual should not be (or feel) excluded because of his minority-group status. Nor should the Jew or the homosexual incline to favor "his own." The theater needs all the
points of view, all the orientations it can muster. And if it falls
victim to a single group's control, either by conquest or default, it
will suffer for it.

In most of the kinds of right-wing theater that I have been
discussing — Broadway, off-Broadway, touring companies, music
tents — the *kinds* of plays are controlled by the producers, rather
than by creative people. The intellectual-emotional makeup of
these producers — the ideological-philosophical identity of right-
wing America — governs their choices.

It means a belief in God, a respect for law, a love of country, a need for order, a sense of family, a concern with appearance, a willingness to be organized, a recognition of the good in social responsibility. It means an interest in melodic music, representational art, story fiction, rhymed poetry. It means a taste for hamburgers, Chinese food, pizza and ice cream. It means a belief in cornerstones — of marriage, social systems, maturity. It means an acceptance of the various interdenominational, nonsectarian, middleclass values, ranging from the Ten Commandments to the Boy Scout oath. And, in general, the ethical foundation upon which Western society is built.

Within this ideological framework are a number of reform ideas and sophistications — the most recent left-wing ideas to have been assimilated by the right wing — such as the evil of racial prejudice, the worthiness of illegitimate children, alcoholism as a disease, juvenile delinquency as society's fault and responsibility, insanity as mental illness, and so on. Despite their apparent worthiness these are nearly all platitudes, many of them ill conceived. They represent the comfortable ideals for a comfortable society that has lost the interest, and consequently the power, to think for itself. They also represent past progress.

A subdivision of this right-wing form of sophistication is the material communicated by television, magazines and the movies. This means a vague awareness of inconsequential New York fads six months after they have become passé — pop art, underground movies, discothèques, dance steps, new drugs, and so on. They provide new twists for old situations in comedies, presumably making them up-to-date.

The theater of the right wing reflects these social, ethical and moral patterns. Its dramas project traditional moral structures, its comedies appeal to a traditional sense of humor, its musicals appeal to traditional entertainment tastes.

There is a pattern of audience behavior in New York that is commonly described as the very cause of the theater's problems, and while it is a symptom rather than a cause it should be mentioned in this discussion, I suppose, although it really is not terribly important or worth a fraction of the space it receives in mass magazines, sensible monthlies and Sunday supplements. This is the phenomenon variously described as "hit or miss" or "hot ticket" theatergoing.

As mentioned earlier, the audience that remains for drama on Broadway is too small to support right-wing drama and too old or ignorant to understand the occasional left-wing drama. As a result, this right-wing audience is interested in only the musical and the comedy, and within that, only the musical or comedy that receives *rave reviews*. It sees a *status* in attending such productions early in their runs.

As for dramas, the right-wing audience will no longer turn out in force for the most widely acclaimed right-wing play. There is a popular argument that Broadway audiences are not interested in drama merely because none of them are any good. This argument is both facile and insupportable. For example, the 1963-1964 Broadway season began with two British productions, Jean Anouilh's *The Rehearsal* and Arnold Wesker's *Chips with Everything* — the former impeccably presented, the latter electric in a traditional, dramatic way. The plays received wonderful reviews but neither ran very long. Why did they fail?

They failed because there *is* no audience for right-wing dramas.

The questions then arise: can the right-wing audience be "blamed" for rushing to its comedies and musicals? Can the left-wing audience be "blamed" for staying away from the right-wing theater in general, and therefore virtually all of the theater? These audiences, after all, are merely following their tastes — everybody's privilege — and are depending upon critics of their own wings to accurately reflect those tastes (as indeed they do). The only way for Broadway drama to regain public support is by regaining the left-wing audience, and the only way it will do that is by regaining left-wing theater.

The right wing is capitalizing on the division; having been handed control of New York theater, it is insisting upon greater and greater conservatism. The critics must not merely recommend the musical or comedy, they must call it the greatest of the century. Concomitant with this insistence upon right-wing extremity has been the forcing of the critics, by these audiences, into an abandonment of their duties. With few exceptions, the critics of this wing have become the slaves of their readers growing prone to rave-or-pan notices; far from being too powerful, they have little power to speak of and, ironically, it is spoken of constantly.

According to popular mythology, the right-wing critic has make-or-break power over the Broadway theater. At the very start, drama must be excepted (cf. *The Rehearsal* and *Chips with Everything,* cited above). The most enthusiastic reviews will have little box office effect on any right-wing drama, and it is only when the left-wing audience is aroused that a play will have any real success on Broadway. Even the God drama, once the safest of right-wing bets in the days of *J.B.* and *Gideon,* has become a very long shot.

In the case of the musical or the comedy, the New York daily newspaper critics can produce financial success or failure, but only under very special circumstances: if the reviews are unanimously favorable or if the *Times* is unfavorable. In all other circumstances, business is unpredictable, depending upon such factors as drawing cards in the cast, pre-opening promotion, business conditions and the weather. There is also word-of-mouth, meaning that bad news is passed from one person to another like a venereal disease, or that word of an artistic production gets piped into the left-wing underground. The musical *Skyscraper* was an example of the former, John Osborne's *Inadmissible Evidence* and Pinter's *The Homecoming* of the latter.

The relationship of reviews to business has nothing to do with what those reviews said (and certainly not with the productions' value) other than whether they were "raves" or "pans." In fact, for the purposes of critical "power," reviews could be reduced to a yes or no. This is all the right-wing audience is interested in.

Perhaps this can be called power, but if so, it is power of an extremely primitive nature.

A critic's power should lie in his ability to persuade his readers to see anything he considers worth seeing. That does not mean the production he considers superduper. The readers should be convinced to see the production upon which the critic has equivocated and recommended *despite* the equivocation. Readers should *not* be encouraged to decide for themselves. They obviously cannot and do not wish to see *everything*. They should be educated, influenced, led. The critical responsibility, in any case, is toward the *theater* and in assuming that responsibility the critic must have the strength to effect what he believes. Not mere attendance or nonattendance, but the respect for theater values by both audience and creators.

A critic's power lies in his ability to command the respect of the theater. His opinions about creation and execution, ideology and purpose, passion and provocation; his vision and his sense; his analysis is of the existing theater and its possibilities should be taken as a guideline to what will be attempted and how the present can serve as an education for the future.

His power should lie in his posture as the loyal opposition — the defender of the theater from the people who practice it, go to it, attempt to shape it to their own purposes and prejudices. If the practitioners give and the audiences receive, it should be the critic who bestrides them, preserving the holiness of the theater between. Are the creators betraying the theater? The critic must berate them. Are the audiences defiling it? The critic must condemn them. He must demand that those who are in it be worthy of it, do their best by it, follow it to its own greatness. He must insist that those who enjoy it enjoy it on their highest levels.

The right-wing critics have abandoned this power, overwhelmed by the extreme division. No longer involved with a theater that should be vitally thriving between change and tradition, they have been pulled along with the rightward swing and have abandoned their true responsibilities.

Left-wing critics have a greater power (in the most important sense), but because they are so alienated from mainstream theater, it is seldom obvious to the public. The left-wing critic can draw a left-wing audience to a left-wing production; he will be respected by left-wing theater people. But his theater concerns are so severely biased that his perpetual, hammering rejection of the right wing has become a cranky and ineffectual whine.

A healthy theater demands critics with real power. Only with powerful criticism can a theater be pressed toward greatness.

But if left-wing audiences are so estranged from Broadway, what is one to make of the phenomenon of the preview?

The preview was conceived to minimize the expense of out-of-town tryouts, which were the traditional method of ironing the wrinkles out of a production before submitting it to the New York critics. The testing in New Haven, Boston, Philadelphia or Washington had long gone unchallenged as the normal route to Broadway.

The out-of-town system made some sense. Away from New York and family, the cast, the director, the playwright and everybody else concerned with a play could concentrate on the work and only the work. Twenty-four hours a day were devoted to reworking the lights, rewriting the second act, recasting and redesigning.

Virginia Woolf came in on a 1962 shoestring and had no money for travel expenses. It chose to try out in New York and previews as we know them today were invented. They introduced a theater for playgoers who were willing to gamble along with the producer. Playgoers who were eager to fight against — to engage with — drama that could be respected.

The result was a theater alive with reaction. A theater where audiences would fight back. Would walk out. Would shout approval or invective. They were not, perhaps, thoughtful of the pressures on performers. They were not, perhaps, mindful of the fact that the play was unfinished. But they were vital.

The people at these previews were a strange crew in the theater. They were nowhere to be seen once a production opened. They were new, unrecognized, strange. They were the lost excitement of a living theater. They were the homesick expatriates, the estranged lovers. They were the audiences of the left wing.

Why did they come? And why did they disappear after the official opening? Producers are baffled. Serious plays that sound left wing draw eager left-wingers during the previews only to find them gone after the negative reviews that invariably greet the première. This situation occurs repeatedly, some examples being the Broadway production of Brecht's *Arturo Ui,* Terrence McNally's *And Things That Go Bump in the Night,* Paddy Chayefsky's *The Passion of Josef D.* and any Edward Albee play. I am not suggesting that these productions were *good.* Some of them were dreadful. But they sounded *possibly interesting, possibly modern,* to the left-wing theatergoers.

Distrust of right-wing critics is one of the reasons these left-wingers attend previews. They want to be able to judge for themselves before reading the daily reviews (evidently they trust the negative reviews once they are published). The low-price ticket is offered as another reason, but I really can't accept that, since balcony tickets for plays are not terribly high priced anyhow. But the possibility of discovering an exciting play on their own and an *adventure* associated with previewgoing certainly plays a part in this phenomenon.

In any case, the left-wing audiences at the previews prove that they do exist. While producers from Broadway to Lincoln Center remain frustrated by their inability to draw these left-wingers during the regular runs, they are unable to grasp the real cause of the problem. The cause lies in the wing division and the estrangement of these left-wing audiences.

CHAPTER THREE

The Left Wing

THOSE audiences that are rustling up involvement at the Broadway previews of left-wing plays — grappling, wrestling, building up a pulse beat — are the beginning of the theater's tomorrow. Just the few streaks in a still-darkened sky, but streaks shining and bright.

On March 2, 1966, the *New York Times* ran the following story under a Paris dateline:

> An audience of second nighters, composed of Comédie-Française subscribers, greeted Eugène Ionesco's latest play, *La Soif et la Faim* (*Thirst and Hunger*), with a storm of disapproval tonight.
>
> Indignant cries of "Enough! Enough!" broke out during a brainwashing scene in which a prisoner is tormented into reciting the Lord's Prayer.
>
> Loud objections to the objections followed and for almost ten minutes the actors were inaudible, though they continued playing, drowned out by the uproar.
>
> At the evening's finish when the actors came to take the curtain calls, boos, catcalls and whistling sounded over the applause.

Imagine a demonstration like that at any nonpreview performance in a Broadway theater (or, for that matter, in *any* American theater). Impossible because the Broadway theater is almost entirely occupied by right-wing plays and right-wing audiences, comfortable together, one providing what the other comes to be provided *with*. The drama is docile and so is the theatergoer.

What this Parisian fracas illustrates is the direct confrontation of left-wing theater with a right-wing audience and, within *that* audience, a direct confrontation between the left-wing and the right-wing theatergoer. It is precisely the attitude that a healthy, functioning theater compels. Albert Camus once defended the slashing of a painting by a violently idealistic student on the grounds that such concern is more important than any painting. So long as the theater is a fat, comfortable place where fat, comfortable people find the fat, comfortable plays they seek, that theater will decay.

The left wing represents the challenge — the opposite. It is antagonistic to every norm on every front, whether it is proposing a change in dramatic form, in point of view, in scenic design, in acting or direction. Because it is so separated from establishment American theater, it has been driven ever leftward, seldom projecting its innovations, never able to have them practiced. The left wing is proposing changes for a theater that is out of earshot.

So long as there is a single man who does not care about what the producers want, what the audiences want, what the institutions want — who cares only about what *he* wants for *his* theater, there will be a left wing. So long as there is one man who cares about a particular play that he has just *got* to write or direct or act in, there will be a left wing. So long as there is somebody disgusted with the Way Things Are — in *any* phase of the theater — there will be a left wing.

The left wing is building a dam in the face of an onrushing current. A dam that repeatedly crumbles, finally holding well enough to divert the roar to a slightly different course. Where somebody else is building a dam.

On Broadway, where the powerful right makes its home, the left wing has folded its tents (or has had them folded for it). With its audience adrift, the critics antagonistic, the producers baffled, the directors of another generation, the left wing finds it virtually impossible to put a drama into production. Edward Albee is the only consistently produced left-wing playwright in today's American theater and the primary reason is that he has his own left-wing producing company behind him (Richard Barr, Clinton Wilder and Albee himself). Albee even has his own left-wing director in Alan Schneider. The wing split is so extreme that all of this is necessary for a left-wing playwright to be performed on Broadway on a regular basis.

The left wing's antagonism to Broadway is total. From its point of view, commercialism is rampant, the theater is a product manufactured for sale to matinee ladies and benefit parties. The *idea* of theater is dead, replaced by a plastic object *posing* as theater.

The left wing means to destroy this plastic object. It is plotting the murder of traditional dramas and plotting is not the left wing's forte, which may be one reason for its fumbling of the crime. It wishes to eliminate not merely the mysteries, the thrillers, the courtroom dramas and the message plays, but the very modes in which these plays are written. It is sick of the "well-made" play, dismissing it as *badly* made and according to an obsolete formula. The separate matters of content and style represent to it a theater that is both senile and corrupt. It is after a new theater for its time, conceived in new ways of thinking, new areas of knowledge, true culture and fresh consideration of old and new problems in living and in art.

Art is the key word, because the left wing is rooted in it. For the left wing, the theater is a sacred place where great and wonderful things happen. It seeks the what-is-the-point?, the where-am-I-going?, the what-is-my-identity? It is after what right-wing critics call the "eternal verities" — beauty and truth. Childish? Usually. In most cases, the playwright dipping for depth will come up with a handful of warmed-over Kafka leaking through his fingers. But how can he be condemned for it? And how can we ask him to seek nearer, more easily attained goals? Well, we do, and when he complies we get more frequent, limited successes. Not commercial successes, necessarily, but "nice" plays. A pretty song is preferable to an awful opera. Isn't it? Such is the lure of the right-wing Lorelei.

The left wing has turned away from realistic, didactic plays that seek or provide answers to social questions. Straightforward content has become repellent to it. It does not conceive of its plays in terms of message delivery services but as theater works — plays that *happen*. When there is an idea behind the play, it is implicit. The concentration is on Theater.

This is just as well, since playwrights are not the brightest people in the world, in either wing. When they attempt to be specific their reasoning turns top-of-the-head, their information hazy, their thought habits sloppy. Their critical intelligence generally collides with the outer limit of their education, as soon as they attempt particular remarks on particular subjects. (This is most obvious when a playwright attempts to discuss his own play. See Miller on *After the Fall;* Albee on *Tiny Alice.*) But it is partly understandable — a playwright is a specialist not in elucidation but in exemplification: his mind is drama trained and so inclined toward instinctive and reactive thinking — the metaphor — rather than toward proposition and argument. He is a demonstrator. His concentration is on the theatricalization of an attitude. And so the play that suggests, through parody, irony or wit, some point of view will seem more intelligent than the play which tries to provide a solution or alternative.

But in appearing to concentrate on style as against content, or at least in combining them, the left wing has found itself criticized by traditionalists: how can there be art without content? It is a foolish criticism, too easily answered (why can't there be?). In the first place, a play with an implicit content is not a play without content. In the second place, a play needn't have a content in the first place. Art is its own reason — it exists because it exists.

This is the thought behind the trend away from realism, the increasing abandonment of the script as a play's bible, the growing attention to production detail and directorial creativity, the inclusion of choreographic or group movement (as opposed to individual speaker movement) and the tendency, in the construction of dramas, toward full-production theater.

Left-wing dramatists have found the discipline of the realistic play too restrictive and untheatrical. They look at life through art, not "realistically" (which they consider *unrealistic*) but imaginatively, honestly finding life *itself* unrealistic — seeing the organized outer lives that people live as social camouflages for their disorganized inner lives. They also use comedy as a necessary adjunct of drama, and while they refuse to write comedy for comedy's sake, nearly all insist on humor as the underbelly of drama. Finally, they are seeking a place where theater — the special experience of the stage — *happens*. As a result, the director's role has become increasingly significant.

He is the man who lifts a play from the script and transposes it to the living experience. He takes what you read and makes it into what you see. It isn't merely a matter of getting a cast to read lines in a believable manner and blocking out the movements requested by the playwright. It is, in the fullest sense, creation itself. Examine almost any play and you will find the barest of stage directions. This is likely for two reasons: First, a playwright is imagining his drama as he is writing it, and a mind's stage is very little like a theater's. Second, a playwright may be theater oriented, but his work is literary. He cannot write a performance. It is not enough to note an entrance here and an exit there. How is that entrance made? What does the character do while he is on stage? What is he doing while somebody else is talking? What happens to everybody else on stage at that moment? How fast does he speak, how fast does he move? What about music? And most of all, what will everything be like? The shape, the color, the action, the *sensation?* The questions are endless and the answers must come from the director.

A play does not exist on paper — it is only secondarily literature. There are works that read well, but play badly. They therefore fail their purpose. Plays do not exist as they were meant to exist until they are brought to life on a stage, in the theater, before an audience. They must be plucked from the page and be made into scenery, lighting, actors, movement. The play's purpose is to be *played*. And it is the director who makes it play.

The left-wing director is an interpretive artist, somewhat like a musician who is given a musical score and performs it his own way. He re-creates. He does not merely do *King Lear* but *his King Lear,* finding new ideas in it, new points of view, new ways of doing it. The play worth reperformance is like any classic — it is unceasingly provocative. The left-wing director is provoked.

There are examples of such director's theater, although not very often and only in the further left of the resident theaters. John Hancock directed a *Midsummer Night's Dream* for the now-defunct Actors Workshop in San Francisco (and later took it with him to the Pittsburgh Playhouse). Based on the radical theories of

Jan Kott, the Polish Shakespearean analyst, it shook loose the traditional magic-love ideas and replaced them with grotesquerie, sex and evil. Backing the stage with a black, vinyl-like tarpaulin, Hancock dressed his cast in primary-color satins and scored the production with brooding Mahler set against the standard Mendelssohn. He cast a six-foot actor in drag as Helena, long blond hair flowing past his rouged cheeks. The other characters were similarly strange — Puck as castrated, Hippolyta as a Nubian slave and so on. As it turned out, these bizarre trappings never made any thematic sense and the actors were incapable of handling the poetry, but that is not the point. Hancock's attitude was provocative and original. Such experimentation is bound to maintain vitality and lead, finally, to a success.

Another example was Douglas Seale's production of Max Frisch's *The Chinese Wall* for Center Stage in Baltimore. This play is very early Frisch and is embarrassingly modeled on Brecht. Its anti-bomb message is overwrought, simplistic and stale. But it is a play of great fun and imagination and Seale grasped its spirit, turning it into a stage circus, blasted through with music, irony and the gaudy colors of the carnival. It was pure show.

Far-left directors go even further with this, creating their own productions. Julian Beck and Judith Malina with the Living Theater, Joseph Chaikin with the Open Theater, Peter Brook with the Royal Shakespeare Company.

Of the sporadic left-wing plays that reach Broadway, the most consistent producer is David Merrick, who, from a theatrical point of view, is schizophrenic enough to qualify for commitment. Mr. Merrick produces under two auspices — the commercial, of course, and the nonprofit through the David Merrick Arts Foundation. If there are a few signs of left-wing–right-wing interaction in Broadway drama, it is Mr. Merrick's foundation that provides most of them.

On the right-wing side, Merrick typifies the conservative producer. His musicals are seldom adventurous — you will find only *Gypsy* embodying any innovations. His comedies are always the most manufactured, the least inspired, specifically geared for right-wing consumption. As for dramas, he will seldom present a play on a commercial basis.

On the left, his foundation specializes in serious, original, artistic and *imported* dramas (the importing is in part a bet-hedging, relying on European productions as tests, and partly a reflection of the paucity of polished, valuable, original American plays). They may not always succeed in what they attempt, but they are given first-class productions. Without him, most of these plays would never even be produced on Broadway. Among the Merrick Foundation productions were the revival of Brecht's *Arturo Ui,* the plays of John Osborne, Peter Weiss's *Marat/Sade* and Tom Stoddard's *Rosencrantz and Guildenstern Are Dead.*

Compare this with the work of Kermit Bloomgarden, a very left-inclined Broadway producer who always presented his plays under the regular profit system. Mr. Bloomgarden, a man with a genuine desire to present fresh, adult theater, hurtled into the wing division, and after futilely sponsoring left-wing plays for right-wing audiences, was virtually forced to abandon his activities.

Why can Merrick work the left wing on Broadway and not Bloomgarden, or other well-intentioned leftists? The most important reason is the foundation ploy. Merrick can afford to take risks since any losses are tax deductible; Bloomgarden and the others have to account to investors. There are other reasons: Merrick is a hard-nosed right-wing producer and the lessons he learns on the right are applied to the left. He will never kid himself. He will not be carried away with a play's artistic pretentions when it is perfectly obvious that the pretentions are unfulfilled. It is easy to become enthusiastic about a play that is really daring, but those enthusiasms cannot be allowed to overpower good theater judgment.

It is such judgment that Merrick uses in selecting plays for foundation production. Osborne's plays are bad commercial bets in a right-wing theater but they are good plays, important plays, plays that must be produced. Merrick — at least the foundation Merrick — has the sense of responsibility and the judgment to select and produce them.

A season-long episode in 1964-1965 provided another example of the left wing on Broadway. This was the experience of the Actors Studio Theater. Lee Strasberg had come to the conclusion that left-wing theater had to be reintroduced to Broadway and that he was the serious theater's savior. His taste, he decided, was artistic and his motives were indisputably pure. Figuring that it had a right-wing appeal in its big-name roster, the Studio decided that the time was ripe for it to function as a producing entity — something it had wanted to do for a long time.

Granted $250,000 by the Ford Foundation, which was matched with funds raised by Roger L. Stevens — a right-wing Broadway producer and later director of the right-wing National Council on the Arts — the Actors Studio Theater presented five plays. It is interesting to see the kinds of plays chosen and the manner in which they were produced, because this is a full-scale example of the naïveté of a left-wing producing agency.

The opening shot was a twenty-one-gun salute to the Studio roster, throwing some of its biggest names into a revival of Eugene O'Neill's *Strange Interlude:* Geraldine Page, Ben Gazzara, Pat Hingle and other box office people. The "all-star" production of the unwieldy drama was nonstaged by José Quintero, at that time the reigning O'Neill director, on his way downhill after a brief period of good work and great promise.

Although terribly old-fashioned, *Strange Interlude* was left wing for several reasons: first, because it was in oblivion despite being a major success in the career of America's major playwright; second, because it represented an innovation at the time it was produced (an innovation that was correctly rejected by the right wing). When the play was written, in 1925, O'Neill was impressed with psychiatry and forcibly superimposed it on his play. Because such a playwrighting mistake — patently overlaying a theory — is so crude, it is difficult to understand how it was swallowed at the time but in any case 1964 showed its devices of asides to reveal the character's thoughts as both dramatically and psychiatrically primitive. They were laughable — so laughable that Gazzara (most unprofessionally) could not resist breaking up each time he was called upon to follow such stage directions as: *"thinking uneasily,* 'Mustn't look at her . . . find an excuse to get away . . . and this time never come back!' "

From the point of view of 1964 right wing, *Strange Interlude* was backward. For the Actors Studio Theater's first production, it provided flamboyant roles for the big names and a stubborn, though predictable, public resistance.

The next production was James Baldwin's *Blues for Mr. Charlie.* Mr. Baldwin was the pride of the Studio's playwrighting unit. The hottest literary name at the moment, he was riding the best seller list, not for his fiction (which was presumably his métier) but for his essays on the Negro antagonism with American racial conditions. These essays, particularly *The Fire Next Time,* had come after the first major burst of organized Negro impatience — the sit-ins, the Freedom Riders, the flare-ups in Montgomery, Little Rock, Birmingham. For the first time, America was aware of the Negro and was frightened by him — could no longer pacify him with platitudes. Organizations — CORE, SNCC and the rest — sprouted daily, each outdoing the other in hate and militancy, which became the test of their popularity.

Baldwin had moved toward such extremism. Though inexperienced as a playwright (he had written *The Amen Corner,* a perfectly awful play, some years earlier), his celebrity gave him privilege.

Blues for Mr. Charlie was a mess. Badly organized, with some stretches of theater excitement, it was meant to say exactly what its title implied ("Mr. Charlie" being traditional Negro slang for the white man): the white race must be decimated. Producer Strasberg and director Burgess Meredith toned this down, making things even more confusing, since the play then seemed to lead up to a point that never materialized.

The AST's next production came soon after, with Strasberg apparently eager to spend as much money as quickly as he could. This was June Havoc's *Marathon '33,* a recollection of Depression-era marathon dances looking more like a two-hour Studio improvisation than a play.

Then, another new play, James Costigan's *Baby Want a Kiss,* an attempt by a basically right-wing playwright to do a comedy in the then novel and faddish surrealist style. Mistaking the outer look of Ionesco for the whole, and not knowing how to use the style in any case, Costigan wrote a ridiculous and hopelessly boring play. As things happened, it became AST's only commercial success because of its movie star (Paul Newman and Joanne Woodward) drawing cards.

The final Studio Broadway production was a revival of *The*

Three Sisters, giving Strasberg his first chance to direct since 1951. It proved that he *did* have a talent and that he really understood Stanislavski. Chekhov, however, as any right-wing producer could have told Strasberg, is a Broadway loser. Chekhov folded.

AST also produced a brilliant comic opera off-Broadway called *Dynamite Tonite,* and it will be discussed in a later chapter. All that need be said about it for the moment is that it received a hysterically violent pan from the right-wing critic for the *New York Times* and closed on opening night — an act of unforgivable cowardice on the part of the Studio (it would have been economically senseless to buck the press notices, but a *single-night* closing is an insult to a serious work).

What can be said of the Actors Studio Theater's strange season on Broadway? It displayed all the dangers inherent for a left-wing producer in the right-wing theater. The AST was stupid in spending its half-million dollars so quickly, stupid in not accurately gauging Broadway economics, stupid in not realizing that the only possible chance for left-wing theater to survive financially would be through repertory. It was, finally, stupid in losing all objectivity in selecting plays.

Yet, what must be made of these five plays is that they represented genuine left-wing theater on Broadway at the time. In every case, AST's productions were contrary to the right-wing rule. *Strange Interlude* was the kind of work that *should* have been revived — just as the lesser plays of any artistic playwright should be revived. America cannot continue to let its more serious plays die after initial Broadway runs.

Blues for Mr. Charlie attempted new things with time and music, and its point, after all, *was* strong stuff. The stylistic novelties of *Baby Want a Kiss* have already been mentioned, and a revival of *The Three Sisters* is hardly the sort of thing for which New York right-wing producers are noted. *Dynamite Tonite* was the most left-wing of all, as well as the most exciting, despite its derivation from such plays as Brecht's *Mother Courage,* Hasek's *The Good Soldier Schweik* and Green-Weill's *Johnny Johnson.*

All five of the AST productions qualified as left wing. They were the kind of theater that the right wing steadfastly refuses to produce. And they qualified on another level. In every case, they represented a special and left-wing attitude toward the theater, an attitude of stage vitality: that magic comes first. Especially in the case of *Marathon '33*, the AST productions were involved in the happening of a theater event. They were original — not simply "plays" — comedies or dramas. They were involved with stage life: the creation of a whole new world in a theater, the putting of life there, the making of a show. The curtain would rise to transport the theatergoer not to just around the corner or into a familiar living room, but into somewhere dreamed up by somebody with a vision.

The Studio season also managed to demonstrate the severe limitations as well as the qualities of its members, revealing these with especial fairness because the plays, after all, were chosen by the Studio itself. The method was never displayed better than in *The Three Sisters,* a play written especially for the Moscow Art Theater and its Stanislavski system. The Studio concentration on Stanislavskian "inner truth" had its greatest opportunity for expression here and Strasberg capitalized upon it. His direction was all inclusive, according to Stanislavski's instructions, from a sense of ultimate power. Every phase of the production was controlled.

Furthermore, the "reality" that is the aim of the Studio style found its ultimate applicability in the Chekhov style, just as the Moscow Art Theater had found sixty years earlier. This was perfectly logical, since the Stanislavski system was bound up with Chekhov's playwrighting and *The Three Sisters* was indeed commissioned by him and MAT. Moreover, of all the Chekhov plays, none is more concerned with "inner beingness" than *The Three Sisters*. It is, after all, *about the thoughts* of its characters. Their thoughts are its *plot*. So if the art of this great playwright was rooted in basic psychology, it could find no better expression than in an acting school devoted to precisely the same "science." The Studio's was the finest Chekhov seen in New York since the Second World War — finer even than *The Three Sisters* done by a decaying Moscow Art Theater in 1965 during a season at the New York City Center. For sheer "reality" — sunlight streaming through gauzy windows, flowers fluttering in the breeze, a real group of real people at a real party, it was incomparable.

The Studio's other productions were not so Method oriented and so the performances faltered. Geraldine Page's personal intensity was marvelously effective as performance, if not acting, in *Strange Interlude*. Newman and Woodward revealed a major Studio weakness — comedy playing — in *Baby Want a Kiss* (although Woodward was substantially superior to Newman). *Marathon* was a completely unactable nonplay and the company merely improvised it. *Mr. Charlie* exemplified the Studio's school of self acting rather than character acting. Rip Torn played Rip Torn, Pat Hingle played Pat Hingle, and so on. *Dynamite Tonite* was largely played by non-Studio people and so is not applicable. Only *The Three Sisters* displayed any genuine acting and the entire company was superb.

Whatever the problems, the Actors Studio episode on Broadway represented left-wing theater that was predictably doomed to failure because of the hostility of the entrenched right wing.

Insofar as Broadway comedy is concerned, the left wing is so alienated — so disgusted with the fake sophistication that the right wing grinds out — that it is inoperative (the only exception that comes to mind is Murray Schisgal's *Luv*). Left-wing playwrights, by and large, dismiss the comedy-as-such as a theater for hacks despite the artistic tradition that began with Plautus and Aristophanes. The oddest thing about this left-wing abandonment of the comic form per se is that it came at a time when all comic hell was breaking loose throughout the country. The fresh intelligence of postwar America, out of which the present left wing springs, has been roaring itself silly over the endless absurdities in political, social and intellectual life. Reactive intelligence is bound to be expressed in scornful high spirits and this humor is displayed wherever serious people gather. But while America has been on a giddy, bright, wacky and critical laughing jag of the most unholy proportions, its dramatists have kept their intelligent fun off the stage.

When you consider the humor in the novels of Nabokov, Beckett, Nathanael West and, to a lesser degree, Heller, Friedman and Donleavy; in the Beatles movies; the comedians like Peter Sellers and Jonathan Winters and the late Lenny Bruce, you realize the virtual absence of grown-up humor on the stage.

Postwar American humor is new *in kind* and widespread. It is not limited to intellectuals but is part of the brightness afoot. Its fun is with the worst of popular culture — the phenomenon of camp that breezed through mid-Sixties America was but a single example of the humor that lighted up a growing country with a fresh instinct for the ridiculous. We had turned clever (not just word-witty but idea-witty), and a mocking, nitwit, irrational fun was everywhere. Except in the theater.

The only consistent theatrical left- right-wing relationship on today's Broadway is in the musicals. It is there despite the near-total ignorance of them by the left-wing audiences, which persist in dismissing the form as essentially and incorrigibly right wing.

The first of the new interwing musicals was Leonard Bernstein's *West Side Story*. From that point began a series of exciting productions which followed the theory of production theater. Instead of a story proceeding with regular interruptions for a dance, a song, a production number, constructed according to the old standards of musical staging, the work developed as an entity. Music never began or ended, dances were not separate "numbers." Instead, all movement was choreographic and music was continuous, winding in and out of the dialogue. The piece was a self-enclosed ball, all elements relating to and emanating from its core. It moved and spread, like a flowing stream. And most significant of all, it involved sophisticated composers and choreographers. The hack tune-smith, the song-and-dance director were through. The deep excitement available only through musical technique was finally applied to the theater and the song was over.

The memory of the traditional musical comedy lingered on. Its grand, no-business-like-show-business tradition was too strong, too good a kind of theater to just disappear and it deserved a respectful phasing out. It had provided years of fun and, like any right-wing body, did the polishing that made the theater ready for the next innovation. But while its Tin Pan Alley composers were still writing stock AABA, thirty-two-measure songs for the bulk of the right-wing musicals, there were limitless, free-as-creation areas for the educated composer applying training and talent to the theater needs of the new musicals.

It is because these new musicals are benefiting from right-wing influence that their development has been so smooth. Perhaps in no other theater form is Broadway craftsmanship so evident. The supporting creative people such as arrangers and orchestrators, dance music composers, choral arrangers and musicians are superb professionals. Scenic designers are accomplished artist-engineers, conceiving complicated combinations that swivel and flash with computerlike efficiency. To watch a Broadway musical unfold is to see a large group of people doing assorted, demanding jobs, each requiring a different set of technical educations, and doing them all with instant coordination. When you realize that these teams must synchronize eight times weekly, you begin to understand the formidable proficiency they require.

The combination of this proficiency with artistic imagination and fresh theater ideas is what moved the left-wing musical innovations into the stream of progress.

There would be no sense in pretending that this new musical theater has already dominated Broadway. It has taken a firm hold, but the vast majority of the musicals remain right wing — smooth and occasionally very entertaining, but constructed according to old schemes. There is a "book" — that is, a play or story as such, into which songs and dances are interpolated. These are fitted for scenic needs — there are only so many major sets you can have, only so much time to change them. Small, slide-on wagon sets are used for small, slide-on numbers. The big dances are only beginning to get out of the nightmare or dream ballet rut (nightmare means the lighting is basically green and dream means it is basically yellow — otherwise the choreography remains the same). Of these old-fashioned musicals, most are worthless, thrown together in a haphazard confusion that multiplies with out-of-town trouble. The professionals keep it all very sleek and shiny but the shows invariably emerge as rubble heaps with Lucite coatings.

Off-Broadway, once the home of the left wing, still has its reputation for the adventurous, but with little justification. It is far from being the right-wing capital that Broadway is, and while one can still see productions of significant and forgotten plays of the past (Brecht's *Baal*, Dylan Thomas's *Under Milk Wood*, Wedekind's *The Awakening of Spring*, Webster's *The White Devil*), such productions have become more and more rare. Ironically, off-Broadway is without left-wing comic influence and its regard for musicals is as self-blinded as most theater intellectuals'.

Furthermore, the once-strong left-wing dramatic influence that provoked the production there of the important contemporary playwrights — Genet, Ionesco, Pinter and, most of all, Beckett — has dissipated. It was the left-wing influence of off-Broadway's *The Threepenny Opera* in the Fifties that pushed Brecht into his present acceptability, but that influence has waned. Ionesco and Genet, who were receiving regular off-Broadway productions in the halcyon years prior to 1963, are no longer seen. Beckett (and we) are fortunate in having the producing combine of Barr, Wilder and Albee presenting all of his plays.

An obligation that off-Broadway should fulfill but doesn't is in the revival of American plays. The new American play is produced, runs and is closed, never to be seen again. This is an absurd system. There may be no reason to reproduce a weak new play, but when a provocative or unusual one is given a poor production, it should be tried again. And when it is done well, there is all the more reason for reproducing it, especially if it can be done another way (if it is good, it *should* suggest varying approaches). Only Barr, Wilder and Albee have attempted revivals in any systematic way, regularly reproducing Beckett and Albee.

It is preposterous, of course, to classify Albee with Beckett, and Albee would most likely be the first to admit it. Still, he is a serious playwright and his work cannot be "folded" as if it were a summer stock comedy. It must be kept alive and for it to be kept alive it must be performed. So long as the right wing dominates our theater, this cannot happen.

Albee, Wilder and Barr are very much alone in this enterprise — as alone as they are in the promotion of experimental drama. Renting the little Cherry Lane Theater, they made a solitary left-wing stand. Between their own productions, they first presented a repertory season of surrealist plays. They supported workshop productions of left-wing playwrights whom they had been encouraging in their own playwrights' unit. It was an expensive effort and a thankless one, but it was ideal left-wing behavior.

Perhaps commercial producers cannot be expected to donate

their profits to theater needs — Barr, Wilder and Albee are willing to invest in the theater's future out of sheer dedication, but should such dedication be asked of a private producer? Perhaps, but why aren't the resident theaters doing such work? Could they be looking for the same drawing cards as the commercial theater?

This is part of a continuous, self-defeating reasoning. By accepting the proposition that "audiences would not be interested," such theaters justify the "economic necessity" for producing plays with "broader appeal" and provide no reason for a left-wing audience to come, which in turn substantiates their theory that there is no left-wing audience at all. The theater must lead taste, not follow it.

One of the few places you will find such leadership is the American Place Theater, which began operations in 1964, with the tremendous assistance of Ford and Rockefeller foundation grants.

Things didn't look so promising in the beginning, with the organization of APT under what seemed a very illogical premise: it meant to encourage playwrighting by nonplaywrights — an intention having the neatly groomed look of organized culture. Where was the sense in producing plays by novelists, poets and sociologists?

Instead of a theater devoted to dilettante approaches toward developing American drama, New York needed a place where left-wing playwrights — people who had already committed themselves to the theater — could further develop. Playwrighting is not merely another literary form, to be tried by anybody who can write even a good novel. It requires special technique, special interests, special sensibilities. A man is a poet, a novelist, an essayist, a short story writer. Each demands its own form, its own disciplines, its own dedication, its own talent. APT was promising subscription audiences, free of critic pressures, but to whom was it promising these audiences? And for what?

Wynn Handman (artistic director) and Sidney Lanier (producer) organized the American Place Theater to present the serious, original, left-wing plays that were not being produced in New York, on- or off-Broadway. Believing that the then current writers for the theater were of little talent, they decided to encourage the participation of writers who had already proved themselves artistically respectable in other fields. Their idea was to transfuse talent to the theater and to encourage writers by producing them, even when their work was admittedly flawed.

The theater place that they made was a *writer's* theater. This was entirely against the modern theater's grain. American theater, particularly the resident theater, has been moving away from the play as the *written word* and toward the play as a *production*. This has diminished the role of the playwright. APT's devotion to the writer went directly counter to the left-wing trend.

Mr. Handman insisted upon respect for the playwright. He believed that the author must have a theater that produces his play as he visualized it. If that proved impracticable, APT would compromise, but always leaning toward the *playwright's* concept. In general, APT decides playwright-director disputes in favor of the writer, and directors are chosen with an eye toward their general compatibility with him.

I find this a conservative attitude but I appreciate it. I think, too, that every trend needs countermovements to provide balance. The plays that APT has produced, while indeed tending toward the literary, have by no means been untheatrical. In fact, APT shattered such fears with its very first production, Robert Lowell's *The Old Glory*.

The Old Glory was comprised of three plays based on short stories by Nathaniel Hawthorne and Herman Melville. Because of overlength, one of them (*Endicott and the Red Cross,* based on the Hawthorne story) was dropped, and the program opened on November 1, 1964, with *My Kinsman, Major Molyneux,* based on the Hawthorne, and *Benito Cereno,* based on the Melville.

Molyneux was an artsy-craftsy exercise in graduate school neo-Genet — a mixed-up and generally unintelligible vision of colonial America dressed up in irrelevant, surreal clothes. *Cereno* was a slightly overwritten but stunning play, building a shattering dramatic climax from a clear insight into American intellectual and racial history. It was a marvelous example of original left-wing orientation blended with right-wing professionalism of production and direction (by Jonathan Miller). The critical pattern is really so predictable; the rightists rejected it, the leftists overpraised it. (*Benito Cereno,* incidentally, was turned down by every major New York producer, including the Repertory Theater of Lincoln

Center. That should be a fair enough indication of New York's right-wing orientation. The play has since been produced by several resident theaters.)

APT's second production, like the first, seemed a tacit recognition of the illogic in seeking first-class, fresh plays from nonplaywrights. For while APT was presenting staged readings of works by novelists like Robert Penn Warren and Philip Roth, it appeared to recognize, *in the scripts themselves,* that the playable works were coming from writers experienced in and committed to the theater.

Ronald Ribman was a poet who dedicated himself to the theater. His first produced play, *Harry, Noon and Night,* was written in the surrealistic style that characterizes nearly every new-era drama. It was rooted in the broadened intelligence, genuine education, art and humanism that characterizes the postwar left wing. Like *The Old Glory,* it was given a guaranteed six-week run at APT's theater in St. Clement's Church. Like *The Old Glory,* it was subsequently moved off-Broadway following the six weeks. Like *The Old Glory* (although much more severely), it was rejected by the right-wing critics, although unlike it, it was also rejected by the left-wing critics. (I am sorry, but I cannot explain this according to the well-known, all-inclusive and generally formidable theory of the wings. The rejection by the left-wing critics was out of simple misjudgment.) *Harry, Noon and Night* was the best new American play produced anywhere in New York that year.

It was about an American painter gone unstable over a number of things — that the only painting he could do well was Norman Rockwell realism; that he failed to follow in his brother's air-force-pilot footsteps; and a variety of childhood problems only vaguely hinted at. But basically Harry, the painter, lost his mind (although not his intelligence) because he was fouling up his life and knew it. Young and just barely begun, he was through. Now his life had become constant mockery, half mad and half sardonic.

The play was arranged as a trio of scenes: first showing one variation on Harry's theme as he puts-on a stupid American soldier while envying his easy virility with a German prostitute; then another variation, mixed with lunatic humor, as Harry's roommate plays the lavish homosexual for the pilot-brother, now a superconventional but content civilian; and finally Harry's breakdown, coming in a final scene that mashed together the elements of the lost life in a grinding whirl of theatrical fury, lacing excitement with heartbreaking pity. It left open the question of whether Harry could survive his own tragedy — whether he could ever go home to be what he was — whatever he was — to a place where nothing dies and it is always summer.

This marvelous play was closed after two weeks.

APT opened its next (1965-1966) season with a play by William Alfred (again, no newcomer to the theater, although his adaptation of *Agamemnon* was, at that point, unproduced and he was teaching English literature at Harvard). *Hogan's Goat* was a play so incredibly dated that it appeared, for half of its first act, to be a parody of turn-of-the-century melodrama. For the second half of that act, I found myself tempted to give the playwright credit for precisely mimicking the look of late nineteenth-century American theater in order to produce the very *stage feeling* of the period. Unfortunately, the remainder of the play confirmed every fear: Alfred was truly, *nonchalantly* ingenuous — his clichés were innocent; his greased-moustache villains, reformer heroines, purple climaxes were all meant seriously. His play was a self-parody and he didn't know it.

Neither did the right-wing critics, and they predictably raved about this extreme right-wing play. (What was a right-wing play doing at APT? The only possible explanation was that it was *so* right wing that it had turned completely around, walked behind the scenery and come out the other side as left.)

Alfred's gushy, flatulant imagery was hailed as poetry and his Irish American barroom reminiscences and shamrock-Catskill sentimentality were taken as historical reflection. *Hogan's Goat* was a smashing right-wing success, going on to enjoy a long off-Broadway run.

Newness returned to APT with *Jonah,* a play by Paul Goodman, the sociologist, city planner, novelist, dramatist and professional left-winger. There is no sense belaboring the point. *Jonah* was impossible, a playing of the Old Testament story in Jewish dialect, directed in the giggling faggot style developed by Lawrence Kornfeld at the far-left Judson Poets Theater. It was also shabbily constructed, hooking music and dance into a script that provided no

hooks, much in the same manner as a right-wing Broadway musical. The entire business was effete, amateurish as only the far left
can be, and terrible (to give you an example of pure leftism, Goodman insisted on amateurism as an *aesthetic*).

APT's next production, however, once more proved its importance, and the left-wing sense of Mr. Handman. Ribman's second
play, *The Journey of the Fifth Horse,* demonstrated the tremendous talent that had been at work in *Harry, Noon and Night.* Again
the fresh qualities that lie at the core of left-wing playwrighting
provided theater in the new style. Again there was the foundation
of language sensitivity and an awareness of classical dramatic construction. Again there was the electric current of stage vitality. And
again there was the philosophical point of view that ran through
Harry — the sensitivity to human vulnerability.

The Journey of the Fifth Horse was drawn from Ivan Turgenev's
Diary of a Superfluous Man, a mediocre novella primarily notable
for introducing into Russian literature a character type that would
be subsequently developed with greater artistry by greater writers:
the antihero.

But Ribman used Turgenev only for the inspiration. The original
novella was the diary of a man who died of ineffectuality and loneliness; a man who so desperately needed to be needed that he
forced himself upon people. His vulnerability was self-defeating.
Ribman introduced a publishing house where the chief reader had
precisely the same ache (really Harry's ache, in its own way). The
reader, however, was one step more neurotic than Turgenev's superfluous man. He masked his sadness with cruelty and sarcasm, a
defense mechanism against rejection.

Journey of the Fifth Horse had the reader's life parallel the diarist's, one happening upstage on a rise, the other downstage and
below. It was geared as an imagination-hallucination of the reader,
with the people in his own life drawn parallel to those in the diarist's. And at the very end, as the diarist reaches out a hand to the
reader — his partner-in-tragedy — he is refused. The reader, so
wretched from rejection, is afraid to love even himself.

In a sense, *Journey of the Fifth Horse* was not so complete as
Harry, Noon and Night, although it had a similar beauty and
power. The second play was much more ambitious and the com-

plexity of its construction provoked staging problems which Ribman was not quite ready to solve. Still, it too was the finest new American play of its season. It proved beyond question that Ribman was well into his own bright future. It is a future that is our own theater's.

The overall value of APT lies not so much in the plays it has produced as in its influence as an interwing element. It is finding the audiences who will support the serious theater of tomorrow — it is providing them with a theater on their level. And because Lanier and Handman are in the lovely position of being able to choose the best of the left-wing plays (since the right-dominated theater ignores them), it will be their own fault if they do not succeed. They have in fact been succeeding quite well.

Another aspect of today's left-wing theater is the Negro — as actor, as playwright, as thematic force and as the controller of "Negro theater."

The Negro actor's problems in American theater have been too well documented to demand elaboration here. While the arts have traditionally been liberal, the Negro actor was limited to playing the roles he played outside of the theater: the menial, the servant, the fool, the illiterate and so on. Occasionally, a well-meaning playwright would write a play "about" the Negro, but it was usually condescending and smug: standard liberalism.

The new intellectualism of today's left wing is riding the tide of sense that rose up against the old bigoted traditions to demand fair, color-blind casting in the theater. Unfortunately, the tide is rising only to fall back and leave right-wing ignorance a little damp but still dominant. Broadway producers and directors are left inclined "personally, but how far can I go?" We have the token Negro in the chorus, along with his obligatory Negro partner. There are Negroes in non "Negro" roles — lawyers, businessmen, etc. — but it is all very minor. The few Negro actors (such as James Earle Jones and Roscoe Lee Browne) who have developed despite the restrictions are still hard pressed to find regular work in New York, but at least they are hopeful — unlike their predecessors, who had left disgustedly for Europe.

One of the first instances of genuinely race-ignorant casting on Broadway was for a mildly amusing right-wing comedy by Bill

Manhoff called *The Owl and the Pussycat,* a two-character love story. Diana Sands, a Negro and an excellent performer, was cast as the girl, opposite Alan Alda, who was (and remains) white.

That the producer of this play beat his breast over his own broadmindedness was evidence enough of our continuing inability to confront racial issues with relaxed objectivity. More interestingly, the play displayed the problems that will ensue when a theater allows irrelevant considerations (such as determined liberalism) to interfere with its own artistic needs.

The problem in *The Owl and the Pussycat* lay in its refusal to make any mention of the fact that the girl was a Negro. In this way, a fundamental need of the play's realistic genre was completely disregarded, for as soon as the curtain rose it was apparent that Miss Sands was colored, Mr. Alda was white and, presumably, that difference was related to the play. When the couple argued (their bitter arguments were a major part of the story) without racial references, the audience could not help but anticipate a racial slur. It is impossible to imagine a genuine battle between a Negro and a white without mention of race, and if the playwright or director refuses to raise the issue, the audience's mind, conditioned by prejudice, will include it for itself. A self-styled liberal once told me that the girl's race *was* recognized in *The Owl and the Pussycat* when the boy called her "an animal." One might argue that this is the *audience's* problem and not the playwright's, but it is a theater-defeating argument.

Now as it happens, *The Owl and the Pussycat* was not written to be interracially cast — it had nothing to do with race. Without reflection upon the playwright, it was undoubtedly written with white players in mind (and the actress originally announced for the girl's role *was* white). But in refusing to make even a passing reference to Miss Sands's color — a reference that would have cleared the audience's mind, intellectually if not emotionally, of the color difference — *The Owl and the Pussycat* emerged as a play with something missing, as if it had been cut during tryouts with no adjustment of references to the deleted material.

The problem in this play (in the racial respect) lay in the ignoring of the theater's need to keep a realistic story realistic. The reference to color was left out because of the insistence of either the author or the producer upon proving that "race makes no differ-ence." This is naïve. The theater is no place to project personal — and worse, platitudinous — convictions unrelated to the work it-self. *Of course* there could be a love story between a Negro girl and a white boy. *Of course* a play written about a nondescript couple could be interracially cast. But there is no sense in refusing to make mention of it, even in a passing remark. Anybody would notice color except somebody absurdly *refusing* to notice, as if noticing was in itself "wrong." What is more noticeable than color?

Such is the problem when a left-wing idea (the reform of casting bias) is being impressed upon the right wing — it takes a long time for it to be properly and naturally understood.

In the right wing of Broadway, the Negro actor is only beginning to be hired as just an actor. He is still the Negro playing the Negro. It will take the development of a great deal of sense before he will be accepted simply as another professional.

On the other hand, Negro actors face fewer problems working the classical literature. The theater adjusts to this naturally. A pe-riod play takes an audience an extra step away from reality and allows a greater freedom in casting. Period costumes and classical styles help an audience accept what it rejects in the contemporary. After a while, an actor's complexion is forgotten, at least if the production is working, and a Negro Cordelia, for example, can manage quite nicely without an explanation of how a white Lear happened to father her.

The artistic directors of the theaters that produce classical drama — the resident theaters — being left wing in social and moral as well as theatrical matters, have realized this and pro-ceeded to correct the injustices of the past. They are far ahead of right-wing theater in the employment of Negro actors. Unfortu-nately, however, their eagerness to right wrongs has led them, in many cases, to relax their already slack acting requirements. Inade-quately trained Negro actors are often given work when they would be quickly rejected if they were white. This is an insulting favoritism.

Particularly, many Negro actors have never taken the trouble to rid themselves of accents. In the production of *The Changeling* by the Repertory Theater of Lincoln Center, a supporting actor rang out the Middleton-Rowley Jacobean English in unmistakably Ja-

maican dialect. Joseph Papp, whose New York Shakespeare Festival has done so much to train actors, and who has higher standards
than most artistic directors, will hire Negro actors with thick
Southern accents when he would not even consider a white actor
who had such problems. If well-meaning directors relax qualifica-
tions for Negro actors, the actors will suffer. They are also insulted
by measurement against lower standards.

The major Negro-related left-wing theater has come to be called
"Negro theater." This must not be confused with the folk theater
that can be found in Pigmeat's skits at the Apollo Theater on 125th
Street in Harlem or in the plays of Langston Hughes. It is the new
Negro theater of change, born of and afire with the drive of the mid-
twentieth-century Negro revolution.

Although Genet's *The Blacks* seemed to begin this Negro theater, a white playwright could never really be classified as a part of
it. It is impossible to feel Negro if you are not Negro. The movement really began with Lorraine Hansberry's *A Raisin in the Sun*
(though it is basically a right-wing play) and Ossie Davis's *Purlie
Victorious.*

There was little craft but great intensity in this left-wing movement, fueled by the outdo-each-other extremism of groups that
were exploding the Negro community. As the excesses of the Black
Muslims, Mohammed X and the Lenox Avenue violence mongers
were stretched to appeal to the most vulnerable instincts of frustrated Negroes, Baldwin and then LeRoi Jones wrote plays to
match. Hatred was the instinctive reaction to white maltreatment
and hatred appealed to playwrights looking for gut art.

If *The Blacks* painted this hatred in the poetry of a grotesque
Negro requiem for the white race, *Blues for Mr. Charlie* and the
later Jones plays used it in the simpler styles of simpler minds:
outright murder and overblown philosophizing.

Jones's first produced play was *Dutchman,* which opened on
March 25, 1964, at the Cherry Lane Theater. Written in self-
defeating fury (whether real or worked up), it was a dull and
sloppy work, relying on a stock climax (a murder) for most of its
drama. It was about a vicious slut who alternately entices and
taunts a well-dressed, well-spoken, would-be white Negro. Finally,

she murders him as, according to Jones, the white race will murder any Negro who would be white.

This playlet was warmly received by the right-wing critics, its message appearing neatly liberal (they missed its bloody implications in their eagerness to be tolerant) and its surrealism was mild enough for low-level comprehension. Six months later they were horrified by what was basically the same message, much more apparent in Jones's pair of one-acters, *The Toilet* and *The Slave.* These were no worse than *Dutchman,* and presumably the critic who liked the one should have liked the others. But suddenly the point was spelled out — Jones was out for blood.

The Toilet, written before *Dutchman,* was the better play. Set before the urinals of a Harlem high school washroom, it was about a group of Negro adolescents preparing to punish a Puerto Rican student for having made homosexual propositions to their leader. Leo Garen staged it choreographically, working wonders with verbal and physical rhythms. When it was done, the Puerto Rican boy was beaten and bloody, his head cradled in the arms of the Negro leader. For Jones, Negroes and Puerto Ricans were natural brothers and belonged together in their joint battle against the white race.

The Slave was less involved with the tools of the theater. It was a wishfully intellectual exercise, dressed in ludicrous dialectics. In attempting to philosophically justify a racial vendetta, it was only an exhibition of sloppy rhetoric.

The Toilet and *The Slave* were rejected by the right-wing critics not on the basis of their theatrical worth but because of their themes and language. *The Toilet* was written in the legitimate vernacular of the high school washroom, matching the graffiti on the wall, four-letter word for four-letter word, and enriched by a true poet's ear for word values and rhythms. For the right-wing critic, it was "filth." Never-in-my-life-have-I-heard-such-language, and so on.

The Slave was berated for its point, rather than for its dullness. As a matter of fact, while its message was wildly left wing, calling for annihilation of the white race, its delivery was in the straight, old-fashioned style of right-wing reform drama.

Jones has very little talent for the stage. Whatever power there was in *The Toilet* (and there was a great deal of it) was as much the director's as the playwright's. The crudeness of construction could be corrected only by concentrated study and practice, and Jones was too carried away with his missionary zeal for that. The pity was that his own true intelligence had stumbled over a familiar artistic perversion — the vision of art in the primitive.

There was another curious left-wing aspect to the production of *The Toilet* and *The Slave*. In his obsession with the racial war, Jones stacked the St. Marks Playhouse opening-night audience with Negro youngsters. Rough youngsters. The only white people in the house were the critics. The playwright intended — as Brecht had intended — that his plays would drive the boys to attack the whites and start the revolution *on the spot*.

Aside from the viciousness of the plan and the condescension toward the youngsters, Jones had no basis for the conceit. His plays were too boring and anyway theatergoers — especially youthful ones — park their senses of reality with the ticket taker. If Brecht could not provoke audiences to action, Jones hardly could. (Be that as it may, a bottle flung at me on my way out of the theater must have attested to some small success on the author's part and I hereby credit him with it. I am also grateful for the bad aim.)

Jones subsequently took his talents to the Black Arts Theater, a subprofessional Harlem group dedicated to racial violence through the stage. This appeared as one of our rare instances of left-wing comedy when it turned out that President Johnson's war on poverty was financing Jones's war on whites. Worse (and funnier) still, it was financing Jones's dirty words, prompting poverty-war master Sargent Shriver to well-publicized outrage.

The Negro theater keeps in the left wing, with plays like Adrienne Kennedy's *Funny House of a Negro,* Edmund White's *Blue Boy in Black,* and Douglas Turner Ward's *Days of Absence.* They are all bitter, all out for blood, all reflecting the confused attitudes toward the racial conflict that are found in left-wing circles. These plays are usually surrealistic in style. In every sense — thematically, stylistically and in general crudeness of presentation — they are left wing.

An incidental left-wing aspect of Negro plays involves language. Until 1960, drama had been written in the stultified tongue of the right wing. This meant a fair approximation of everyday language, inclining away from the poetic (which was dismissed as "artificial") and toward the stage-realistic, as revolutionized by Ibsen. To be sure, some slang was allowed; in fact the average right-wing comedy would have been a scene shorter if each "son of a bitch" were deleted. But the language of the street was forbidden.

It is preposterous to deny a writer specific words. Words are his tools. Words are his choice. The natural reaction of the right-wing critic to street language is to accuse the writer of "trying to shock," but such an accusation is only a rationalization of the critic's discomfort and embarrassment. Such discomfort and embarrassment is the critic's problem and not the writer's. If an artificial environment has created taboos, the environment must be corrected. An art form must not be limited because of the backward traditions of right-wing morality.

Yet such traditions, such morality rule our theater. The right wing's violent resentment of the language in *Blues for Mr. Charlie* and, to a far greater extent, in *The Toilet,* indicates the extremity of the right-wing syndrome.

The introduction of street language seemed to come with the Negro theater left-wing movement because of the themes and milieus with which these playwrights were dealing. The sidewalk in any big city is cluttered with Anglo-Saxonisms, especially in slum areas. By the time you get to Harlem at least every other word is an obscenity and it would be silly for a play set there to avoid them. How silly this can become was exemplified by *West Side Story,* whose hoodlums sang Stephen Sondheim's ersatz-dirty lyrics ("When the spit hits the fan"; "Krup you!").

There is no need to defend *any* language in the theater. Nor is there any need to defend a playwright's right to use it. I cannot think of a single instance in which a left-wing playwright used it gratuitously. I would add the same for right-wing plays except that the "bastards" and "son of a bitches" in the comedies are largely unnecessary and should be minimized because they are such clichés.

Another left-wing change in theater language is toward clean, modern, poetic dialogue. Nowhere is this more beautifully displayed than in the work of Beckett. This is the language of music, the words flowing and bounding, the content woven between. Tennessee Williams remains left wing in this respect. It is also found in Pinter, whose every word is calculated for nuance, flow, meter and implication within the theater milieu.

Finally, there is the left-wing return to a tradition — the use of English for its richest, most adult purposes. Edward Albee is leading this movement in the United States, not yet master of the tongue but improving with each play. And John Osborne in England. Together they are picking up the threads of refined English that run through all of drama.

With the removal of the barrier to natural vulgarity on the one hand, and the growth in poetry and the return to refinement on the other, the left wing is working toward freeing an English language which the right wing had for too long smothered with staid, merely workable dialogue.

Left-wing disagreements range from literature to politics, from philosophy to popular music, from intermarriage to incest. The most prominent would be atheism, but perhaps atheism is in the right wing already, if covertly. Establishment religion in America is so entangled in hypocrisy that it is difficult to tell just what is pretense and what is honest. Atheism may very well be the modern American religion, but as far as appearances are concerned it must, I suppose, be categorized as the major plank in the left-wing philosophical platform. There is yet to be a right-wing drama with an underlying theme of atheism or an attack upon the frustrations and intellectual dishonesties involved with organized religion as well as the self-deceptions, evasions and easy solutions in private religion.

Oddly, there are also few dramas centering on the *greater* value of religion, and this is probably because American-style religion is more concerned with appearance, ritual and acceptance than it is with the varieties of holiness, morality and philosophy. When a right-wing drama is involved with religion, it is sentimental and related to social or cultural aspects of practice rather than to serious matters of devotion. It is difficult to recall a genuinely religious drama in New York. Only Graham Greene's *The Potting Shed* and

T. S. Eliot's *The Cocktail Party* come to mind. Such plays cannot hold a commercial candle to such establishment works as Robert Bolt's *A Man for All Seasons* or Archibald MacLeish's *J.B.* Pure religion is as left wing as atheism.

Left-wing morality is based on the ideal. It demands truth, honesty, purity, and at the same time will overlook any human failing except hypocrisy (a definite small-mindedness, and I mean that, on its part). While demanding charity and responsibility in social areas, it insists upon selfishness and egoism in the personal, managing to be anarchistic and communistic simultaneously. Such contradictions are inherent to the left wing, botherless since it is blithely without the rationality and wisdom of the right wing. It cannot live with the criminalities in establishment society and follows the revolutionary line that unconditionally accepts abortion and free love; it rejects capital punishment and restrictive divorce laws. It is ardently pacifistic and mortified by nuclear weaponry and military thinking. It has no patience for stupidity, materialism, cruelty, greed, overweight, bad teeth or right-wingers, nor for really thinking through any of these complex questions. It is eager for new horizons and new experiences: narcotics, hallucinogens, opiates, barbiturates, marijuana and banana skins. Typically, the left wing is interested in the immediate rather than the deferred joy.

The left wing is oblivious to — contemptuous of — the ordinary relationships that identify right-wing life: country, community, friends, family. I cannot think of a single left-wing play that is involved with the family relationship as a blood bond (except Pinter's *The Homecoming,* and there the bond was frightful). In fact, it is difficult to think of a left-wing play that even *includes* any family relationship, except in parody (Ionesco's *The Bald Soprano* or Albee's *The American Dream*).

As for marriage, the unhappy one is a theatrical staple, left *or* right wing. After all, what drama is there in contentment? The only difference between left- and right-wing plays with respect to marriage is that the right-wing play will keep the marriage bad for plot purposes and then patch things up for the happy ending, while the left-wing play will just keep the marriage bad.

In any case, left-wing moral structure is basically that of the young and the true, carrying with it the last word in modernity and the first in immaturity. It has in it the grain of tomorrow's truth and absolutely no fertilizer.

The left wing, comprised as it is of diverse rebels, can never be as consistent as the right. It is constantly rejecting, constantly proposing, constantly rejecting again. It is so busy finding imperfections that it has little time for cures. Its identity lies in antagonism rather than in defense or solution.

Its ruling concern is art. Any compromise is sellout and right wing. In this is the source of both its weakness and its strength. The left wing will not permit itself the easygoing, nice play. Modest theater is obviously more achievable than great theater and its pleasures would be foolishly dismissed. But without the drive to greatness, there would never *be* greatness. The left wing's progress may be stumbling, but its goal is absolute.

Its greatest weakness is in directors. It is the director who provides the smoothness of execution and draws the ease of performance that takes a production past the "professional" barrier. But as soon as directors develop to the point of being able to do this they usually move rightward. Seldom are they idealistic enough to remain with left-wing theater.

The only director with right-wing assurance who is staying with left-wing Broadway drama is Alan Schneider. Mr. Schneider has staged nearly every Beckett production in New York. He has staged all of Albee's Broadway plays. He directed Joe Orton's *Entertaining Mr. Sloane,* an exciting play that ran briefly on Broadway in the fall of 1965. Other Broadway left-wing directors come and go, usually discouraged by the inhospitality they find there. Tony Richardson remained awhile to stage Brecht's *Arturo Ui* and Tennessee Williams's *The Milk Train Doesn't Stop Here Anymore.* Michael Cacoyannis did *The Trojan Women* for the Circle in the Square, Terence McNally's *And Things That Go Bump in the Night* and John Whiting's *The Devils.* Cacoyannis is not a terribly talented director. Peter Brook manages to keep "clean" only by visiting occasionally to do such things as Dürrenmatt's *The Physicists* and coming in with the Royal Shakespeare Company now and then with left-oriented productions such as *King Lear* and *Marat/Sade.* Mike Nichols was hemmed in by his very success with right-wing comedies even while directing several left-wing plays (*The Knack, Luv*). José Quintero was waylaid by an apparently insoluble personal problem, moving not rightward but downward after doing brilliant work with O'Neill's *The Iceman Cometh* and *Long Day's Journey into Night.*

There is almost nobody left to direct the few left-wing plays that get to Broadway and as a result they are directed by right-wingers who invariably misunderstand and botch them (Joseph Anthony's direction of Saul Bellow's *The Last Analysis;* Fred Coe's direction of Jack Richardson's *Xmas in Las Vegas;* Peter Kass's direction of David Rayfiel's *Nathan Weinstein, Mystic, Connecticut*).

Ironically, there are a number of left-oriented directors fully capable of staging such plays. They have developed in the resident theaters. Relaxed by the varieties of classical theater, and with perspectives freshened by their work with different *kinds* of plays, they are alive and eager, inventive and knowledgeable. They include William Ball, America's finest director, and his American Conservatory Theater; Douglas Seale, who does anything from André Obey to Max Frisch at his Center Stage in Baltimore; Gordon Davidson, who nourished UCLA's Theater Group on high standards and art (and who was rewarded with a minor position when Theater Group was moved into the Los Angeles Center Theater Group complex); Stephen Porter and Mel Shapiro, who shuttle among resident theaters; Brook Jones of Cincinnati's Playhouse in The Park; Jacques Cartier, the talented and creative director of the Baltimore Stage Company; André Gregory, whose Theater of the Living Arts made Philadelphia's theater life amount to more than a diet of right-wing Broadway tryouts until he left; Edward Payson Call, the free-ranging associate director of the Minnesota Theater Company and later the American Conservatory Theater.

Any of these men could be called into New York for a left-wing play if the material, resources and conditions were artistic enough for their uncompromising standards.

Even more desirable would be an exchange of these directors among the resident theaters. In nearly every case, they initiate and spearhead their companies and then direct progressively fewer plays as they become more involved with administrative and producer chores. Their rooting in creative work should be regularly revitalized and there would be no better way for them to do it than to visit other companies and guest-direct. Too, as some of them develop special treatments of particular plays, they should stage them elsewhere. As conductors have their own interpretations of various composers (the Toscanini Beethoven, the Bruno Walter Mahler, the Szell Mozart), theater directors should have their own Pinter, their own O'Neill, their own Shakespeare.

The left-influenced musicals on Broadway are in much better directorial shape, befitting their healthier situation. That they demand choreographer-directors makes this all the more remarkable. Jerome Robbins, who brought these new musicals into their present, prized situation as the only interwing Broadway theater, is by far the ranking leader and the only director with the deep background in both ballet and theater necessary for ultimate musical theater development. Gower Champion is not so creative or artistic, and his understanding of the new form is limited, but he has a formidable ability for staging the most complex schemes so that they roll smooth and easy. Others just beginning to come into their own are Joe Layton and Peter Gennaro.

Among scenic designers, so many are eager to try the new that as a group they can be classified as interwing. However, too many are willing to grind out the hack if it is demanded and this removes them from uncompromising leftism. Perhaps only Rouben Ter-Arutunian, Boris Aronson, William and Jean Eckart, and Ming Cho Lee are leftists, and even the Eckarts, whose primary-colored, Mondriaan-like panels were once fresh, are settling down into repetitious ruts. Oliver Smith, who seems responsible for every last Broadway musical and a fair share of the comedies, is in an extraordinary position. He is without a doubt the supreme technician, able to achieve effects that belie the storage, mechanical and logistic complications involved. He can design sets of extraordinary artistry, utilizing the most advanced stage equipment. He will use simple, rollabout scenery if it best fits the situation — for example the stylized, lithographic sets in *Hello, Dolly!* Yet he will also design massive, vulgar sets for massive, vulgar musicals (like *Bajour, Sherry* or *The Girl Who Came to Supper*). Perhaps it depends upon his stable of assistants.

In any case, the scenic designers who work Broadway are un-

matched for sheer talent and technique, and they represent the
finest aspect of the right wing. When they are allowed to indulge
their left-wing tendencies they display a dazzling combination of
originality and polish.

Like left-wing directors, the left-wing actors are those who are in
the oldest, most traditional stream of classical performance. They
are in the left wing not because they are seeking innovation, but
because they are in the minority, because they represent something
that is not present in the right wing. Left-wing actors are estranged
because of the demand for *personality* actors by the right-wing
plays. Such "acting" is demeaning to them, insulting their equipment, just as the plays themselves insult their sense of the theater.
How they have managed to acquire their skills must be credited to
their own integrity and perseverance, for there have been no American repertory theaters for them to learn in. Many developed their
technique in English or Canadian repertory companies and the
handful of American resident theaters that existed before 1960.
Otherwise, their development is due to their own drive, seeking out
the broadest variety of character roles; eliminating their personal
characteristics; developing, solitarily, the tools of their art: diction,
physical control, intellectual discipline, familiarity with materials,
comprehension of the ways of the stage.

There are not many but they are there: Christopher Plummer,
certainly the finest actor in America and the only one capable of
handling the heroic roles in the dramatic literature; Michael O'Sullivan, who managed within the space of two seasons to give brilliant performances in diametrically opposing roles — the director
in Pirandello's *Six Characters in Search of an Author* (off-Broadway) and the title character in Molière's *Tartuffe* (at the Repertory
Theater of Lincoln Center); Lester Rawlins, an actor forced to
take workaday roles in workaday plays off-Broadway, who uses a
tremendous talent to make them rise beyond their own limitations.
And just beneath these, James Ray, Frank Langella, James Earle
Jones, Michael Higgins, Ed Flanders, Roscoe Lee Browne, Anthony Zerbe, J. D. Cannon, Douglas Watson, Patrick Hines, Jon
Voight, John Colicos. Left-wing actresses are rarer still — Rosemary Harris and Zoe Caldwell are the only American actresses of
any real stature, and Carrie Nye, while not in their class, is sub-

stantially accomplished. Except for a handful of actresses working the resident theaters, like Ellen Geer at ACT and Lois Smith in Philadelphia, there is nobody.

With the desperate lack of repertory companies to train such actors, where can these people receive their education? Schools and studios do not (and probably never can) provide it — acting can only be learned in performance. Plummer worked repertory theaters in Stratford, Ontario, in Edinburgh and in Stratford-on-Avon. O'Sullivan crisscrossed America for whatever serious theater groups he could find — the Ashland Shakespeare Festival, the San Francisco Actors Workshop, the Milwaukee Repertory Theater, the American Conservatory Theater. Rawlins came out of Washington's Arena Stage. Rosemary Harris played with England's Old Vic and was an organizer of the Association of Producing Artists. Zoe Caldwell played at Stratford-on-Avon and with the Minnesota Theater Company. Again and again, the training comes from repertory, where roles of every period, every size, every style are played regularly.

This is the only way for an actor to learn — in the prolonged playing, under expert direction, of varying roles in the dramatic literature. It is only in such acting that the art of becoming somebody else — of taking the playwright's part — of understanding the needs of the stage — can be acquired. An actor must develop his craft, his vocal instrument, his dramatic intelligence. He must *know* the plays, *know* the periods. He must have a repertoire of parts the way a pianist has a repertoire of concertos and sonatas. And most important of all, he must have the experience, the chance to act, changing roles regularly and playing heroes, buffoons, fools, grandfathers, adolescents, kings and peasants.

As for the American playwrights, except for Albee there is not a single man being regularly produced on major stages. Except for Schisgal, there is not a single man writing left-wing comedies. This is the extent of the right-wing domination of our theater. Whatever new left-wing theater comes to America is found in sporadic Broadway and off-Broadway incidents and, mostly, English imports.

Nevertheless, our revolution is beginning. Despite the general beating down that they receive from right-wing Broadway producers and directors and right-wing critics, the left-wing playwrights persist. David Rayfiel, Jack Richardson, Jack Gelber, Ronald Ribman, Arnold Weinstein, John White, Jean-Claude van Itallie, Lanford Wilson and a handful of others are developing their imaginative and thrusting talents despite the stupidity of the current schism. The Rockefeller Foundation is doing important work from a left-oriented vision that is wonderfully surprising. Some of the most talented young American playwrights, Ribman and Weinstein among them, have been given the grants necessary to continue their work. Who knows how they would have survived — or whether they would have persisted in playwrighting — without foundation assistance?

These playwrights, and the others preparing for our new theater, must keep writing. In them is the new. The tomorrow. And that is the essence of the left wing. It is our future and the theater's. But today that left wing is estranged and rejected, restricted from development and refused influence. The present cannot be real without a sense of both the past and the future. Our entrenched, established theater present has no touch, no sight, no sense of either.

CHAPTER FOUR

So Long Broadway

THE most significant left-wing influence on postwar American theater has come in an explosion of resident companies, theater-building, the development of modern artistic directors for them, and a frightening new force — the American Subsidy.

Perhaps the most accurate description of these theaters is that they are "outside of New York." Their attitudes, purposes, levels, accomplishments and makeup vary too greatly for any other. They have been called regional theaters, but the term is resented as being too reminiscent of the Thirties movement in community theater. They have been called repertory theaters, but that is inaccurate since only a fraction of them perform in repertory (generally speaking, the summer festivals play in repertory and the winter companies in series, giving a single production for four or six weeks and then replacing it with another).

There have been attempts to redefine "repertory theater" to cover this loose assemblage of diverse companies. These are attempts to capitalize on the magic of the term "repertory" since it has come to represent something indisputably good. But the term cannot be defined to suit particular wishes. Repertory means *the daily change of program* and that is the only thing it *can* mean.

I am sticky about this because I believe the repertory system to be necessary if a theater is to produce great plays, particularly unpopular ones, and is to establish a company capable of performing them well. With the repertory system, the number of weekly performances of a play can be varied according to box office demand. This provides the chance to produce a work that, if played for a four- or six-week period, just could not draw enough business to justify its expense. With the repertory system, the production of an avant-garde, obscure, forgotten or inconsistent play becomes economically feasible. The more commercial work can support the less commercial one.

The repertory system is also extremely helpful as an acting tool. The actor who plays different roles each night is given the opportunity to polish his skills at characterization and reap the benefits of variety. He plays in different periods, in different styles. He is no longer subject to the stultifying drone of performing the same part, night after night, eight performances a week. He can come back to a part with a fresh attitude, not having played it for two, three or four nights. The system also makes smaller roles more acceptable to the talented actor because he works with the knowledge that although tonight he may be Guildenstern, tomorrow he will be Woyzeck.

The repertory system also promotes *ensemble performance*. This is another theater catchphrase, abused and misconstrued. The company that is performing in ensemble is a company that is working as a team, interacting, weaving, blending. It is opposed, naturally, to a company that is working as a group of stars and bit players, unfamiliar with each other. The player who is working in ensemble is always speaking, reacting, moving in relation to his fellow players and to the production as a *whole,* and it is the production itself that is the guiding purpose of the individual's work.

Repertory is helpful for ensemble performance because it keeps an unchanging group of actors at work together for constant periods during which different plays in different styles are juggled. With such assorted challenges and a constant dependence upon teamwork, the actor learns to function as a member of an artistic *corps* rather than as a lone craftsman. And while the solo performer may seem more attractive and eye-catching, it is really the company performance that will present the most satisfying theater experiences. It is not my-goodness-what-an-actor! that we are after. It is my-goodness-what-a-company! And only after you have witnessed a company trained in ensemble work, such as England's National Theater or Royal Shakespeare Company; Canada's Stratford Shakespearean Festival; East Germany's Berliner Ensemble; or (to a lesser degree) William Ball's American Conservatory Theater and the APA — that the rich theater pleasures of group performance become apparent.

Finally, the repertory system provides extra benefits for the audience. The theatergoer who is not interested in a particular play need not stay away for the duration of its run. He will be quickly cured of an interest in stars, becoming more accustomed to a *company* and a *play,* and will finally settle into seeing *theater*.

If a term is desired to cover all resident theaters, something other than "repertory" will have to do, for the plain fact is that only a fraction of the theaters play in true rep.

"Resident theater" is as good as any. Unlike the commercial theater, which works on an individual production basis, hiring specific directors, actors and supportive creators for each work, these theaters have a permanent artistic director, a designer and an acting company of from eight to twenty or thirty. They and their theater are the city's and they are meant to be part of the cultural climate, I believe the expression is. Regarding "professionalism," most of the actors in the resident theaters across the country are not only Equity but reasonably capable and the physical productions — costumes, wigs, scenery, lighting — are generally craftsmanlike. So the *look* of the productions, from the point of view of technique, is polished enough to be considered professional.

While the resident theater is inherently left wing in its purpose, choice of plays and theatrical attitude, its growth has been so rapid and its dependence on subsidy so great that it has become part of a quasi-official establishment that threatens to mutilate it during its formative years.

After the movement into theater by the Ford Foundation in 1962, with grants totaling $6.1 million given to nine resident companies, this country jumped into subsidized theater on the giant and haphazard scale on which it seems to do everything. Joining the foundations were cultural centers, state governments, private citizens and, finally, the federal government, with the formation in 1965 of the National Council on the Arts. This totality — the American Subsidy — was the direct stimulus for the boom in resident theaters that started early in the Sixties. It also created a new kind of theater person — the artistic director who hustled the big-time subsidy circuit.

In city after city, theaters sprang up — sometimes organized by private groups, sometimes prompted by the municipal government, sometimes originated by a transient director. Large quantities of money were raised, a company was organized, a theater was fitted out (with a new and larger one promised soon). Then, with a board of trustees pledging to cover all *reasonable* deficits, the theater began — and generally on a very smooth level, presenting classic plays. It was instant institutional theater.

There were serious problems in this birth process and institutionalism was a crucial one. Institutions are official. They are prone to sterility. Involvement with a large organization prompts bureaucracy. Community stature causes creative obesity. There is a pressure to be inoffensive, an inclination to be sleek, proper and bland. A living theater begins to mummify and decay. There are other problems. For one thing, the artistic director becomes a local official and, beyond that, a supermodern fund raiser. He gets involved with school systems because student audiences are guaranteed customers. None of this has any place in creative professional theater.

There can be no greater loss to the artist than that of self-reliance. Once he becomes dependent upon outsiders, he can no longer be free. Healthy creation is creation from inner drive, unfettered by extrinsic influences. It must be for its own sake, for after all, art has always been an individual act, a personal expression. Artistic directors, driven to form their own resident theaters by the need to fulfill a personal expression, are threatening to become art bureaucrats at worst, or simply are diverted from the theater to administrative, official and financial chores. Whatever drive pushed them into resident theater is being subverted into administration, fund-raising and public-relations hustling.

Patronage has always provoked artistic troubles. While Europe's governmental subsidies descend from what was supposed to have been a golden time of aristocratic support for the arts, patrons were not the sensitive cultivators they are cracked up to have been. Michelangelo and Cellini were both pressured by the Church. How many artists were forced to paint idealized, absurdly costumed portraits of their patron saints? Bach had to write his *Goldberg Variations* because his sleepless patron thought that a different nightly variation would cure his insomnia. Countless composers were commissioned to write pieces to celebrate transient occasions (the Handel *Water Music* and *Fireworks Music* being the most famous instances). Mozart wrote many letters complaining bitterly about having to use talentless singers because they were patrons' favorites.

The governmental subsidy that evolved from European patronage proved relatively benign but unavoidably bureaucratic, as any government function will. Herbert von Karajan's troubles with the Austrian government led to his resignation as director of the Vienna State Opera.

Still, patrons in Europe, from royalty to government, were generally interested in satisfying their personal taste rather than in controlling the overall direction of art. This is because art was part of the cultural fabric, which is hardly the case in the United States, where the cultural fabric is as yet unwoven. Here, whether you are dealing with politicians or with massive foundations that form grandiosely muddled schemes for national cultural development, the sources of subsidy could not have been more clumsily devised.

The romance of the left-wing artistic directors with the right-wing American Subsidy apparatus that supports them makes the condition of our resident theaters a very peculiar one. Whether the directors will be pulled rightward into computer-age art or the subsidizers drawn leftward into the beginnings of an American artistic awareness remains to be seen. There seems little basis for optimism.

There are so many varieties of resident theater as to defy classification, but they have a primary trait in common: they are producing many of the great plays that lay dormant all the years we relied on Broadway for our theater. Broadway is dedicated to the new work. Its commercial identity all but precludes the revival of classics. The touring companies of its financial successes had provided virtually the only theater that existed in the United States. With the exciting spurt in education in the postwar years — with the emergence of the new intellectuals and their concomitant frustration with the existing right-wing theater — a number of young, left-oriented directors began emerging in search of a new theater: a theater where they could work with important plays and where they could make statements of their own.

In many cases, they were forced to look elsewhere by a Broadway theater that rejected new ideas and newcomers (or at least placed formidable odds against their breaking into New York theater). Others were just idealistic. They followed the trail forged by a small group of pioneers who set out, in 1954, to build a left wing.

At that time, Tyrone Guthrie was being convinced by Tom Patterson, a Canadian newspaperman, that an English-style summer Shakespeare festival was artistically and commercially feasible in a lonely, flat stretch of Canada about halfway between Toronto and Detroit.

The difference between the Stratford Shakespearean Festival with Guthrie and the small, classics-oriented theaters beginning around America could not have been greater. For people like Margo Jones in Dallas, Herbert Blau and Jules Irving in San Francisco, Nina Vance in Houston and Zelda Fichandler in Washington, the theater was hardly more than a dream held together by half-a-shoestring. They were desperate idealists willing to work for little more than satisfaction, with any actors available. For Guthrie, the theater would be a million-dollar house importing the very biggest English theater names, of whom Guthrie himself would be the first.

There were other differences. Guthrie's theater was to be strictly Shakespearean, strictly proper, strictly repertory, strictly professional. He was an experienced, respected, established director. The fledgling American resident theaters were run on ten parts drive to one part technique.

Nevertheless, they were left-wingers all. In their broadly divergent ways they were out to change the state of things, doing the plays that were not being done and doing them in ways untried.

From these two streams developed the resident movement that is streaking toward the powerful American right wing while being battered by the multitude of problems it has itself developed.

Individual resident companies may be identified as left or right wing despite the fact that the force that brought them all into being originated from the left. They have conservative or liberal tastes, directions, motivations and identities. For example, the Stratford, Connecticut, American Shakespeare Festival is very right wing and

the Living Theater was very left wing. In some cases the wing division exists within the structure of a resident theater, as in the clash
between a progressive director and a conservative board. There are
theaters designed as summer festivals, theaters designed as artistic
revolutions, theaters aligned with giant cultural centers.

It is ludicrous, therefore, to include a massive, wealthy theatrical
institution in the same "resident theater" classification as a struggling independent theater. It is impossible to compare the Broad-
way-slick professionalism of Stratford, Ontario, with the analytical
experimentation of the now-defunct Actors Workshop or Philadelphia's Theater of the Living Arts as it was under Gregory's direction. If there is any kind of a movement to which these theaters
belong, it is only a general trend leftward for varying reasons.

What must be remembered is that while the resident theater phenomenon seems to have been born full grown it is very, very new,
and for all of its impressive financial support its vitality is far from
proved. By 1967, while there were some thirty-five theaters operating, most of them were no more than five years old. Also, while
these theaters were producing important plays, their choices were
conservative, and left wing only because of the absurd extremity of
the Broadway orientation. A theater that is consistently doing
Shakespeare, Shaw and O'Neill (the general fare for most of these
companies) is hardly audacious. This is comparable to a symphony
orchestra programming only Brahms, Tchaikowsky and Beethoven. The comparison is apt, because the institutionalization of
these theaters is much like that of the symphony orchestras, whose
war-horse programs are directly due to the influence of their right-
wing boards of trustees. Like those of the orchestras, the theater
choices are classical but they are too safe and too repetitious.

Nothing really crass, mind you. There are a few companies that
revive *The Seven Year Itch* and *Harvey,* but such fluffy theater is
generally beneath their artistic dignity. The bulk of the plays lie in
midcultureland. The reason for the popularity of O'Neill, Shaw and
Shakespeare is obvious enough. O'Neill is America's guaranteed
great playwright and many of his plays are easy to take. *Ah!
Wilderness* is a good example. *The Iceman Cometh,* however, is
not done. *Long Day's Journey into Night* sometimes, but while this
frightful spilling of a playwright's blood is (with *Iceman*) one of

the two greatest O'Neill works, it can also be taken as a conventional enough family drama.

The Shaw is even more conventional and still easier to take: *The Devil's Disciple, Major Barbara,* and so on. Hardly anything to challenge an easygoing mind. Considering the mass of seldom if ever performed Shaw, it is dismaying to find only his most popular works performed.

But there is virtually no Lorca, Strindberg, O'Casey. Of Wilde, only (and continuously) *The Importance of Being Earnest.* Little Greek tragedy and barely any Büchner or Ghelderode. Of Pirandello, it is almost strictly *Six Characters in Search of an Author.* On the other hand, there are plenty of contemporary dramas, apparently to satisfy at one and the same time cultural yearnings and popular taste. Nearly all of Arthur Miller's plays are done and many of Tennessee Williams's. They are guaranteed box office. There are some productions of Albee's *Who's Afraid of Virginia Woolf?,* Kopit's *Oh Dad,* Osborne's *Luther.*

That is not to fault these plays. Many are worth reviving and American theater cannot continue as a place where plays have a Broadway run and die. But where are the new classics, the important plays of our age? Resident theaters have unjustifiably accepted a reputation for doing the dramas that are presumably "too artistic, too uncommercial for Broadway." Could it be that such plays are also too artistic and too uncommercial for resident theaters?

Brecht's name is usually thrown out as the basis for this reputation and his plays are certainly produced on the circuit. Unfortunately, they seem to be produced out of conformity. One season everybody may do *Mother Courage* and the next *Galileo.* Producing Brecht has become the easiest way for a resident theater to prove itself artistic and his currency is the most negotiable of any left-wing playwright today.

Samuel Beckett is just not produced except for a *Waiting for Godot* here and there, and an occasional *Endgame.* This is incredible. Beckett is one of the ultimate playwrights of this century. Pinter gets an occasional one-acter on a program with Ionesco to lip serve the theater of the absurd. But practically no Genet, Dürrenmatt or Frisch.

There are a few theaters more vital than the rest. The Theater

Company of Boston does Camus, Arden, Stein, Beckett; Baltimore's Center Stage does Pinter, Anouilh, Frisch, Behan, Obey, Pirandello; Lincoln Center does Büchner, Sartre, Brecht, Lorca. They are exceptions.

The programming is inhibited by right-wing forces in the shape of trustee pressure and director rationalizations that they are "training" their audiences. In general, the artistic directors of resident theaters are educated and serious people who have strong inclinations toward the artistic left. They are convinced, however, that their audiences will not come to left-wing productions, even though some of their more ambitious colleagues have proved otherwise. Whether trustee conservatism or director hedging is the cause of the middle-class programming, the result is invariably an older, safer, right-wing audience and an ever-strengthening resistance to the left. The longer a director keeps his theater away from left-wing productions, the more difficult it will be to ever lure back the audiences for them.

None of these right-wing influences, however, is in the category of the financial forces themselves. "American Subsidy" means those forces and the massive power behind them. To understand its influence, importance and frightful danger, one must first examine its beginnings.

Two events prompted those beginnings. The first was the passage of the Internal Revenue Act of 1954, which allowed tax deductions for contributions to nonprofit, educational institutions. It was this act that moved theaters to go nonprofit, elect a board of trustees and abandon forever the problems, responsibilities and freedoms implicit in self-support.

The other event was the first major foundation step into wholesale grants for theaters. Since 1957, the Ford Foundation had been giving grants to theater people for specific purposes — for playwrights to write works for particular resident theaters, for directors to work at particular theaters, and so on. In December of 1959, it gave its first bulk grants to resident theaters themselves: $559,000 divided among New York's Phoenix Theater, Houston's Alley Theater, Washington's Arena Stage and San Francisco's Actors Workshop. The grants were designed to "guarantee annual contracts of $200 a week for three years to a nucleus of ten actors in

each theater." But with the big $6.1 million bundle in 1962, Ford
moved out of specific-purpose grants and into full-scale help for the
resident theater itself. Henry T. Heald, president of the foundation,
said at the time, "Since its initial venture into the arts in 1957, the
foundation's assistance has been limited to talented individual artists and to experiments and demonstrations seeking new avenues
and standards. We are now carrying our program into a new dimension." So the grants were given for general, broad purposes,
described vaguely as designed "to help professional groups reach
and maintain new levels of artistic achievement and financial stability." With this step taken, the other, smaller subsidizers began to
follow suit: the Rockefeller Foundation and the soon-to-be-created
National Council on the Arts. Exit private theater. Enter public
theater.

Ford's 1962 grants ranged from $2.1 million for the Alley The-
ater to $100,000 for Fred Miller's Theater in Milwaukee. Other
recipients were the Minneapolis Theater Company, the Actors
Workshop, the Actors Studio Theater, the American Shakespeare
Festival and the Theater Group in Los Angeles.

The subsequent history of these grantees is curious. Fred Mil-
ler's Theater folded. The Actors Workshop lost Herbert Blau and
Jules Irving to Lincoln Center, and along with them most of its
Equity (though semiprofessional) actors; it finally collapsed (and
Blau, of course, subsequently resigned from Lincoln Center).
The Actors Studio Theater blew its $250,000 (and the other
$250,000 in matching funds) through disorganization, bad plan-
ning, foolish spending and poor judgment. The American Shakespeare Festival became even more of an artistic joke. The
Mummers Theater — an abysmally amateur, Bible-belted company — was not even able to use its funds for four or five years
because of difficulties getting land for a new theater (the premise of
its grant). Even more striking, Ford sent a young man named
David Lunney to work with the Mummers Theater on an administrative fellowship. While in Oklahoma City, Lunney studied the
area's potential for supporting a theater of the size the Mummers
meant to build. He found a crucially undersized population, but
more than that, a population of which about one-third was actually
discouraged from going to the theater by the Baptist Church. If

that wasn't odd enough, Ford never even bothered to ask his opinion and even granted Mummers an extra $535,000 in 1967.

However, the grants marked the beginning of Ford's involvement with American resident theater on a wholesale basis. Being
the largest of the foundations, it assumed the leading role, and
under its humanities and arts program, directed by W. McNeil
Lowry, it stepped up its activity, riding the attitude that the world
revolves about it. Amusing as this self-importance is, it carries with
it a frightening weapon — the means to shape, affect and control
the very direction of theater development. Soften that a bit — I
really don't think that this foundation, for all of its misguided good
intentions, can ultimately control progress. It is much too confused
and pompous, and civilization manages to survive anything. However I do think, despite its clumsiness, that Ford manages to help
somewhere, if only slightly. *Something* has to come out of all those
releases, all the talk, all that money. Doesn't it?

But Ford's involvement with resident theater is consuming and it
positively resents anybody else interfering with its baby.

In 1961, Ford created its most subtle and effective device for
influencing American resident theater: the Theater Communications Group. This was no longer the giving of funds to help an
independent theater while insisting that no strings were attached.
Ford had actually formed the organization itself and then granted
the funds to sustain it. TCG was given a four-year grant of $244,-
000 to "improve cooperation among professional, community, and
university theaters in the United States." While the ostensible aims
of the group were kept purposely vague, it was clear that TCG
would be a working part of American Subsidy. Mr. Lowry cited
examples of what TCG might do: "Community-theater directors
who want to 'go Equity' would be given funds to work and observe
at professional regional theaters that have already made the transi-
tion. Heads of university drama departments would be enabled to
find professional apprenticeships for their students. Producers and
directors seeking front-of-the-house or stage personnel would get a
chance to study community, summer-stock or academic theaters at
first hand. The most hopeful prospects will be brought together for
auditions in at least one center each year. Broadway directors, producers and actors will go out to reach the young people before they

are lost to view in New York or Los Angeles, and attempt to give them a more realistic idea of what the theatrical profession requires of them or holds for them."

In this plan for control over every aspect of American resident theater, from universities through producers, directors and actors, you might say that the Ford Foundation seemed to be mildly interested in having a slight effect upon it. Or, as Mr. Lowry put it, "In short, the Theater Communications Group will perform a variety of cooperative tasks, and the group's field director *will keep the whole of the American theatrical circuit under constant survey.*" (Italics mine, megalomania Ford's.) And to kick that home, before the four years of that first grant had transpired, Ford gave another $795,000 in 1964 on a five-year grant.

The value of TCG must not be denied. It really does provide a variety of extremely useful services. Directors are helped to see how other resident theaters are solving problems similar to their own. The auditions provide central clearinghouses for acting talent. The play-distribution service makes scripts available to all members (although this service is largely restricted to plays that have already been performed by one member and TCG, admittedly, is not doing much to move *new* plays through its members' hands). The organization's specialist in subscription drives and fund-raising — a man named Danny Newman — is a master of his science and has come through for many a theater whose subscribers had been defecting or whose supporters had grown lax.

But TCG, too, has all the faults of any purely administrative organization. It is cold and faceless. It tends toward the filable and the organized. Worse, it is bitchy and that is one of its more obvious reflections of the Ford Foundation that is pulling its strings. The organization will hold grudges against particular theaters and particular directors; it will withhold membership for reasons that are apparently arbitrary, quietly using its services as a lever for a theater's conformity to Ford policies. In 1967, it reduced its membership to thirteen theaters — thirteen Ford pets.

TCG is Ford's finger in the American resident theater pie. Through it, Ford can and does influence the intertheater movement of actors and directors, guide the administration and organization of theaters, even provoke the plays that are produced. Behind it,

and behind Mike Mabry, TCG's cool, efficient, noncommittal field
director, looms the cool, efficient Ford Foundation. This is how
Ford itself considers its theater role:

"Between the establishment of the Ford Foundation Program in
Humanities and the Arts in 1957 and the kick-off of the Guthrie
[Minneapolis Theater Company] in 1963, the Ford Foundation
served as the focus of experiment for what the critics and drama
reporters now call — but we do not — 'the repertory theater
movement.' [The humility aside, it is interesting how little credit is
given the theater people themselves, but then Ford, like the rest of
American Subsidy, is not *theater* and does not recognize theater
people as specialists in their own business, to be left to do their
own work.] Money had less to do with this than the organized way
in which the Ford Foundation went into staff work in the field,
visiting people and institutions and organizations and companies in
the arts in more than a hundred communities in the United States
. . . The concept underlying what the Ford Foundation was doing was that in the United States there should be some offset to the
'hit or flop' economics where the serious play, the new script, the
serious young actor, was being forced out by economic and budget
exigencies of the producer."

The quote is from a sort of white paper issued by Mr. Lowry on
July 1, 1965. It indicates not only the speaking-of-itself-in-the-
third-person pomposity but also the power inclinations of the foundation. Presuming to alter the pattern of American theater (and of
American culture in general), who is there to criticize it, control it,
even stop it if necessary?

The Rockefeller Foundation, having one-eighth the endowment
of Ford, is necessarily smaller scale. It is also comparatively left
wing. Ford considers itself America — grants are given to established people for respectable projects based on traditional principles. Rockefeller, whose theater work was supervised until mid-
1967 by Dr. Robert Crawford, goes determinedly leftward. It helps
left-wing playwrights. It gives to left-wing companies. Dr. Crawford became carried away with enthusiasm where Mr. Lowry
speaks down from a celestial throne. That does not mean that
Crawford was any the more qualified to judge or play God to the
American theater's congregation, but at least he admitted to laity

(his field is Islamic history). He depended upon advice from theater people and that put him a step ahead of Lowry. Besides, the
Rockefeller Foundation gave me a very nice grant.

What, then, are we to make of these foundations? Are they responsible, constructive, altruistic private organizations, spontane-
ously generated to fill social and cultural needs on a supragovern-
mental basis? Or are they self-appointed twentieth-century deities,
bizarre and overgrown versions of the clumsy, interfering do-
gooder? Are they in fact trying to convert money into goodness?

The foundations see themselves as cultural heroes, attacking the
right wing. But in the sheer grossness of their attack, they are be-
sieging not only the right wing but the theater itself. They are drowning the theater of the individual in the process of creating the theater
of the community. They are creating a right wing of their own.

When Mr. Lowry writes or speaks of the theater, it is about a
theater that does not present plays or house actors. It is not the
theater as a stage occurrence but only as an institution, a cultural
entity. Always as some antiseptic, organized thing. For Lowry as
for the Ford Foundation and the subsidizers generally, the plain
excitement of theater has been sterilized out as if it were a disobe-
dient, undisciplined kind of vulgar germ that cannot fit into the
neatly bound organizational schemes which are so close to their
hearts.

Still, they were giving the money and as they did the new directors were moving toward true theater and away from Broadway's
right-wing kingdom. Theaters sprouted everywhere, immediately
incorporated as nonprofit and educational. The older ones re-
formed, carefully packing their boards with assured friends. The
newer ones took whatever boards they got, guaranteeing themselves trouble.

All were geared to play the subsidy game. They represented a
theater so financially secure that small companies like Philadelphia's Theater of the Living Arts could build a $100,000-plus defi-
cit within its first eighteen months of operation and not only
blithely anticipate its subsidization but look forward to a nice theater coming down the Main Line. Center Stage in Baltimore, which
had nearly folded in 1964 under its original director (Edward J.
Golden, Jr.), switched gear, went nonprofit and moved smoothly

into American Subsidy. Subscriptions more than tripled from the
1100 at the end of the 1963-1964 season; total audiences went
from 26,000 people for eleven productions to over 40,000 for eight
productions. By 1966 it was a happily dependent theater with another juicy deficit, another source of income (it was perhaps the
only theater in the country receiving *state* subsidies) and another
new theater on the way.

The successes of the Theater of the Living Arts and Center Stage
were directly connected with the hiring of Ford Foundation-trained
business managers. These young men — while being perfectly
charming, personally — were trained by the foundations for the
American Subsidy game in much the same way as the Nazis trained
their Hitler Youth.

The same thing went for the older, fatter cats, except that in
those cases it was the artistic director who learned to play the
money game. Finally the subsidizers came to the major conclusion
that financial help could not be predicated on the theaters ultimately becoming self-supporting. They had always insisted that at
75 percent of capacity a theater would pay its way. Now they decided that subsidy was going to be a continuing and permanent
need. This in the face of resident theater audiences nearing the sold-
out point. Not even full houses would pay the rent.

Within this short period of time — only four or five years, really
— the artistic directors of these theaters had gone from independent leftists fleeing Broadway philistinism to ultramodern institu-
tionalists who knew every trick of the rightist American Subsidy
game.

Whether these theaters really could never be self-sufficient will
never be known. Zelda Fichandler, the artistic director and creator
of Arena Stage, claims that her theater had always managed to pay
for itself. When the modern style of patronage arose, she decided
that self-sufficiency was no longer possible, even with the company
playing to 95 percent of capacity in its new, 752-seat house.

The Arena Stage is a good, professional theater producing important, artistic plays. Its selections might be more adventurous, its
character less institutional, Mrs. Fichandler's interest in the classics
more vital — but things could be worse. Couldn't it have continued

on its own? Perhaps not. Will its involvement with American Subsidy be debilitating? Probably.

How is the subsidy game played? Among the tricks is knowing
how to play ball with trustees, with politicians, with foundations.
Nobody, after all, gives money for nothing. The National Council
on the Arts is involved with dozens of politicians, each with constituencies that they would like to please. It insists on school-
production programs. It must approve the plays to be presented and
sometimes even their directors. There are foundation vice-presi-
dents who pass on grants. They are terribly sincere, terribly responsible, but they are essentially bureaucratic dilettantes with pseudo-
sociological visions of national culture. There are state art councils
doing important work in getting theaters to tour schools in the provinces. This is fine for the schools. It is harmful to the theaters, which
are considerably less than eager to be adjuncts of school systems but
need the money. In too many cases, the school performances lead
directly to right-wing pressure from authorities to do standard and
acceptable classics, and that means Shakespeare, Shakespeare,
Shakespeare. And finally, the theater's own board of trustees becomes involved in what works are being done and why, frequently
applying enough pressure to affect the kinds of plays produced. In
fact, many directors' contracts give the boards some veto power
over plays.

Because of all of this, the running of a resident theater becomes
a highly institutional job requiring political dexterity, trustee-
juggling, foundation infighting, tea-time community relations and,
not least, boxing out the other resident theaters in the power pattern of American Subsidy. As an example, in the jargon of resident
theater, the Arena Stage, the Minnesota Theater Company, the
Alley Theater and the American Shakespeare Festival are known as
"the Syndicate." From the regularity of their grants, they appear to
have a direct line to the Ford Foundation. It begins to appear as if
the play itself is becoming an incidental interest. From that point of
view, the resident theater movement is far more right wing than
Broadway ever was and the obstacles it places in art's way seem far
tougher.

As a result, the artistic directors have become smooth at conning subsidizers. They need the money and will do anything to get it. Sometimes they will actually walk into a foundation office and offer to make any artistic adjustments necessary to qualify for a grant. Usually, they are more subtle and are aware that a foundation must be led to believe that it is exercising no control before it will approve a grant. So they will connive and hustle with icy suavity. They are a new breed of infighters and only the wiliest survive. Most are wily enough, being young, clever and ambitious. Besides, there is so much money floating around. They claim they are doing it all for art's sake, but they are beginning to preside over official theaters, dispensing official drama. It may be from the important literature. It may even be professionally executed (in fact, professionalism has become so common that they are no longer defensive about it and seem ready to condemn *Broadway* as amateur). But in their brief lifetime, these theaters have become cynical and sometimes hypocritical. They have also begun their damaging effect on individual talents.

The first near victim of American Subsidy was William Ball, the finest director in America. By the time he began his American Conservatory Theater in 1965, Ball had already demonstrated a dazzling virtuosity, staging anything from grand opera to *Six Characters* to *Tartuffe*. Ball's technique was formidable, his imagination apparently unlimited. But he was more than a first-class director in the modern style. He was a visionary. In the left-wing directing that was sweeping through Western theater, he was not only the most talented but also one of the most revolutionary. His contemporaries were creator-directors with firm rootings in classical techniques. They were all concerned with getting a stage moving, adding their own idea to a play, working with rhythm and choreography. They were all interested in the theater as *show*. It was Ball who brought all of these tendencies together at peak excitement, peak invention, and then went back to fundamentals, insisting upon training new actors for the new theater. He wanted more than a company. He wanted a conservatory.

Just why he assembled so large a company (140 people including administrative personnel) and began organizing classes before he had a home is incomprehensible; just why he accepted a temporary offer by Pittsburgh of two theaters (one of 540 seats, the other of 350) makes no sense at all; how he expected to maintain such a company is beyond understanding — unless you realize the fanaticism of Ball's belief in his idea and his dependence upon American Subsidy. I doubt whether there is a single director in America so wound up in the new kind of theater, so messianic. The company and the conservatory were his dream.

It was only with a permanent company, constant training and a continuity of existence that Ball felt he could implement his concurrently traditional and radical theater ideas. His taste in plays does not run to the left wing ("I don't care how often the plays have been done; if they are done well, brilliantly, they are recognized and admired for their brilliance") and the most radical plays he has done go no further left than *Tiny Alice, Endgame* and *Six Characters in Search of an Author* — hardly comparable to the erotic-grotesque *Midsummer Night's Dream* that John Hancock did at both the (late) Actors Workshop in San Francisco and the Pittsburgh Playhouse; or André Gregory's production of Rochelle Owens's *Beclch* for Philadelphia's Theater of the Living Arts; or Jacques Cartier's *The Balcony* with the Hartford Stage Company; or Douglas Seale's *Titus Andronicus* and *The Chinese Wall* at Baltimore.

But Ball's left-wingism goes deeper than production styles even while it is applied to right-wing play selections. It goes back to ultratheatricality — something that was put aside when Stanislavski influenced the whole theater world into psychological and visual realism. Ball finds modern, right-wing actors much too restrained — vocally and physically. They are mild, cautious, afraid to tear themselves loose and break out into yelling, jumping, wild gesturing. He is training them to discipline flamboyance and then apply it to productions that he stages with all the devices of grand opera, ballet, mime and magical, full-throated theater. Combining these primary theater colors with an unrelenting demand for such basics as voice control, diction, movement and facial expression, and pumping them up with the inspirational effect of his own genius, he blends directorial creativity with respect for a playwright's purposes. This respect is not always very noticeable and that is one complaint that has been lodged against Ball. He is also not terribly interested in attaching modern political or social significance to his productions. Frankly, I am with him on that point — and even more with him in his absolute devotion to one major end: the creation of vivid theater experiences.

Accepting Pittsburgh's offer, he agreed to present eleven plays for repertory performance. They were prepared in little more than the time necessary to adequately rehearse a single play. The choices were almost cynical, geared to appeal to a broad range of audiences and subsidizers — and offered on a choose-your-favorites basis — from Albee's *Tiny Alice* to Goldoni's *A Servant of Two Masters,* from Williams's *The Rose Tattoo* to Shaw's *The Devil's Disciple.* A couple of plays that Ball had recently directed in New York (*Tartuffe* and *Six Characters*) were done to ease the rush-rush burden.

But Pittsburgh is a strange theater town and the Pittsburgh Playhouse a peculiar operation. The city has never been able to support any sort of theater and, in fact, could not even carry two perform-ances of a bus-and-truck *Half a Sixpence.* The Playhouse's two theaters — the Craft and the Hamlet — on the other hand had been financially successful, offering semiprofessional productions of things like *Mary, Mary* and *Bye, Bye Birdie.* Much of its success was credited to a popular, private restaurant on the premises. I think that should give a fair idea of Pittsburgh's cultural tend-encies.

The Playhouse's board of trustees finally admitted that its thea-ter was not presenting the sort of plays that would keep Their City in tune with the times, and so the offer was made to Ball.

But the board, you see, was still of the *Bye, Bye Birdie* mental-ity. Unable to understand serious theater and completely unin-formed about new methods of administration, it watched ACT's audiences dwindle — and perhaps even gloated over it. The business executives who sat on that board gave negligible help. Ball's irritation grew. His impatience with the importance granted the private restaurant did not endear him to them, and his insist-ence upon exclusive artistic control was resented. Within six months he and his company were forced out and the experience of his successor John Hancock was almost identical.

Now he had sets and costumes for eleven productions stored at Carnegie Tech, and a New York building donated by ANTA to house rehearsals and classes while a new home was sought. The company studied — daily classes ranging from first- and second-company rehearsals to the peculiar "Alexander technique" (a pat-ent-medicine kind of antigravitational theory that Ball picked out of a *Village Voice* ad and that he himself called "crazy" but which managed to work wonders for body sense). There were classes in voice, scansion, fencing, movement. Mind you, *everybody* in ACT has to take these classes, secretaries included. Then the Rockefeller Foundation came through with a $160,000 grant, to be adminis-tered by Carnegie Tech's drama department. That was in March of 1966. It looked good.

But Ball's dream was too expensive. He needed more than $160,000. He needed a ten-million-dollar endowment and a home theater provided by a city willing to give it without strings. A city willing to benefit from the presence of a driving artistic director and the first fully trained company of actors in America.

Ball was frantic. He spent increasingly less time with his com-pany. The classes were allowed to run themselves. Morale was rid-ing on a belief in Ball himself, a belief that bordered on the fanatic. He flew to Washington to beg money from the National Council on the Arts. They promised and then cut, cut, cut. By the time they were through the money was too little and too hamstrung to help. (The stories about the National Council on the Arts are wild enough to be true. They range from a President Johnson eager for a Texas resident theater to get a big grant, to the necessity of council approval for new plays and directors, to the tying of the grant to the touring of schools in a powerful Congressman's home state).

Ball flew to Phoenix, to Milwaukee, looking for someone to take in him and his dream. They wanted him, yes, but not the dream. Couldn't the conservatory be disbanded, the company elimi-nated? Couldn't he come alone? No, he couldn't.

But, you see, it isn't their fault. It isn't the *National Council's* fault. You *expect* them to behave that way. They are pure right wing. It is *Ball's* fault for letting the whole American Subsidy game swallow him up. He had *depended* upon it instead of upon himself. Twenty years earlier he wouldn't have begun a company *or* a con-servatory with no money. He would have started a small theater, relied on himself. These days he depends on the game.

Rule number 569: do not ride your dream on the American Subsidy game. Dreams do not ride on games.

The American Conservatory Theater nearly fell apart in the spring of 1966, with Ball that most bitter of men — the frustrated visionary. Just before he swung a National Council on the Arts grant good for a few more months, he was near collapse, his eyes sweeping the country for just one more city with a theater to offer, one more deal to swing. He hadn't directed in months. He swore, as before, that he would never go to Broadway (he had rejected dozens of offers). He spoke of leaving the theater forever. Finally, the frenzy of his drive paid off. The company played a brief summer engagement in 1966 at Chicago's Ravinia Festival and drew both critical applause and good audiences. Meanwhile, Ball was off to San Francisco, talking to cultural leaders who had already murdered the Actors Workshop there with inadequate subsidization. Having lost a home-grown and reputable theater, they followed the usual irony by helping another. Ball finally swung his support and ACT found a home, at least for a while. Then, both the Rockefeller and Ford foundations jumped on the success with thumping grants. Ball could let out his long, well-earned sigh. For the moment.

But this was the result of a personal drive, an extraordinary obsession. Ball's trouble was rare. Most resident theaters are getting as much in subsidy as they need. It is unfortunate that his maddening problems occurred to so extraordinary a talent, but it wasn't surprising. To swing with the American Subsidy you have to be a charity hipster, and Ball was too insistent upon absolute power over his company. His dedication, his concern with art, nearly forced American Subsidy to pull the carpet right out from under him. He is not surefooted yet.

The development of the American Subsidy is typical of our country. America jumped into the financial support of art without knowing anything about it, spending money like mad, doing everything on a gigantic scale without even bothering to learn anything about subsidy's dangers, effects and controls. In 1960 we were practically without a noncommercial theater and within five years the theaters had joined the symphony orchestras and art museums on a superinstitutional cultural binge.

The relationship of the resident theater people with Broadway is one of love-hate. On the one hand, from the trustees through the artistic director and minor players, they are antagonized by commercialism. *Their* theater is the *real* theater — the *artistic* theater. On the other hand, they are bitterly envious of their Broadway counterparts. Their smugness is defensive and they don't completely believe in their avowed superiority, inwardly giving in to the feeling that the "real" theater is New York's. They feel as if they are working in the provinces, painfully aware of the minimal national or New York publicity they are given. Their actors are convinced, no matter what their own and their theaters' accomplishments, that the only "professional" theater is Broadway's, and in many cases they ache to play Broadway, make it there and then return, just to have "proved" themselves — to have Played the Palace. People like Christopher Plummer, Kate Reid and John Colicos of Stratford, Ontario; Douglas Watson of the American Shakespeare Festival; Zoe Caldwell of the Minnesota Theater Company and Stratford, Ontario, have done just that.

Whether they return to their companies out of dedication or out of the need for the steady work they cannot get on Broadway is conjectural. Unfortunately, it is doubtful whether they understand the genuine importance of resident theater. For all of the noisy resentment of New York, actors across the country instinctively recognize Broadway as the major theater of America.

That instinct is not illogical. While our country has foolishly developed its theater as commercial and in a single city exclusively, there is nothing unusual or problematic in the development of that theater in a single city *primarily*. Every country, always, has its intellectual-cultural center of gravity. It is where the major artists congregate — where they study and work and communicate. It is where artistic and intellectual developments ferment. France has its Paris and England its London. America has its New York and to deny that is to ignore reality.

Because New York is where American creative life is centered, the actors and directors of the resident theaters feel isolated from fresh trends. They are outside the modern theater dialogue, relying on inbred self-analysis and inadequate journals. Even then, they merely read about the new — they have no one to argue with, no productions to see, no criticism to receive (although in America

provincial criticism is generally better than it is in New York). It is
difficult to work away from the center of activity. Resident theater
development is restricted because of this and is perpetually threatened by provincialism.

This is but one of many problems faced by these theaters. Yet, a
need for audiences is not one of them. The subscription lists grow,
thanks to high-power promoting. If the success of TCG's Mr. Newman even half matches his reputation he is a formidable symbol of
the anonymous efficiency of the American Subsidy components. It
doesn't seem to make a difference which theater he is helping or
what kind of drama that theater presents. It doesn't seem to make a
difference where the city is or what its intellectual climate may be.
Newman, like TCG, like the whole system, practically guarantees
95 percent of capacity.

Is it really possible to build audiences through a formulated
scheme of tea parties? It is. Oh, if only it could happen on Broadway. It can't. The resident theaters are part of the whole system,
playing the receivers to the American Subsidy's transmitters. Modern subscription sales methods are like big-time fund-raising methods. You may not know exactly who is going to donate how much,
but you know that, according to the percentages, the fund is going
to be approximately such and such.

Still, while these audiences may be treated as numbers, they are
humans, and they seem to be at least as interested and as argumen-
tative during intermissions as their New York counterparts. As well
they should be. Whatever the devices in recruiting them, the plays
they are given are superior, and are usually as well produced as any
in New York. In certain important respects, these audiences are
better off than New York theatergoers, seeing eight or ten excellent
plays a season.

The superior financial stability of these theaters as compared to
Broadway need hardly be emphasized. The cost of a Broadway production is enormous, with comedies and dramas generally running
toward (and soon upward of) $150,000 and musicals sometimes
going over the half-million-dollar mark. Such amounts are obviously difficult to raise, proportionately more so if the production is
left wing. A musical with a Richard Rodgers score and a star like

Mary Martin is pure right wing and needn't worry about financing (as a matter of fact, Mr. Rodgers and Miss Martin will finance it themselves). An inventive play by an unknown will need months and perhaps years of coaxing backers to put in twenty-five or fifty dollars each, and even Tennessee Williams has financing problems these days.

Out in the relatively left wing of resident theater, there are no such problems. The director of a resident theater can plan his Chekhov, Brecht, Shaw, Shakespeare, O'Neill, Miller program and relax in the certainty that the bills will be paid.

Once a resident theater recognizes financial reality (that is, the one-fell-swoop solution of its economic problems) it loses its independence. It becomes dangerously interested in the tastes of the subsidizing forces and of its audiences. But what *is* the "taste" of a subsidizing force, or of an audience? If polls were taken, the audiences might select Broadway hits and the subsidizers popular classics. But what they "like" is what they are conditioned to like. As they become familiar with literature, their tastes change. It is the way of education — the way of left-wing influence.

In their sensitivity to economics, artistic directors are prone to forget this, intent upon immediate assurance of full houses and deficit financing. They will do *Cat on a Hot Tin Roof* rather than *Camino Real*. This is not part of any conscious attempt to water down the artistic purity of their theaters, but it has the same effect. Directors will shy away from steady diets of the art theater they would like to do, using "balance" as a justification. It is a justification that is partly reasonable and partly a rationalization for bowing to wing pressures. A financial crisis at the Pittsburgh Playhouse — a notoriously right-wing resident theater — was cured by emergency fund-raising and a shameful concession demanded of its director. John Hancock, though a leftist, promised to do plays of *broader appeal* and canceled plans for Brecht's *Saint Joan of the Stockyards*. Before the season was over he was asked to resign. Trustee pressure caused similar concessions from Jacques Cartier at the Hartford Stage Company.

In going along with the right-wing interest in popularity, the resident theater is really no different from any commercial theater. Its motives for attendance may be different (existence as opposed to profit) but the behavior is identical: pandering to lower tastes instead of insisting upon the ideal.

Is it really pandering or are resident theaters simply being realistic? Suppose an artistic director programmed Aeschylus's *Oresteia,* Jonson's *Volpone,* Büchner's *Leonce and Lena,* Tardieu's *Lovers in the Metro,* Kleist's *The Prince of Homburg,* Pirandello's *Enrico IV,* Beckett's *Krapp's Last Tape,* Green-Weill's *Johnny Johnson* and Ronald Ribman's *Harry, Noon and Night.* Would the 75 or more percent of capacity audience upon which his theater's very existence depends be reliably there with subscription checks in hand? Doesn't the director *have* to consider such matters? I suspect that if the audience trusted the theater it would come. If the plays were as good as we believe they are, they would work. Once the theater starts catering to the audience's presumed taste the trust will slip away. "Education" of theater audiences is largely rationalization.

The only way a true theater can exist is when it is working on the basis of honesty. Plays must be produced only because they are believed in and because a believer wants to do them. Integrity, conviction and ultimately high standards are the minimum disciplines. Adventure and dedication are the minimum motives. The theater must exist for its own sake. The decision as to what plays to do must be completely free: "what I want to do" and not "what they want to see." Once the decision-making process is affected by "will they like it?" it is contaminated. There can be no theater greatness unless the theater is committed to it.

In this respect, the Broadway theater is sometimes purer than the resident theater. The private financing of Broadway compared to the American Subsidy-hustling makes the commercial theater look absolutely pristine. The standard of values may be right wing but within that standard the producers invariably select plays on the basis of their own convictions. They present what they believe to be good. They have learned that it is impossible to pretest a play's money-making possibilities.

The director of a resident theater may argue that even a steady diet of Shakespeare, Shaw and O'Neill is preferable to the packaged imbecility that often passes for Broadway theater. In a sense he is right. But his programming, like a play, must be judged by its own standards. For what a noncommercial theater is meant to be, safe-played programming is as repulsive as the plastic Broadway production.

Realizing the threats in subsidy, the government, the foundations and an enlightened citizenry must assume the responsibility of support without interference. It is not easy to give responsibly, but it is necessary if the gift is to fulfill its purpose. When John D. Rockefeller organized the Rockefeller Foundation he expressed the fear that it might do more harm than good. The fear was justified. The director of a resident company must be given his freedom.

One way to ease this nagging problem is to relieve artistic directors of their fund-raising responsibilities, for even when resident theaters have executive or business managers to handle financial matters the directors are often involved, whether in speaking at cocktail parties or in direct confrontation with the boards of trustees and fund sources. With this confrontation comes the clash between left and right wing in American professional resident theater. Just how severe this clash will be depends upon the leftness of the director and the rightness of his subsidizers.

It is most depressing in theaters that were originally created by the director and then went nonprofit to qualify for American Subsidy. In these instances, the director was forced to give up some control to the board of trustees that he had to name. In most cases, obviously, he stacked the board with friends, but this was not always possible. The more money he needed, the more alien trustees he would have to permit to be named.

On the other hand, resident theaters that were begun by a city or group of citizens (such as the Repertory Theater of Lincoln Center, the Seattle Repertory Theater or the Pittsburgh Playhouse) had boards before they had artistic directors. This made for even more right-wing boards.

This, then, is how the resident professional theater fits into the overall American theater scheme: it is left wing in general artistic stance, providing a kind of theater — the classical literature — that is rejected by the established powers. It is also strongly bound to a right wing of its own: the new but formidable forces of the American Subsidy. It has little effect upon the mainstream (Broadway) theater, especially in regard to new plays. It is also so young and so

beset with problems of its own that there is no chance of its altering
the American theatrical balance in the near future. Still, it is the
major left-wing influence on modern American theater because of
the dedication and taste of its artistic directors. We see the bestrid-
ing influence of right-wing Broadway with a flurry of interwing activity among the musicals. And we see the beginnings of a resident
professional theater that can potentially provide a balancing influence if it is not swallowed up by institutionalizing pressures.

The most significant aspect of resident theater is that its plays
are chosen by an artistic director, as opposed to the commercial
theater, where they are chosen by a producer. The controls are in
the hands of a creative theater person rather than an outsider. The
director is a trained participant whose taste is usually rooted in the
left wing, whose background is usually in classical theater. The
Broadway producer is basically a businessman who may be hooked
on the theater but for whom theater is a "show." In his own way,
he too is *of* the theater, and in a sense his outsider status gives him
a better perspective on whether a production is *working*. This is a
trivial advantage when balanced against the general level of producer background and education in artistic matters. The producer's
aesthetic too often rests in the proudly uneducated cliché "I may
not know what is good, but I know what I like."

Unfortunately while resident theater artistic directors may know
what is good, between their subjugation to subsidizing forces and
their inclination to follow patterns, they tend to do war-horses.
When they move out of the masterwork rut they do the same Unusual Plays as each other. They also concentrate on only the most
famous plays of less advertised playwrights. There is little interest
in producing forgotten playwrights.

A director should be adventurous enough to try the untried. He
must be excited by personal discovery. Merely because nobody in
his *city* has done *Six Characters* is not reason enough to stick with
it. Even if he believes it to be Pirandello's finest play, and even if he
is aching to do it himself, it is not reason enough. He must realize
his role in the overall American theater. He should try *Enrico IV*.
Resident theater programming is just too repetitious and faddish.

Another trait of the resident theater artistic director is his conviction that he and his theater must have an *identity,* or a *point of view.* This can be taken to mean a number of things. It can mean a company style of performance. It can mean a thematic homogeneity of repertoire. It can mean nothing more than taste. In general, though, it means what Herbert Blau meant when he developed the credo school of resident theater at the Actors Workshop.

Blau, who inclines toward phrase-making, calls theater "the public art of crisis." He believes that his theater must commit itself to a liberal ideology specifically relevant to modern social and political history. And by specifically, he means *specifically.* He admits to being "in the habit of seeing analogies between the slightest gesture on stage and the fate of nations." He says that the Actors Workshop "couldn't proceed to the question of style . . . until we knew what gestures were credible in the Cold War." Mr. Blau saw references to Vietnam in Büchner's *Danton's Death* — not general references but *particular* ones. He will say, "Taken with Cuba and the Congo, the [Caryl] Chessman case gave a social mooring to the obscurantism of Genet." He will describe the 1956 Actors Workshop production of Brecht's *Mother Courage* as "a thoroughgoing criticism of our reigning foreign policy, Mr. Dulles's Brinksmanship."

The quotes are from Blau's book, *The Impossible Theater,* a loosely disassembled collection of claptrap littered with philosophical and political name-droppings. My point, however, is not to discuss this book, which really ought never have been published. My point refers to his idea, and his idea is that a resident theater should have a relationship to its contemporary world, a way of looking at things, an extratheatrical motive for selections and a method of projecting this attitude into its productions.

The matter is not that Blau does not seem to understand the issues he raises or even that his approach to politics is muddled. It is that he is imposing transient political situations upon plays that were never meant to bear them. His concern for the theater itself seems secondary and he is not willing to produce a play that was written to exist as theater magic. "The drama," he writes, "is a postlapsarian form born of the Fall. And its commitment to Action — the price of atonement? — makes it responsible to problems of choice and identity. If the theater is an insubstantial pageant, its merit depends on the degree to which — by projecting their changing appearance — it clarifies the disruption in our lives."

Forget about the incomprehensible sections of that quotation and the word "postlapsarian" (I can't find it in any dictionary). But note the reference to theater as an "insubstantial pageant." The extremity of this attitude, implying a rejection of the theater as a pure art form, is striking indeed.

Yet, while it is extreme, so are most left-wing attitudes in their first statement. Other resident theater directors, while refusing to go as far as Blau, have been deeply affected by his measuring the merit of a play by its relevance to modern life. They have been fashioning it, right-wing style, into a viable and more reasonable tool that could be profitably applied to the theater *so long as the theater itself came first*. They are still inclined to see the drama as an event in itself and the creation of that event as their purpose. With Blau's pure left-wing idea absorbed, they found a method of selecting plays. Not, as Blau would have it, in the plays' reflection upon the CIA, or McCarthyism, or Ecumenism, or The Bomb. But as an *aesthetic* — so that there would be some artistic cohesion to their programs.

Still, many of these directors insist upon too-strict contemporary applications of the plays they choose, and while their social and political ideas are generally admirable their reasoning is happily uncomplicated by subtleties. They just follow the going collegiate line. As it happens, they usually keep their references in mind rather than in the productions. There are seldom overt attempts to overlay extrinsic references upon the plays.

The point-of-view syndrome is really part of the broader theatrical development in directing: the left-wing conception of the director as a creator. It is a conception running through nearly all of the modern British and American resident theaters.

Peter Brook and the Royal Shakespeare Company's *King Lear* was a perfect example. When Mr. Brook's company visited New York in the spring of 1964, it presented the now-famous Samuel Beckett *Lear*. Brook, stimulated by the Jan Kott theories, had seen striking similarities between Lear's senseless destruction by an empty world and the desolation in Beckett's *Endgame*. He saw both plays' consideration of the human condition as senselessly painful.

Frankly, I see this in neither *Endgame* nor *Lear,* but that makes no difference. *Brook* saw it and it was a perfectly valid way *to* see it. He drew a stunning, unique and at the same time curious performance from Paul Scofield, who began the play with an uncontrollably shaking arm and a wavery vocal production that had him sounding as if he were underwater. As the evening progressed, it seemed as if this manner was being used to indicate periods of madness, and if that was meant, then Scofield and Brook saw Lear as mad to begin with and the division of his kingdom as a lunatic attempt to buy love. This makes some sense since a king would have to be out of his mind to prematurely chop up his territory or to completely misunderstand the obviously saintly Cordelia from the very start.

However, Scofield did not play the madness as rant, and his Lear was marvelously underplayed — a great relief from the bombast the play generally elicits. It had the white sensation of Beckett. So this Lear was akin to Hamm, of *Endgame.*

There are several superficial similarities between the plays, one of which is in the opening scenes. As *Endgame* opens, Hamm is seated "in a dressing gown, a stiff toque on his head, a large blood-stained handkerchief over his face, a whistle hanging from his neck, a rug over his knees, thick socks on his feet." The look is familiar as still another Beckett way of imprisoning the human body to set the mind free. It is also, on the visual level, reminiscent of *Lear.* Hamm seems very old because of the blanket and the socks, and the toque is crownlike. His chair is much like the throne Lear assumes in most productions.

The opening lines can also be likened to each other. As *Endgame* starts, Clov, who is Hamm's servant and cellmate in life's prison, begins with an expression of futility. ("Grain upon grain, one by one, and one day, suddenly, there's a heap, a little heap, the impossible heap. I can't be punished any more.") In a moment, Hamm is casually agreeing. ("Can there be misery loftier than mine? No doubt.") It is a wonderful example of Beckett's comic humanity yawning in the face of tragedy. The king's first line in *Lear* is equally hopeless. ("Meantime we shall express our darker

purpose . . . to shake all cares and business from our age . . .
while we unburdened crawl toward death.")

Later in *Lear,* similarities again arise, especially in the storm
scene, with the king mad and ravaged by fate, control over his own
existence having proved impossible. This is only an *apparent* similarity, however. Beckett's futilitarians are *never* defeated. (Beckett
people do not die; even in *Play,* where they are imprisoned as ashes
in funeral urns, they are chattering away. They, like we, go on. Go
on because, after all, don't we?) Too, Shakespeare's *Lear* howls to
the wind — even if Brook-Scofield's didn't — and a Beckett character absolutely *never* howls. He accepts *everything* with spirits
high, and very complacently. That is the great, silent irony.

Whether Brook was "right" or "wrong" makes no difference. I
don't consider *Lear* a great play and find it amusing that directors
make fads of one or another of the tragedies. But the Shakespeare is
art and as art it will draw different reactions from different people.
Brook's version exemplified the free-swinging energy of modern,
leftist directors; an energy that he would magnificently demonstrate
a couple of years later in his production of Peter Weiss's
Marat/Sade, to whose devastating power he added a choreography
and rhythm of his own.

It is an exciting development, this leftist directing, and it will
bring to the great plays a wholly new vision and a vital theater
existence that will make them fresh with each production. It demands a theatrical depth, a background in classicism and a creativity never before expected from a director, a knowledge of materials
and a sense of totality never before considered. While today's right-
wing director is an experienced and formidable craftsman, schooled
in the important areas of polish, psychology and realism, he is
hampered by his sense of fidelity to a script. Today's left-wing director has added to this the contribution of a creative artist.

Another aspect to resident theater's left-wing direction is the
awareness of team acting, reactive acting and choreographed
movement. Players are treated as a group, working together to create an ensemble that could not be achieved by solitary effort. They
work with each other, not as star, featured player, supporting
player and extra, but as an interweaving combination.

Reactive acting, while a traditional dramatic discipline, has been forgotten because right-wing directors spend all of their time with the actor who is speaking, neglecting the one who is listening. Look at nearly any Broadway play and you will find a stageful of actors leaning against doorways, standing on staircases, sitting on sofas, waiting near ashtrays while somebody is reading his lines. They are nearly frozen. The leftist director is altering this, making them listen, react. They may not be speaking, but they are *alive*.

He is also having them move — having the play move — in continuous patterns that are both logical and rhythmic. The static environment of the average right-wing production may be the biggest single reason for its consistently boring tone. There is nothing so good for stage life as activity — something, after all, is supposed to be *happening* on a stage.

The left-wing director who is emerging from the resident theaters is more aware of such staging creativity because of the plays that excite him. They present staging challenges entirely different from those to which right-wing directors have grown accustomed. And they provoke entirely new ways of looking at any kind of play from any period. A growth in directing cannot be limited to a single style of playwrighting. This growth is in basic theater. It is going to enrich the entire range of dramatic approach.

Resident actors are only at the beginning of their education, but they *are* at the beginning. In April of 1966, Actors Equity revealed that for the first time there were more actors working in resident theater than in New York. It sounded like the millennium. It was merely the start.

But it was a start that was desperately needed. Up to that time, resident theaters had been having a difficult time luring actors from New York. The big problem was the conviction that, art notwithstanding, Broadway right-wing theater was the only real theater. But there were other problems: young people who want to act have always come to New York, where the schools, the theaters, the chances were. Once there, they settled. It was home. Besides, once you become accustomed to living in New York, it is difficult to imagine living anywhere else. Why move out to Nowhere when the big break may come tomorrow?

This made no sense. Employment opportunities for actors in New York are absurdly small. The kind of work that *can* be gotten is not merely useless but downright destructive to the development of acting craft. Actors recognized this but never really believed it. Their homes were filled with theater literature and their minds with show business.

The booming resident theaters changed this. At first it was necessary to practically shanghai actors out of New York. Then things grew easier. Actors began realizing that what they had been saying about the importance of serious theater was really true. Salaries began rising and recruiting became less haphazard. The TCG auditions enabled resident theater directors to see actors on an organized basis rather than go looking here and there by chance. For the actors, it was a chance to be judged by intelligent standards rather than on the lunatic pounding-the-pavement, calling-on-producers, knowing-the-right-people basis of New York.

The question we now face is how these actors will develop in the resident theaters. The answer depends mostly on the quality of direction under which they will work. Obviously, the playing of major and minor roles in a variety of styles and periods is an essential part of an acting education, but is this the playing they will do? If their company is uneven, the director will be repeatedly forced to cast his more competent players in major roles, depriving them of the benefit of careful, minor playing. If the company is dominated by local stars, actors will have no chance to move up to larger roles.

If the company presents its season in series rather than in repertory production (and nearly all do), the actor will not be required to master a number of roles for regular performance, one for today and another tomorrow. He will be that much deprived. If the actor is lured from one company to another, neither he nor the company he leaves will have much of a chance for the continuing development of ensemble style that requires stretches of mutual interplay.

The "luring" of actors by one company from another is usually less kindly described as "raiding," and it is a mean and destructive practice. It is not general but it is common enough. The contract for resident theater actors allows a very short resignation (or dismissal) notice. In an effort to correct it, the League of Resident Theaters contract was devised, permitting an optional secure, season-length contract. But few resident theaters, or actors, were eager to exercise this option, being uncertain whether the actor (or the theater) would prove satisfactory. As a result, even the LORT contracts are breakable.

A resident theater must plan its schedule on the basis of the company. Reality demands that players be capable of the roles and what is the sense in scheduling a great play if the company is incapable of it? Special, one-shot actors can be jobbed in but (a) this cannot be frequently done, (b) it is expensive and (c) it subverts company development and morale. When another company swoops in and bribes an actor with salary increases, it can wreak havoc with a schedule. One of the most unpleasant instances of this happened in the fall of 1966, when Philadelphia's Theater of the Living Arts was playing a two-week guest engagement at the Yale School of Drama. Yale was beginning to organize a professional resident theater of its own, and while the Philadelphia company was playing there two of its major actors were offered considerable raises to defect. They did, crippling their company at season's start and forcing the cancellation of one production for lack of a proper lead. The impropriety, of course, was as much the actors' as it was Yale's. Perhaps all's fair in commerce, but by engaging in such practices the resident theater places itself in the commercial category, instigates salary wars and cuts its own throat. And that's if you choose to ignore ethical considerations.

These are problems in the handling of actors. Then there is the matter of training. I have yet to see a training program that really works. It seems to me that the only way for an actor to develop is through constant work, *on the stage, in performance.* Acting schools in the United States have been largely useless, perhaps even detrimental. On the university level, they have been conducted by theoretic, nonprofessional faculties, working entirely without the stimulus of prove-it standards. In every sense, it is academic theater. The acting schools in New York exist to suck off the young and the stagestruck. It is generally a tossup as to whether the students have had more or less practical experience than the teachers. As for the acting conservatory in conjunction with a professional theater, I have yet to see its value proved.

The English assume that an actor good enough to hire is an actor who has already perfected his craft. The English classical director takes it for granted that the professional actor has developed fundamental technique. Perhaps the only way for an actor to receive basic training is through an apprenticeship program with a repertory resident theater. Insofar as formal classes are concerned, the possible value is limited and whatever *can* be taught there (diction, vocal control, movement) can nearly always be better taught in practice, under a strong, knowledgeable, communicative director. Acting is learned in the doing, and one hour on stage is worth thirty in the classroom.

There is still another problem in acting for resident theaters: although the best way to develop discipline and versatility is in the performance of different roles in varying periods and styles, the only way to best produce a particular play is in the concentration of energies on *it* and its author's work. That is, Shakespeare will be best produced by a company specializing in Shakespeare. This presents a conflict between the development of acting versatility and the virtue of specialization.

It is true that a Shakespeare company will develop actors well schooled in basic stage disciplines and generally able to handle nearly any kind of play. The occasional non-Shakespeare productions at Stratford, Ontario, prove it (they have done a marvelous *Cyrano de Bergerac* and an excellent *Cherry Orchard*). Undoubtedly, they could do respectable Restoration comedy, Molière and surreal theater. But for definitive Restoration or Molière or Brecht or any specific style, a company experienced and bred in that particular tradition cannot be matched. The resident theater producing a single Shakespeare play a season will not be able to give it more than a perfunctory presentation, even if it is the Minnesota Theater Company with a Shakespearean director as experienced as Tyrone Guthrie.

Naturally, few resident theaters are willing to limit themselves to a single playwright or period. Shakespeare, because of his institutional status, festival appeal and box office value, is by far the most popular playwright for such exclusivity (but obviously he is an exception, being the World's Greatest Playwright). Brecht managed to get himself a Berliner Ensemble devoted strictly to his own

work. Various countries have national companies to specialize in
the local Golden Age.

But for the nonfestival, ordinary resident theater in America,
how can a restriction to a single playwright or period be economically or even culturally justified? Which board of trustees and
which audience will put up with it? Or which artistic directors, for
that matter? These directors are young, eager and admirably eclec-
tic in their tastes, eager to stage the great plays of all periods. They
may believe that a true Brechtian style demands consistent performance of the Brecht literature (and most of them do believe it),
but will they do it themselves? And will their audiences support
them? For that matter, how could you justify the only serious theater in, say, Baltimore, spending all of its time on surreal theater, or
Greek classics?

It is a dilemma. Acting versatility, which is necessary, will develop only through general experience, while perfection will only
develop through specialization. At this point in American theatrical
history, our major problem is the development of broadly qualified
actors and the revitalization of the too-long-ignored theater classics. We will have to delay the development of specialists and press
for the resident theaters to go repertory.

The need for true repertory cannot be overstated. Most artistic
directors are eager to go into it, but there are a number of practical
problems involved. There must be storage space for the various
sets. There is a considerable expense in their daily change. There
must be adequate time and space to rehearse several productions
simultaneously. The theater must be able to afford a permanent
company large enough to cast its various plays (at present, smaller
resident theaters maintain full-time companies of about ten players,
jobbing in extra people for occasional big-cast productions). They
are also afraid of being saddled, all season long, with a weak actor.

Such problems will have to be solved before genuine repertory is
possible. However, they *can* be solved. In most cases, the theaters
aren't rep because the directors haven't gone ahead and tried it. A
ballet or opera company wouldn't dream of not performing in repertory, and even an organization as tightly budgeted as the New
York City Opera Company manages semi-annual repertory seasons. One of the most practical solutions is in the use of imagina-

tive, nonrealistic half-sets capitalizing upon creative lighting to minimize storage and set-changing problems. Conservatism of design is consequently a practical as well as an artistic handicap.

At present, the primary repertory companies in America are the summer festivals, and they are repertory for a commercial reason. They are geared to transient business. They must schedule on the basis of tourists who are in town for a few days, and wish to see several productions. There are only a handful of winter repertory companies, mainly Ball's ACT, Ellis Rabb's APA and companies in Seattle, Atlanta, St. Louis and New Orleans.

For the winter companies, the artistic directors' interest in rep is restricted by their inability to convince their boards of directors that it is worth the added expense. Again, a simple left- and right-wing collision.

A both gratifying and irritating area of left-wing activity among resident theaters has been the development of stage shapes, away from the proscenium and toward the arena, but particularly the open, apron or thrust stage.

I have no intention of getting into the development of theater and stage shapes. There are many excellent books on the subject (particularly those of Richard Southern). It should be sufficient to say that the thrust stage has become very fashionable in both English and American resident theater. This fashion began with the festival theaters in Stratford, Ontario, and then Chichester, England, whose stages jutted out into deep-dish, bowl theaters that rose steeply around three sides. Tyrone Guthrie, who designed the Stratford (Ontario) Festival Theater with Tanya Moiseiwitsch, exported the shape to Minneapolis, and Jo Mielziner adapted it for the Vivian Beaumont Theater in New York's Lincoln Center. Virtually every new theater since built for an American resident company has used it in one way or another.

It is, of course, a fad. Not that the theaters themselves are ill conceived. In fact, they are marvelous, allowing excellent viewing for all audience members, bringing the play into the house, giving the director much more space (and depth) and encouraging movement. But different plays have different needs and it should be remembered that with the Restoration, the proscenium stage *replaced* the apron stage and was considered an improvement at the time. All of this is simple left-to-right movement. The proscenium stage is on today's right wing and the thrust stage is moving quickly from the left to replace it.

But the big thrust kick is no longer the revolution it was when Guthrie was fighting for it. Today it is merely the thing to do, whether or not an artistic director has a need for or even an understanding of it. It is a pity that many of these new theaters will be unable to perform the kinds of stage tricks that the proscenium stage permits. The "picture-box" look, so scorned by thrustists, is a magical look — a terrific theater look. The wonders it can do with scenery and lighting are unavailable to the thrust stage.

Just as an example, in the summer of 1965, productions of *The Cherry Orchard* were staged at both Stratford, Ontario, and Minneapolis. Both have thrust stages. The Chekhov is devoted to absolute realism. It is *about* realism. It demands a stage look faithful to life's — the daylight streaming through the windows must look real as real; leaves must flutter in the breeze; a parlor must look, in every detail, like a parlor. Such stage design is impossible on a thrust stage, which severely limits furniture, flats and props. And the picnic scene had to be played on a stage bare except for a sad little prop log. This can be ruinous for Chekhov.

Faddism in general should be avoided and the headlong plunge toward thrust stages is unfortunately prompted by bandwagon-joining rather than individual, considered thought. It is encouraging that some of the newest theaters are being built to work as either proscenium or thrust.

The resident theater explosion, too, is faddish. Every city wants one, every director wants one. There is sloppy preparation, organization, subscription-selling and trustee selection. And the whole business is ultradependent on the giant balloon blown up with the funds of American Subsidy. Resident theater represents a strangely self-contradictory phenomenon that is peculiarly whole-hog American. Left wing in theater purpose and taste, it was executed through massive right-wing influence. Whether its imaginative artistic directors will survive the pressures remains to be seen. Whether its current interest in original American plays will subvert its obligation to and identification with the classical theater literature and neglected plays is as yet unknown. But since it is performance itself, beyond all other considerations, that ultimately counts, it is time now to take a look at the resident theaters' work.

CHAPTER FIVE

Now You Can See the Great Plays

THE most artistically and financially successful resident theater in the United States is not in the United States. It is the Stratford Shakespearean Festival in Ontario, a splendid example of right-wing virtues in a cultural vein. Along with those virtues, there are the concomitant right-wing flaws, particularly a lack of excitement, originality and concern. But for sheer professionalism, company depth, maturity and the harvest of training, Stratford shows exactly what a top-level resident theater can be.

Statistically, its history represents the kind of pattern best geared to warm a trustee's heart. True, the 98 percent of capacity audiences in the very first season has never been matched. But from that first year, when forty-two performances were given in six weeks for a total attendance of 68,087 and a box office gross of $206,000, the company was able to move — in thirteen years — to 1965's 129 performances in sixteen weeks for a total attendance of 264,395 (92 percent of capacity) and a box office gross of $984,963, not counting the second-string Avon Theater. That, baby, is show business.

From the tent theater that opened on July 13, 1953, with Alec Guinness playing *Richard III,* Stratford has gone on to its million-dollar Festival Theater. There on the close-cropped lawns, amid the formal gardens, along the Avon River (what else?) where swans gently glide; there where Shakespeare first became a summer festival and where vacations first became cultural; there where costumed bandsmen blare a ritual fanfare as part of the things-to-see tourist image (it is enough to send you tearing back to the nearby men's room); there where Canada has finally achieved the cultural respectability it so desperately craves: *there* is the finest repertory theater on the North American continent — the supersuccess of Tyrone Guthrie, who later marched across the border to declare himself the father of American resident theater.

Without slighting Mr. Guthrie's achievement in setting Stratford's standards and getting it off the ground, it should be pointed out that he really did not direct all that much. In the first season he staged both productions, *Richard III* and *All's Well That Ends Well*. In the next he did two of the three, *The Taming of the Shrew* and the first non-Shakespearean work *Oedipus Rex*. In 1955 he did one, *The Merchant of Venice,* and *Oedipus* was repeated. Skipping a year, he did *Twelfth Night* in 1957 and then *never again staged a play at the Festival Theater* (at least, up until this writing). That is not much directing for a man with the reputation of having established and polished a company.

Certainly, Guthrie must be given the credit for implementing the idea, assembling the basic company, arranging a purpose and master plan and getting the whole thing moving, but the ultimate *establishment* of the festival, the maintenance of its standards, the casting and the control of overall artistic direction must be attributed to Michael Langham, who had been a protégé of Guthrie's along with Douglas Campbell. When Guthrie moved on to the Minnesota Theater Company in 1962, taking Campbell with him, Langham took over Stratford's directorship (until 1967, when he left to assume the directorship of still another summer festival, this one in La Jolla, California).

Langham proceeded to run the festival along the lines of the English repertory companies from which it had been copied. The programming was nicely balanced, each season usually having a Shakespearean tragedy, comedy and history and one non-Shakespearean play. Because of a small turnover, the company became experienced in the Stratford style — Eric House, William Hutt and Douglas Rain were there from the very first season. Bruno Gerussi came in 1954, Tony van Bridge in 1955, Peter Donat and Leo Ciceri in 1960 and John Colicos in 1961. They all remain. Some came and went: Christopher Plummer, Kate Reid, Irene Worth. By and large, the company is stable and long experienced in the Stratford style.

And what *is* the Stratford style? It is no nonsense, straightforward and classical, long on physical activity and short on meaningful drive and interpretation. In short, it is Guthriean. Occasionally it will try a period switch. Although the costumes are opulent, made in the house's roomy substage workshops, there is no scenery — the Festival Theater has a permanent set of a two-level portico — and hardly any lighting dynamics. This is especially striking since the theater is equipped with a magnificent lighting system, surpassed perhaps only by that of the Vivian Beaumont Theater in Lincoln Center. Nevertheless, a typical Stratford production will keep its lighting unnecessarily simple, very *white* and practically unchanging.

It is easy to choose a "typical" Stratford production since the production level and style are so consistent. Everything is generally impeccable and if an individual production is weak (which happens very rarely) or exciting (which happens very rarely) it is neither terribly weak nor terribly exciting. This is classic institutional behavior. For example, the Stratford *Troilus and Cressida* in 1963 was a straight, good production. The play is strange and flawed, presenting certain technical problems to which a company like this and a director like Langham are perfectly suited. Shakespeare is trying to combine two basically unrelated subjects: war and lechery. His major characters are shallow — Troilus is absurdly clean-cut and naïve; you almost expect him to be wearing a Rutgers sweater. Cressida is impossible to understand since she begins as a girl passionately in love and turns inexplicably heartless. Finally, the play never focuses, being part history, part comedy, part tragedy. What to do with it?

Stratford never worries overmuch about such problems. The directors never seek their own, possibly inventive explanations. They just play the play.

So Langham did not attempt to make any sense of *Troilus,* staging it exactly as it reads. Except for one slight change (William Hutt played Pandarus as an old queen with face powder, beauty marks, rings, bracelets and a fan), the acting was straightforward and classical. Peter Donat, looking positively like Michelangelo's

David, was a nobly eloquent Troilus; Martha Henry a beautiful and shining Cressida. What matter why she went bitchy? None to official Stratford.

The *Henry IV* double feature in 1965 was another example of productions going well, no matter what the material. *Part One* is by far the superior play, as complete and balanced as anything Shakespeare ever wrote. King Henry IV has Claudius-like problems as the play begins, unable to forget his complicity in the murder of his predecessor. His sense of guilt continues through the play, eventually being an indirect cause of his death in *Part Two*. But he is also a mature and solitary ruler, consumed with a king's obligations to justice — something that his heir and son Prince Hal has yet to learn. Hal, young and irresponsible, is more interested in drinking and whoring with Falstaff than he is in the duties of a ruler. The play is the first of a trilogy about a king's creation — a trilogy that concludes in *Henry V* with the ideal monarch.

Stuart Burge directed it with Brueghelian color (where would designers for classical plays *be* without Brueghel?) investigating the idea of "honor" against the need for responsible government that meant so much to Shakespeare. Douglas Rain's Hal was much too smug and curled-lip, although his consideration of the language was superb (as it generally is with the entire Stratford company). Douglas Campbell's diction tended toward the sloppy when he shouted (which he loves to do), but his Hotspur was quite correctly self-assured in its tragic parallel with Hal's career. The farewell to his wife ("This evening must I leave you, gentle Kate") was extremely touching, especially because of Miss Henry's soft womanliness. And with Burge's Guthrian pageantry and roar for the battles, it was an excellent production of an excellent play.

Part Two was produced with equal finesse, and so is more to the point since it is an inferior play. A long, fragmented and generally dull history, it was written to capitalize upon the enormous popular success of the character of Falstaff in *Part One*. The result is a play that, like *Part One,* alternates matters of history with broad comedy but, unlike it, does not wed them. In the first play, Falstaff balances against the weight of the crown. In the second, he not only interferes with it but overshadows it.

Burge just followed the play in the Stratford way, handling the distinctly separate scenes as if they were in distinctly separate plays. While he was interested in it as a phase of the Prince Hal trilogy, he was forced to go along with the heavy-handed humor that Shakespeare threw in for the masses — slapstick, burlesque and characters with "funny" names (Shallow, Silence, Mouldy, Wart, Feeble, and so on).

Yet the production proved the wonderful depth of the company, for despite the fact that Shakespeare, no less than a hack playwright, will inevitably botch things when responding to commercial appeal, an ensemble of well-trained actors and a facile director can make almost anything work. The mediocrity of the drama proved the expertise of the company.

But it took the Avon Theater, the festival's converted-moviehouse adjunct, to show up the varsity with a production in 1965 that might have lacked some formal discipline but made up for it with theatrical drive and invention. This was the Bertolt Brecht-Kurt Weill opera *The Rise and Fall of the City of Mahagonny,* which was written in 1927 and was here given its North American première.

Brecht and Weill wrote *Mahagonny* as a multiple parody — of old-school opera, of human "fun." It is a parody of the theater that is designed as entertainment (a kind of theater that Brecht called "culinary") and of the entertainment that humans waste their time seeking. The idea of enjoyment is both its design and its subject matter. According to Brecht, it is meant to be a "moral tableau" to "show up the commercial character both of the entertainment and of the persons entertained." It is supposed to be a condemnation of escapist theater.

As usual with Brecht, his rationale for *Mahagonny* had practically nothing to do with its art. And while his essay on it as "epic opera" is among his most explicit writings on production, this work remains not a mockery of theatrical excitement, but theatrical excitement itself. Very wisely, director Jean Gascon paid scant attention to Brecht's directions in staging the work and musical director Louis Applebaum played down the weak parodies of Wagner, Rossini and Weber to concentrate on Weill's raw and chilling score, easily his most ambitious, and approached only by his extraordinary drama-ballet *The Seven Deadly Sins*.

The result was as cutting, as vicious, as jolting a piece of theater as I have ever seen, staged with all the fury and stuff of the stage that is suppressed at Stratford's main arena.

The lighting went wild. In fact, Gascon was playing left wing to Langham's dominating right at the festival proper. Staged with bursts of color that made for technicolor nightmares and moving in swinging, sliding patterns, it clawed its way through the Avon Theater. Brecht was not yet a line-toeing Communist — only a man furious (if a little overexcited) with man's inhumanity. The city of Mahagonny, while based on an oddly alien picture of America (reminiscent of Kafka's *Amerika*), represented everything he resented in Western civilization — the destruction of morality by materialism and hedonism. Created by promoters as a place for money-making, it became a chaotic haven for animal freedom when a typhoon sidestepped it (Mahagonny needs no typhoons because it is fully able to destroy itself).

At the end, with the hero sagging in an electric chair (he had been acquitted of a murder charge but had not paid a bar debt, and nonpayment of a debt is a capital crime in Mahagonny); with martial music beating in relentless waves; with the "ideals" of the society marching on placards (FOR THE EXPLOITATION OF OTHERS — FOR ETERNAL VULGARITY — FOR THE NATURAL DISORDER OF THINGS); with acid dripping from the stage and brasses rasping against drums, *Mahagonny* ends. Brecht's theorizing had no application. It canceled itself out in overwinding complications. What won — as what always wins — was art itself. Brecht may have thought he knew what he wanted to do, but the only thing that matters is what he did. The opera is the experience of a lifetime.

Such a production, bearing all the marks of left-wing theater (an unusual play, creative direction, intemperance, a certain amateurism, an attitude basically contrary to social norms) should not be taken as hope for a liberal influence at Stratford. It was an exception. This festival is pure right wing and will remain so. Its status is too national, its reputation too established, its ruling powers too staid. But it is nice to rely on its perfection, and it is good to have so superbly trained a company. When any of its members come to

Broadway they can bowl you over with technique. It just is, every so often, under glass.

The Minnesota Theater Company was *born* under glass. And prestressed concrete. Stratford may have begun with sizable backing and governmental support, but it still began in a tent. It was almost an adventure once. The Minnesota Theater Company started with a flashy fourteen-hundred-seat theater, university and municipal support, and a $337,000 Ford Foundation grant that guaranteed subsidies years in advance (Ford anticipated MTC's becoming self-supporting at 75 percent of capacity; this was not to be).

MTC was created to be an all-Ford super resident theater — America's answer to Stratford. The house was embarrassingly copied from the Festival Theater, though smaller. Even the company symbol was almost indistinguishable from Stratford's, as were the intermission fanfares. America, as usual, wanted an end result without bothering about intermediate stages of development.

The problem with MTC was that it did not begin in a tent. Like Brasília, it was built before it was alive. But a theater is not a building; it is a living thing. MTC was the first instance of the prefabricated resident theater company, artificially inseminated by American Subsidy. As a result, it is without its own style or identity.

A company was assembled and the first season's plays — all right wing — were carefully chosen to cover a broad period: *Hamlet, The Miser, The Three Sisters, Death of a Salesman.* Subscribers were enlisted with the sleek efficiency of a Ford assembly line. Sets and costumes were lavish. But no company really existed, as ensemble or as growth from youth. It was an assortment of American-untrained personality actors, headed by three stars: Hume Cronyn, Jessica Tandy and George Grizzard.

Guthrie stayed for only three seasons and in 1965 directed only two of the four productions. He had "established" a company, imprinted the "fine" label on it (misrepresentative and superficial as that label may have been) and emerged with his theatrical sainthood increased by one more degree. Much to his surprise, I am sure, he would have to return to the Guthrie in 1967 to try to rescue it. Money, high-power promoting and novelty can carry a

theater only so far, and MTC in 1966 had run into declining business, critical rejection, defecting actors and a collapse of artistic
standards.

One must concede that Guthrie has done a great deal, as director
and as mentor, for actors, theaters and communities. There is a
great craftsmanship to his directing and he has a wonderful way
with pageantry and battle scenes. His Shakespeare is warmly classical, despite the forays into switched time and locale. But his taste is
much too limited for a modern resident theater.

MTC, like Stratford in so many ways, is like it too in being a
right-wing theater. To start with, it is a summer festival, geared to
attract Midwesterners within a five-hundred-mile radius. It is
planned so that a weekending tourist can get a two- or three-day
sampling of culture, spend some time on the lovely lawn and get
the hell out with maybe an extra program for the hometown dra-
matics teacher. Too big to be flexible and too official to be free,
MTC was conceived, dedicated and exists to be an institution. Having burst full-grown from the brow of the Ford Foundation (it even
took Oliver Rea, one of its first managing directors, from TCG), it
began at once to do standard works in standard ways. Yet in those
standard works it provided the only real theater (and perhaps the
only theater at all) for a large segment of the country. It is doubtful
that many of its visitors would ever have had a chance to see a
professional production of *Volpone* if it had not been for the Guthrie Theater. And certainly not of Brecht's *The Caucasian Chalk
Circle*.

That production, presented by MTC in the summer of 1965, was
perhaps the finest work it has yet done. It was certainly the first left-
wing work it had ever done. Seeing *The Caucasian Chalk Circle* in
Minneapolis was a tremendous event in my life.

The play, like much of Brecht, is in the form of parable, but it is
more than that and is really quite different from most of his work
(it was his last full-length play). While it carries his usual skepti-
cism about the possibility of peace or justice, it at least concedes a
human capability for compassion. It suddenly allows for human
goodness — genuine Christianity — something Brecht never before even admitted existed.

The play is drawn from an old Chinese drama, *The Circle of*

Chalk. It is about two women who claim the same child. A judge instructs the women to tug the infant from a circle. As in the similar biblical tale of Solomon, the woman who does not want the child to be harmed is judged to be the mother ("I brought him up! Shall I also tear him to bits?"). So the moral: "What there is shall go to those who are good for it. Thus, the children to the motherly, that they prosper. The carts to good drivers, that they are driven well. And the valley to the waterers, that it bring forth fruit."

The biblical ring is typical of the play's simplicity as well as being in the standard Brecht mode of primitive wisdom. For sheer clarity and classicism, it can be compared only to Mozart or Shakespeare. In fact, it may be the best example of Brecht as Shakespeare's descendant. What is so surprising is that symmetric art generally produces beauty rather than thrill. *The Caucasian Chalk Circle* has both.

In the play, the infant is the son of an assassinated potentate. Abandoned by his mother, who is more interested in escaping with her possessions than with her son, he is rescued from rebels by the kitchen maid Grusha. This is an act of purity, committed against all the rules of self-preservation. It is done in a world where "motherly instincts can be a suicidal business" — a world where to be good is to ask for trouble. Following a series of adventures as she streaks from danger, Grusha is captured and brought to trial before a judge named Azdak — a manic who rules not by justice (which is impossible on this earth) but by compassion (which, if rarely, is possible). He then conducts the chalk test.

Edward Payson Call, then an associate director at MTC, launched it over the Guthrie Theater's big thrust stage and let it go bounding across, around and right over the sides. The gorgeous Oriental costumes and masks worn by the play's evil characters contrasted sharply with the leathery rags of Grusha and Azdak, and Herbert Pilhofer's songs provided the extra, complementary dimension that music always gives to Brecht. Zoe Caldwell rolled up her Grusha's sleeves and gave one of the finest single performances I have ever seen. Ed Flanders nearly burst apart at the seams in the flamboyant role of Azdak.

Call, in the new directing style, kept the company rolling and weaving and cagily involved the audience in the production. His control was total. In the heartbreaking beauty of the third-person romantic dialogue ("Does the young lady wish to say that someone has come too late?") he maintained a simple tenderness. For the stylized structure he devised stylized staging methods. For example, in fleeing the Fascists Grusha is supposed to dash over a half-destroyed bridge across a frightening gorge. Call had two actors carry small sections of a "bridge" on their backs. Grusha climbed upon the back of a third and then stepped perilously out. As realists, we knew that just stepping onto an actor's back is a touchy thing. As an audience, we were sucked into the magic, helped by howling winds we could almost feel. It was an extraordinary accomplishment. As was the production — a true example of multi-level, interwing theater; a splendid fury matched with the suavity and facility of the right wing.

The rest of that 1965 MTC season was quite another matter. The Balanced Masterwork program (Shakespeare, Chekhov, Congreve) called for a versatile company, trained in fundamentals. The MTC actors were hardly such a company and when approaching, for example, the sheer elegance of *The Way of the World,* they were lost, having neither the style nor the technique for Restoration comedy. Douglas Campbell's heavy-handed direction hardly helped, nor did the inappropriate thrust stage.

But the essential trouble with the Congreve was in the company which, excepting only a few of the actors, was a wonder of bumble. As for the exceptions, the startling thing was seeing Miss Caldwell as the beautiful and clever Mistress Millamant one afternoon after having been electrified by her peasant Grusha the evening before. It was incredible only because American right-wing acting has led us to recognize an actor from one role to another. Caldwell may or may not be beautiful — I'm not really sure — but she can seem beautiful or plain whenever she chooses. As Mistress Millamant she behaved with the willowy control of a lady with absolute composure, as if the whole world were too great a bore for her to bear. She could translate a single word into a series of letters punctuated by individual breaths — an extraordinary discipline of voice and manner.

Such technical aplomb was unusual at MTC. Where Stratford's trained company could turn out a perfectly respectable *Cherry Or-*

chard, MTC transformed Chekhov's humanity into listlessness. Even its *Richard III,* a seemingly perfect play for Guthrie staging, could not work for the shallowness of the company.

No company can do only one Shakespeare play a year and do it well. Nor can it pluck a Restoration comedy out of the dramatic grab bag and manage the necessary high style. MTC has not had the time to develop an approach, a style or a taste of its own. Designed as it was to do plays of any period, it is a company whose aim is to be vaguely but suavely for "all" theater. Such a company will be specifically good for none.

The American Shakespeare Festival at Stratford, Connecticut restricts itself to one playwright but to no greater advantage. It is the single example of far right-wing theater among resident companies and can be fairly called a parody of theater.

The reason that the American Stratford can be called a parody is Joseph Verner Reed, the executive producer who so controls the artistic life of the festival that after running out of directors willing to be directed he assumed artistic control of the operation himself. And Stratford is indeed an operation.

As a summertime, picknicking festival it is incomparable. It is promoted as Easy Culture, Only an Hour and a Half from Times Square. There, on the spacious grounds, Dad can listen to the ball game on his transistor radio while Mom reads *Harper's.* By show-time, everybody is comfortable enough to withstand Shakespeare and is eased through the paneled lobby (in which there hangs a *Richard III* looking exactly like Edward Albee) into the motelly theater with its venetian-blind set and sky-blue cyclorama. By this time, nobody remembers what play is to be done and it really doesn't make any difference, either to the audience or, apparently, to the management.

The American Shakespeare Festival and Academy was not always so. In the beginning, headed by John Houseman, it was worse. Born of a Broadway mentality, it was early dependent upon names rather than a developed resident company. It may have been designed as an academy as well as a theater but it couldn't resist hiring a Katharine Hepburn. It was this company that received a $503,000 grant from the Ford Foundation in 1962.

For a while, early in the Sixties, it shed some of its worst habits and although it returned to them soon enough, things were not too terribly bad. Douglas Seale and Allen Fletcher were sharing the artistic directorship — Seale a well-trained classicist and one of America's most talented, creative and unappreciated directors; and Fletcher a workmanlike plodder. They managed to keep a company of actors together long enough to give them some training and cohesion.

So the American Stratford developed a few actors like Douglas Watson, Philip Bosco and Patrick Hines, and gave some nice performances in 1963 and 1964. The latter was the year for *A Comedy of Errors,* with performances by the visiting Royal Shakespeare Company and Stratford, Ontario, as well as in Connecticut. The one that Seale did was especially inventive, having the Antipholus and Dromio twins played by the same actors. This not only overcame the usual problem of finding look-alikes but gave the production the special kind of brightness necessary for this very early play, which desperately relies on performance to make it work.

Seale did a splendid job that whole season. While his *Henry V* was conceived in a way with which I cannot agree (Seale saw Hal as compassionate rather than heroic), he presented that conception with a consistency and understanding that fully played out his argument. A director can choose any analysis he wishes, and is only obliged to prove it dramatically feasible without distorting the basic material. One need not agree but cannot scoff. For *Henry V,* I would not play down Hal's inspirational speeches, which seem to me necessarily inspiring, but Seale's way was interesting. And James Ray's performance stayed with it, playing for warmth and love rather than for boldness and flaming leadership.

The next season, like 1963, was typified by Fletcher's conservative direction — the kind so appealing to a domineering producer — and it was highlighted by a repeat performance of Morris Carnovsky's Second Avenue *King Lear,* which had been 1964's box office smash. It was with this that Stratford soggily settled back into the depths from which it had briefly climbed during the previous two summers. The production might well have been subtitled *Is This the Thanks a Father Gets?*

Mr. Carnovsky's Yiddish Art Theater performance could not be begrudged its commercial success, I suppose, although I don't see why not. But maybe a little respect for Shakespeare?

To avoid any confusion, the performance was not in Yiddish, but Carnovsky's quivering heartburn basso rumblings, his curling fingers and his grandiloquent gestures were. With sauerkraut robes and facial makeup that ran to silent-movie eyebrows, he seemed prepared, after giving Goneril and Regan their bungalows, to add, "You're entitled."

On the other hand, Patrick Hines — a company veteran who deserved a crack at Lear himself — drew Gloucester with all the sensitivity and insight that experience and talent make possible. It was a performance of the caliber that should be standard for a company with the facilities and backing of Connecticut's Stratford. The role of Gloucester is written in parallel with Lear's. He too is a father betrayed by one child and rescued by another after having been cruelly tricked into trusting the wrong one. He too forced his own fate by allowing his paternal emotions to be capitalized upon: he too believed the worst. He too was trapped by the terrible needs and fears of old age. Lear and Gloucester exist in tandem, one on the majestic level and the other on the human. But while Carnovsky perverted majesty with his potato-latke theatricals, Hines drew humanity with subtle strokes of artistry.

By this time, Stratford was losing many of its trained people. Some, like Seale, left after impossible artistic conflicts with Reed. Fletcher remained with a decimated company, forced to cast half-developed players in leading roles. Right-wing Broadway directors like Joseph Anthony were hired to work with a classical theater for which they were totally unequipped (Anthony did *The Taming of the Shrew* in the style of a traveling Spanish troupe for absolutely no reason at all and in 1966 cut, juggled and revised *Henry IV, Part Two* to so great a degree that the play could not be considered Shakespeare's any more).

By the time that season had rolled around, even Fletcher was gone (to Seattle's Repertory Theater), and Reed was alone with his neat lawns and picture postcards, talking about hiring James Cagney to play Falstaff.

Give my regards to Broadway.

Although Joseph Papp's New York Shakespeare Festival is still another summer theater, it is not a repertory company, having no commercial need to alternate plays.

The Central Park Festival, however, has its own distinctions. It was born of Papp's dream and was, as much as Ball's American Conservatory Theater, conceived in a single man's drive to do what he believed in.

Papp began with a determination to provide free and well-done Shakespeare for the people in New York who could not afford to pay for it. That may sound do-gooder, but he really is that way. To a degree it *was* a bringing-culture-to-the-masses kind of condescension, but it was also a theatrical idealism that is depressingly rare. A television director with artistic inclinations, Papp rounded up a small group of actors who were disgusted with trash and were out of work anyhow — people like Colleen Dewhurst, J. D. Cannon and George C. Scott. Before they were through they were playing to overflow audiences in local parks with a combination of amateur enthusiasm, youthful freewheeling and genuine talent. After a stupid hassle with Robert Moses, the then-reigning Coriolanus of the Department of Parks, over whether the city should be paid for the use (and presumed disruption) of its lawns, Papp managed to get philanthropist George Delacorte to build an open-air theater for him in Central Park and got a municipal subsidy along with it.

At that point, the festival changed, and, more than coincidentally, at the very moment that American Subsidy was developing. With its move to Central Park, Papp's company became a big-money, fully professional theater with budgets passing the half-million-dollar mark. And dependent upon charity financing.

As that financing began to pour in, Papp became more dependent upon *it,* hatching ever greater, ever more expensive plans. Like the other artistic directors around the country, he assumed that subsidy was his due. Like them too, he started his shift rightward from the true left-wingedness that had been his theater's birthmark. He directed less often and when he did it was more conservative and the productions more *swank*. Excitement began to ebb just as finesse began to flow. It was a classic example of left-to-right-wing movement. And Papp began to spend more and more of his time wooing funds from society dilettantes. (He embarrassed the company in the spring of 1966 by participating in a fund-raising dance that featured society hippies in nudie fashions "inspired" by Shakespeare.)

Today the New York Shakespeare Festival is nearly right wing. Perhaps not so far as Minneapolis or Stratford, Ontario, and certainly not so far as Stratford, Connecticut. But rightward it is going.

A good example of this was the *Antony and Cleopatra* in the summer of 1963. It was set with lots of torches (Papp is mad for torches — one day he will set the park afire). Colleen Dewhurst, whose running *schtik* is the earth mother, seemed a perfect choice for the sensual queen. Michael Higgins was a trained actor with a strong quality of vulnerability. They should have been just right for this story of A Man Destroyed. But neither they nor Papp could grasp the play's sense of royal Egyptian erotica along the hot banks of the Nile. While Dewhurst could show the egotistical, vain, selfish traits of Cleopatra, she missed the hedonistic intensity. And while Higgins managed Antony's futile integrity, he never seemed haplessly subjugated. Struggling to rid himself of his passion, he wasn't really unhappy, really ensnared, really tragic.

In terms of public success, the most successful NYSF production in its Delacorte era was the *Othello* that Gladys Vaughan staged in the summer of 1964 (and which subsequently became the initial festival work to move off-Broadway after the summer run). That production, the company's last really left-wing one, gave James Earle Jones his first chance at a major role — his first chance to show the depth that many of us had been insisting he possessed. What he proved was that he would someday play a magnificent *Othello,* but not yet. His portrayal was as confused as it was eloquent.

The most unusual thing about Miss Vaughan's production was its conception of the play in terms of man, woman and sex. Its running theme was desire, its parallel lovers (Othello-Desdemona, Iago-Emilia, Cassio-Bianca) carried in comparative streams of passion. Within these liquid lusts, Miss Vaughan mixed her *Othello* with a twist of lemon, or some bitter fruit. That is, she made Iago a homosexual (as Olivier did, some years ago, to Ralph Richardson's Othello). And so while the Venetian military set was running around in vividly heterosexual circles, the bitchy ensign quietly went counterclockwise. This was not entirely contrary to the play as written. Iago *does* say that during a dream Cassio wrapped a leg around his thigh and kissed him on the lips. Vaughan embellished this by having him actually kiss Roderigo as well, and there was a legitimate dramatic purpose to it: in being homosexual, Iago is able to coolly capitalize on the needs of heterosexuals, being totally uninvolved himself. Furthermore, since Shakespeare fails to provide motivation enough for Iago's extreme villainy, the director is compelled to find some.

Mitchell Ryan played Iago without the standard hand-rubbing, oily villainy. His eyeballs did not barrel from corner to corner as he hatched his scheme. Rather, his behavior was impelled by sexual neurosis and a subsconscious passion for Jones's boorish stud.

Jones was fairly conventional except for his own natural boyishness and a playing up of the beast. In his leaps and thrusts, in his lifting and throwing about of Desdemona (at one point like a rag doll), in his sweepingly long arms and gigantic bounding steps, he was the male — vital and lusty. It hardly compared with Olivier's subsequent performance of a like analysis, which took the jealous madness bubbling past the bursting point into a howl of animal pain, splattering his wounded ego in a careen of nearly nonverbal howls and ripping the crucifix from his throat to reveal the savage he had always been. But then, Jones does not pretend to be in Olivier's class. At Jones's stage of development, the performance was quite respectable and his Moslem touches (a long kneeling bow that had his arms go over his head and out onto the floor, his brow to the ground) managed to combine Othello's social identity with his physical sense.

Another interesting point about this production was Julienne Marie's playing of Desdemona as being not altogether above suspicion. While there does not seem to be any basis for such an interpretation in the play, there needn't be. Valid art will provoke various reactions and a left-oriented director will look for them. A thoroughly right-wing Shakespeare company like Stratford, Ontario's would never conceive of Iago as a homosexual or Desdemona as suspect. That is why it makes few mistakes. A company like the NYSF can dare to see different things (increasingly different with increasing leftness) and will consequently slip more often and occasionally look foolish. It will also, perhaps, find something new to add to dramatic tradition.

However, Papp's company is practically finished with such probing and now inclines toward handsomely costumed things placed, usually, before the striking sets of Ming Cho Lee. The productions are careful, they are smooth, they are mature. For something like the *Love's Labor's Lost* in the summer of 1965, they are lovely, and this may well have been the finest job done by the company since its move into the park.

It is baffling to me why this beautiful and wise play is so seldom performed. In language, it is Shakespeare at his most elegant, swooping from fun and games to shining poetry. Think of the sheer nerve and supreme confidence necessary for him to parody literary affectations when, after all, he was shamelessly addicted to such horseplay himself. To turn and mock the very sport he played — especially when those he was ridiculing were themselves no slouches — demanded exquisite skill at parody and the ability to be beyond it himself (which he really wasn't, as *Beyond the Fringe* demonstrated).

Love's Labor's Lost is not a perfect play, dragging seriously in two sequences, but its combination of wit and substance is adroit and its manner refined. King Ferdinand of Navarre is bright but takes himself a bit too seriously, and his plan to spend three celibate years with intellectual companionship is more of a whim than a real dedication. When he and his presumably scholarly lords are confronted by ladies who are not willing to settle for pseudowisdom, an important point is made in a charming way.

Gerald Freedman's direction was inventive without being distorting, although it came mildly close to ghostwriting. At the close of the play, Don Adriano, a seedy, boastful, flowery pretender, accepts his faults and sadly tells us, "The words of Mercury are harsh after the songs of Apollo. You that way, we this way — *omnes exeunt.*" That *"omnes exeunt,"* of course, was not Shakespeare's *line* but his *stage direction.* If Freedman's use of it was cheating of a sort, it made a wonderfully right conclusion for a play that must be both high-spirited and touching. It was, at any rate, typical of Freedman's creative staging. For example, there is no mention in the text of a Russian dance in Act IV, scene iii; there is nothing to suggest music except a line about "revels, dances, masks and merry hours." It was enough to allow Freedman a dance and, along with it, a funny and spirited scene. And John Morris composed delightful music for the entire production. Incidental music for the theater is usually hackneyed, artificial and trivial. It needn't be, but somehow certain composers seem to have the business locked up and nobody else can get in. David Amram has controlled the NYSF composing for years, writing bland scores that sound Elizabethanphoney no matter what the play. How Mr. Morris wriggled his way in was curious but fortunate.

In July of 1964, Papp expanded his activities to send out touring productions in a mobile theater ingeniously designed by Ming Cho Lee to fold out of a trailer truck and become a small thrust stage, dressing rooms, lighting, generating equipment and seating facilities for sixteen hundred people. If you are interested in ironies by the wayside, twelve days before Mr. Ming's truck made its first appearance the Ford Foundation announced a $75,000 grant to scenic designers Jo Mielziner and Donald Oenslager and lighting authority Edward F. Kook to design a mobile theater. While it is true that Ming's theater was open air and Ford was after an enclosed house, the NYSF unit obviously had an enormous amount of research and development behind it. Why was Ming excluded from the grant?

The best explanation is the usual foundation fuzziness. Another might be Ford's preference for right-wing people (and Mielziner and Oenslager are most assuredly old-guard right-wingers). There is a nagging suspicion of another explanation. It nags because the NYSF has never received a penny in grants from the major subsidizers. Friends of Papp blame it on a foundation view of him as "un-American" (he was once summoned to testify before the House Un-American Activities Committee). I don't know whether to believe that or not, it is so ridiculous, but the foundations' excuse (who needs another Shakespeare festival?) is just as ridiculous.

Because of the festival's dependence upon contributions, mostly from New York City, Papp has become increasingly involved with politicking and fund-raising. Like the other resident theater directors, he built his in a bubble that he insisted could not burst. Like them too, the very existence of his theater became no longer his alone to control. He confidently formulated plans for a two-theater, winter program. The millions of necessary dollars were only figures-on-paper dreams. Certainly, if Papp had waited until the money was raised the theaters would never get built. Certainly, a degree of brazen ambition is necessary to start a great thing. But to conceive of a large enterprise and then expect the subsidizers to pay for it is the weird custom of the American Subsidy situation.

Evidently the theaters are getting built. But when they are, whose will they be? And what will they be?

It is all very fine for the city to be given free Shakespeare. While the audiences at Central Park are obviously capable of purchasing tickets, perhaps they wouldn't come for even a fifty-cent admission price. The system of giving reserved seats to contributors is a neat way of indirectly selling some of the tickets and the "free" idea is Papp's gimmick as well as his social ideal. The price of that gimmick, though, is absolute dependence upon outside sources, forcing Papp to become an annual weeper while his theater grows fat.

Ironically, the mobile theater brought strange reminders of how things once were. On a warm summer night in 1964 the company truck first sprung the theater into Mount Morris Park in Harlem, where sixteen hundred people were seated while countless more lined the fences that isolated the park from the fearful slums that surround it.

Coping with a strange situation (some people in the audience played transistor radios during the performance), the company may not have given the most artful *Midsummer Night's Dream* in theater history, but it surely gave one of the most theatrical. The troupe of young players took theater itself out onto the little stage and sprayed it all over the playground-auditorium. They put on a show as a show *should* be put on; the way entertainment has always reached most people. Jack Sydow staged the comedy with a directness that made more lavish productions seem unrealistically inanimate. Frankly, it is easy to appreciate such things when you are sitting in a crowded park thinking terribly basic thoughts about terribly basic theater. You tend to go artsy, to blow things out of proportion and accept lowness and breadth with a rationalized condescension. But still, I think, there was a real kind of left-wing vitality to that night's *Midsummer* that has been missing in the smoother, better-controlled work at the Delacorte. And it did suggest that perhaps too many directors are staging too many plays, Shakespeare's and others', for *themselves* and their *own* refined tastes rather than for the audiences'.

One last point about the mobile theater. The first year's tour of fifty performances at thirty-nine locations dispelled all foolish liberal notions about art and the slums. The conditions were awful; not everybody was yearning for drama. The audiences were often impossible and more than once the players were threatened with violence in the midst of a performance. It was important for them, for the NYSF and for New York City to learn this. Nothing can be done to improve a condition until that condition is honestly seen for what it is. (The question remains whether the theater should have any other purpose than to be theater.) Papp took his company into some very rough situations and it took a lot of guts for them to do it. Some poor actor may yet be cut up but the work is being done. I think that Papp's mobile theater is one of the few legitimately decent social things I've ever seen a theater company do.

How far is it from Harlem's Mount Morris Park to the Lincoln Center for the Performing Arts? How far is it from a Joseph Papp scrounging up some actors to give free Shakespeare in a local park to the creation of the country's most expensive theater in one snappy miracle of millions? Frank Lloyd Wright once said that the United Nations Building looked like a tombstone. Lincoln Center looks like a graveyard and it is there that American Subsidy seems determined to bury art.

The Repertory Theater of Lincoln Center was created with the kind of money that made the Stratford, Ontario, Shakespearean Festival and the Minnesota Theater Company look like sleazy side shows on a carnival midway. It was designed to be the American National Theater from the moment it opened its doors. Considering the principles, standards and mentalities behind it, there was as much chance of that happening as of an Ingmar Bergman film playing the Music Hall.

Before getting into this marble mess, it must be pointed out that

Lincoln Center is dominated by blue chip New York, which means bankers, industrialists and professional gentry, with their governmental, foundation and high-finance connections and cultural aspirations. Conversely, it also must be pointed out that the Metropolitan Opera House was desperately outmoded; that Carnegie Hall was by no means the ideal concert hall that sentimentalists have since made it out to be; that New York was absurdly without a non-commercial and serious theater; that the New York City Ballet, the finest dance company in America, was housed in perhaps the world's worst (and certainly the ugliest and most uncomfortable) dance theater; and that it would be a very nice thing to have new facilities for all of these in an architecturally cohesive setting.

To build Lincoln Center the place, it was necessary to accept Lincoln Center the idea. The question is whether one was worth the other. In the instance of the repertory theater, since such a theater did not exist before Lincoln Center was built, no case can be made for a good thing having been spoiled. At worst, the possibility for a great thing will have been fumbled.

Given the kinds of people who control Lincoln Center, it came as no surprise that Jo Mielziner, a right-wing Broadway designer past his prime, was asked to design the theater (and model it closely on Stratford, Ontario's thrust stage) or that right-wing Broadway people were named as directors and that they chose their first season's program from right-wing Broadway material. It is difficult to think of two people less qualified than Elia Kazan and Robert Whitehead for the directorship of a major resident theater unless you suggest Jules Irving and Herbert Blau, but we will get to them all too soon.

Whitehead was a successful Broadway producer with a reputation for doing serious right-wing drama. Kazan was the most prominent director on postwar Broadway, brilliant with right-wing psychological drama. Neither had the faintest interest in or sense of either classical or new theater.

So in their choice of Arthur Miller's *After the Fall,* Eugene O'Neill's *Marco Millions* and S. N. Behrman's *But for Whom, Charlie?* for the first season, they were running true to form, programming exactly what Lincoln Center expected. It was Broadway thinking, pure right wing and perfectly in rhythm with the trustees.

The idea of a serious resident company producing two plays that obviously would have been produced on Broadway was preposterous. The whole *point* of resident theater is to present plays that the commercial theater does not or cannot produce.

In their eagerness to begin, Kazan and Whitehead had the temporary ANTA-Washington Square Theater built for two seasons' use while the Vivian Beaumont was being completed. The Repertory Theater of Lincoln Center opened its temporary doors on January 23, 1964, with Arthur Miller's first play in almost ten years.

After the Fall was a great play produced under the worst imaginable circumstances. Left-wing antagonism to the company had already grown well beyond the point of even taking it seriously (an attitude that would soon prove entirely justified). Miller, during his absence, had been built up in the right-wing theatergoers' minds as the Greatest Playwright of the Twentieth Century.

The play went inside its author's mind to find an answer to the confusion of life — for himself and for all of mankind. It came out of that confusion with only a less indefinite uncertainty. If there was some discomfort at being present at so calculated a self-surgery, it was more the chill of being forced to look at something really naked than it was the shallow feeling of embarrassment.

The play was a confession and an absolution. A man called Quentin (too obviously, for "questing") comes forward to tell about his life. The audience is a friend, a psychiatrist, God, humanity, himself. Quentin's life, as it involves his essential being, is brought up to the present, when he is about to marry for the third time. The action of the play occurs in his mind.

The story was glaringly autobiographical, at least as far as the publicized events of Miller's life were concerned. Presumably, if these were facts, so was the rest. It was important to accept this and then forget it, but that proved difficult for a public more concerned with personalities than with ideas. Knowing that Miller's second wife was Marilyn Monroe, it could *not* forget it and refused him the right of any artist to draw the general from his specific experience.

The three women in Quentin's life represent three possible solutions to his guilt (and by extension, that of humanity). With the first wife, a middle-class woman with middle-class demands

("Where were you all night? Why don't you talk to me?") he seeks justification through reason. With the second, a neurotic child needing more love than anyone could provide and who was dedicated to her own destruction, he seeks justification through love. With the third, a sensitive intellectual and humanist, he was to seek justification through forgiveness. Artists have eternally addressed themselves to the question of the purpose of life. *After the Fall* was attempting to answer the same question, only rephrasing it as, assuming that man will always lead an immoral life, how can that life be justified?

The title was drawn from Genesis, out of which humanity had stumbled after its fall from grace, abandoning the paradise of moral purity for the knowledge of sin. For Miller, we must look at ourselves fullface and renounce our self-delusion of integrity. We are not honest. We do not love. And in subtitling the play *The Survivor,* he went one step further; in accepting human fallibility, he demanded responsibility — to pick up and forgive for weakness and work for a relationship with life.

"We are," "life is" plays are usually sophomoric and there is no denying that a great deal of *After the Fall* represented half-assessed thinking. Nevertheless, the intellectual depth, the honesty and the sheer nakedness of it combined with a dramatic power to make it a mental and emotional workout. The play was so moving that it was easy to overlook its beautiful writing and original structure. While there were occasional clichés and intermittent pomposities, the language was generally fine. In construction it was well into the free time and space system that Miller had last used successfully in *Death of a Salesman.* It was an excellent example of right-wing playwrighting.

Right wing, I might add, although Miller was clearly attempting to move into left-wing surrealism with it. Realism is his badge, though, and psychological solution his point. Miller, like all right-wing playwrights, assumes that man is capable of understanding his situation, and that the physical and social sciences, while unable to provide every answer to every question, *will* be able to provide those answers sooner or later. The left-wing playwright works from the premise that the human situation is incomprehensible and that answers do not exist. This, incidentally, is exactly the difference between Jean-Paul Marat and the Marquis de Sade in the Peter Weiss play — a play basically *about* the conflict between the right and left wings.

Because Kazan had stocked the Lincoln Center company with actors appealing to his right-wing realistic theater tastes, and particularly with *After the Fall* in mind, the Miller play was extremely well done. For this very reason, later productions requiring left-wing acting were mangled. Jason Robards was a probing, vulnerable Quentin even though, as it turned out, he didn't understand what the play was all about (later, vulgarly, he called it "pretentious," which is a left-wing cliché and the easiest word in a confused critic's vocabulary, I can assure you). It was to be his last adequate job before succumbing entirely to staccato mannerisms. Barbara Loden made a sensational, giggly Marilyn Monroe, which subsequent roles proved to be not acting but her natural personality. Kazan directed superbly, as well he should have. It was a play written exactly to his style.

After the Fall provoked an avalanche of reaction. A strange combination of movie-star-mad public and intellectuals who saw her as A Symbol rose to protest the invasion of Monroe's privacy, unable to understand that the character in the play was not limited to the person from whom she was drawn. Left-wingers who had dismissed Miller the way left-wingers always dismiss any right-winger brushed the play aside as an overintellectualized conceit. Reams of confused analysis and apology were written, not the least ridiculous of which was Miller's own (at one point he denied that the character had any relationship to Monroe when, aside from the obvious similarities, Miss Loden had been made up to look exactly *like* Monroe).

After the Fall was the only good work to come out of the Repertory Theater of Lincoln Center under the Whitehead-Kazan regime. The second production was *Marco Millions,* third-rate O'Neill that was possibly justifiable for resident theater purposes (a play that would not be commercially produced) but which was unsalvageable.

The final play of that first season was the ludicrous *But for Whom, Charlie?* by S. N. Behrman, a playwright with one of the most unjustified reputations in American theater. This play divided its characters into the Good Guys and the Bad Guys. The Good Guys were Jewish, loved Bach and chamber music, wore cardigan sweaters and suspenders (because clothes-consciousness equals superficiality), were meek, down-to-earth and sensitive. They loved everybody, helped everybody, understood everybody. The Bad Guys were slick dressers and either didn't like Bach and chamber music or said they did but We Know Better. They were clever, devious and socially poised. It was not a finished play. It was a finished-basement play.

Mielziner's split set followed this clever structure. The Bad Guys' part was in 1939 *moderne,* even unto a kidney-shaped sofa. The Good Guys' part was in lovely period decor. My God.

The thunderously negative response to the first season rattled the Lincoln Center powers. For the second season, Whitehead and Kazan abandoned their own right-wing tastes with one exception (Miller's *Incident at Vichy*) and so insured the slitting of their own throats. It was biologically impossible for them to adequately produce the three left-wing plays scheduled — *The Changeling,* a Jacobean tragedy by Thomas Middleton and William Rowley; Molière's *Tartuffe* and Giraudoux's *The Madwoman of Chaillot.*

That season began with the company's most resounding disaster — Kazan's *Changeling.* Ironically, the play was the most properly chosen of all. Almost never performed, although academically respected, it had become a dead classic. If it had not already been dead, this production would have done the trick.

Kazan, a director whose reputation rested upon his undeniable assurance with right-wing plays, had virtually no professional experience in period drama. Insecure and anxious, he staged the Middleton-Rowley as if it were a season's worth of playlets being performed in a city's worth of theaters. What was comic was played broadly, what was serious was played moodily — each scene, one at a time, as if in its own little bottle. And all the while spotlighting symbols — those provided by the play (mirrors for vanity or introspection) and those provided by Kazan (crucifixes everywhere, from small ones in deep cleavages to giant ones spread-eagled over the stage, floating in from *La Dolce Vita*).

The net effect was what it was bound to be — a theatrical Ed Sullivan Show with as broad a variety of acts as possible. And

Kazan's confusion, naturally enough, was reflected in his company, which had been given no consistent guidance or cohesion. Acting styles varied with each performer, at least in those cases where the performers were accomplished enough to have *developed* acting styles. As for Miss Loden, she turned in the most preposterous New York performance since Tab Hunter played a camp Apollo in Williams's *Milk Train.* Absolute sadism to let that girl go on.

Incident at Vichy, the season's second production, was not only the worst play Miller ever wrote but an unforgivable one for the very reason of his reputation. Like *After the Fall,* it was about guilt, but unlike it, it was unable to leave its specific example to make a general statement. The play made the somewhat startling observation that Nazism was evil.

By this time the Lincoln Center trustees had had it. In a personnel change clumsy enough to be worthy of a CIA-inspired South American coup, they tossed Kazan and Whitehead out of the company's directorship a week after the Miller had opened.

Freedom to founder. It seems a wasteful liberty but in art it is as necessary a freedom as any. Without it, there can be no development, no experimentation, no creativity. It was this freedom that was denied the Repertory Theater of Lincoln Center by nonartistic meddlers who felt it necessary to succeed financially, critically, socially and immediately.

Because critical disapproval stung administrative hides and because Lincoln Center was stupidly meant to be Born Great, Kazan and Whitehead were denied the right to fail. They were sacked for not "succeeding." Repertory theater is so new to this country that, at least at the time, there was really nobody who could say this way is right and that wrong. It was obvious that Kazan and Whitehead were badly prepared for the job in matters of taste and experience, but the values that prompted their dismissal were far more inexcusable.

A right-wing board of trustees, like a right-wing producer or director, will not think in terms of growth or development. It lives in a world of guarantees and acceptance. Are bankers, industrialists and administrators to run American art? They are indeed — the official business that American art has become. And who is to be responsible for determining the plays to be performed in a resident theater — the artistic director or a banker, an administrator, a labor and management consultant? (At one point William Schuman, the president of Lincoln Center, actually suggested a particular play and a particular star.) Does the Repertory Theater of Lincoln Center exist for the sake of theater or for the sake of Mr. Schuman and his financial overseers, dabbling in institutional dilettantism?

The only successful production of a legitimate classical play in the first four years of the Repertory Theater of Lincoln Center company came during the lame duck period of the Kazan-Whitehead regime. William Ball, who was jobbed in to stage *Tartuffe,* was completely free of the Center's influence. They needed him more than he needed them. They had to mount the season's final production (the Giraudoux having been canceled).

So Ball, who had every reason to reject the then-current company on the grounds of classic incompetence, was able to cast more than half his *Tartuffe* with outsiders. Here lies the nature of freedom. It is without restriction. In the institutional theater, artistic freedom cannot exist while a director is overseen. Ball's success with *Tartuffe* could never have been accomplished had he been hampered. The already-fired Whitehead and Kazan gave him a freedom that would probably never exist again at Lincoln Center.

His *Tartuffe* was one of the finest examples of interwing theater ever to be seen in New York, a Mozart or Rossini opera heard by an inner ear. Dispensing with the grand, wiggy manner *de rigueur* for Molière, Ball staged the classic with a royal feeling for words and movement, flashing to the heart of the play's matter: the contempt for artifice and hypocrisy, for vicious piety and superpuritanism. And the interest in all-theater fun, rooted in Molière's own ideas of musical staging.

Michael O'Sullivan gave the performance of the season, making the supercilious Tartuffe a wily lecher with stringy hair and legs lumpy and stick-thin. Springing from a chair into which he had just collapsed, he became a dismantled puppet, his arms flying outward, his legs splayed beneath him. His voice careened in falsetto to suddenly drop four octaves into a rumbling grumble, then float into glassiness. In a performance that brought virtuosity to the very brink of excess, O'Sullivan never stepped over that precarious

ledge. He matched flamboyance with control, which is exactly what
Ball demands. This director is not afraid to dive into the wildly
theatrical, but he will never allow himself the self-indulgence that
produces vain sloppiness. Naturally, following this virtuoso display, Lincoln Center decided to replace Whitehead and Kazan not
with Ball but with Herbert Blau and Jules Irving (who two years
later tried to copy Ball's *Tartuffe* with an O'Sullivan-starred *The
Alchemist*. Having no original concept, they failed).

No greater artistic shift could have been possible. Moving Blau
and Irving from coast to coast symbolized the extent of it. They
could not have been moved further. They were as left wing as
Whitehead-Kazan were right. While the company's first directors
were professionals with backward, commercial tastes and no sense
of theater literature, the replacements were near amateurs who
could quickly jot down every play that should be produced by a
resident theater.

Blau and Irving began by scheduling four plays that were almost
everything a resident theater's program should be — Georg
Büchner's *Danton's Death* and Bertolt Brecht's *The Caucasian
Chalk Circle* are two of the towering plays in the theater literature.
The Büchner had not received a New York production since Orson
Welles's Mercury Theater had presented it in 1938. The Brecht
had *never* been professionally produced in New York. The other
plays were Wycherly's *The Country Wife,* a resident theater staple,
and Jean-Paul Sartre's *The Condemned of Altona,* which may be a
perfectly stupid play but could *conceivably* be taken seriously. This
was real left-wing programming.

Blau and Irving dropped the concept of repertory, although not
from the company title, following the trend toward redefining the
word into meaninglessness. In the Whitehead-Kazan days a production would open, run three or four weeks, and then be joined by another. The two would then alternate performances which, after all,
is what "repertory" means. Some weeks later a third production
would open and the repertory would be increased. Blau and Irving
instituted *series* performances, each production running six weeks
and then closing. At the end of the season the "successful" productions were to be revived in repertory. In effect, this is a straight
commercial system, banking on "hits."

They dismissed just about the entire company that Whitehead and Kazan had assembled and brought more than half of their own people in from California, virtually destroying the Actors Workshop.

With this, and some characteristic mutterings from Blau about the political significance of the plays about to be produced, the season began. It was to prove an extraordinary example of left-wing theater without *any* right-wing influence — an unprovoked assault upon a number of great plays.

The siege began with the opening of the crimson, brown and magnificently equipped Vivian Beaumont Theater and the production of *Danton's Death*. In fact, Büchner's great first play was destroyed, and replaced by a leaden, barren, dramaless shell of the important and exciting work it really is. Blau, who directed the production, "adapted" the play to the point of violent revision and defilement. He cut the most vaulting speeches, rewriting them in prosaic static. He dropped essential scenes and blurred nearly all the dark color. In directing it, he seemed a novice, apparently rattled by the awesome versatility of the new theater and unable to use its shapes. As for the company, most of it seemed unprepared for a major work.

The play is, in the deepest sense, about Danton himself and his life-and-death situation. It is perfectly titled—it is about the death of Danton: what that death meant in terms of his attitude toward life; what that death meant in terms of the death of us all; what that death meant in relation to revolutions and history.

It is laid in the aftermath of the French Revolution and is about the bloody infighting among the Republicans that made them the victims of their own cause. It is also about the frightful weakness of man in the face of churning history.

As the play starts, Georges Danton has lost interest in politics. Aware that it is not merely this revolution that is out of hand but that all revolutions will defeat revolutionaries, he has given up. (Büchner himself felt that "the individual is no more than foam on the wave, greatness mere chance, the mastery of genius a puppet show, a ludicrous struggle against a brazen law.") The only thing with real meaning for Danton is life — the flesh, the joy, the love of living things.

His antagonist is the self-righteous Robespierre, who equates pleasure with vice and uses that equation as a weapon for a tyranny no better than that of the defeated aristocracy. For Robespierre, "Morality must rule by fear." His violent asceticism is in mortal battle with Danton's humanism.

In the multiple significances of this, which lead to Danton's suicidal giving up of life, Büchner managed a ranging drama of intense depth and fiery theatrical life. In Blau's inability to grasp either the meaning or the drama (he was more interested in its relationship to the war in Vietnam), the play was butchered.

The season's other productions bore the same fruit — choices of sensitivity, taste, education, culture and adventure, produced with a flabbergasting lack of technique. The company was amateur, unable to perform even the simplest theatrical maneuvers, and the directors were lost in matters of casting, blocking, movement, understanding or controls.

The second production that year was Wycherly's *The Country Wife*. There is no need to elaborate upon the stylistic and technical resources necessary for Restoration comedy or to detail the primitive manner with which this company approached it. There was a typically left-wing attitude involved in this production, however, and it should be pointed out. A left-wing director will invariably refuse to stage a play, any play, in a traditional style. In this case, Robert Symonds (a junior director under Blau-Irving) decided to direct the Wycherly as if it were a *performance* rather than "reality." So the actors first appeared in bathrobes and underwear along with various backstage personnel in work clothes. This was a mere notion, never to be used again once the production got under way. On the extremely amateur level, left-wing directors will do such things, being more concerned with staging ideas than with whether those ideas can really be carried through an entire production. At any rate, the whipped-cream elegance of *The Country Wife* was churned into a hashed mash.

The third production, the Sartre, is hardly worth discussing, and Blau later said that it had been chosen as a concession to probable audience demand for a modern play. If this had been true it would have been a disgraceful example of extreme right-wingery. I choose to think that Blau was rationalizing the production of a play he later realized to be less worthy than he had supposed. If anything, he is too legitimately left wing to cater to presumed audience taste.

The first year's final assault on the great dramatic literature was the New York première of *The Caucasian Chalk Circle.* This gave Mr. Irving his first chance with the hatchet and he proceeded to hack away at Brecht's exquisite play. If it had not been for the sheer strength of the work itself and the excellent Azdak of Mr. Symonds, the play would have emerged unrecognizable. It must be some sort of tribute to Brecht that he could withstand such an attack from an army that had already decimated such theater landmarks as *Danton's Death* and *The Country Wife.*

So ended the first season under Blau and Irving, with no prospects for improvement. Besides, on-the-job training could hardly be justified in a major resident theater. The only sensible decision for Blau and Irving would have been to become administrators exclusively and hire another artistic director. This seemed unlikely, and since Lincoln Center had been horrified by the publicity attendant upon the Whitehead-Kazan dismissal, it seemed probable that Blau and Irving would be retained beyond bearability. Perhaps this was just as well. Revolving-door directorships are more destructive than even the worst of permanent chiefs.

But rules of probability are based on sense and any application of them to cultural centers is doomed to frustration. Having hit artistic rock bottom in their first season at Lincoln Center, Blau and Irving proceeded downhill. Their second season's scheduling again seemed impeccable: Jonson's *The Alchemist,* Lorca's *Yerma,* Brecht's *Galileo* and a new play (Leo Lehman's awkward and dull *The East Wind*). Moreover, the decision to use a guest director, John Hirsch, suggested a new, and wise, policy change. But the execution again proved uncertain and amateur. *The Alchemist* was a mess, a sloppy imitation of Ball's *Tartuffe.* Hirsch's *Yerma,* though unsuccessful, was the first professional production at the Beaumont, but by then the Lincoln Center trustees had once more panicked. Success was too slow in coming. Critical rejection was unbearable. And Blau resigned under pressure. Strangely, Irving — his partner for seventeen years — remained, but the announcements were ominous (and ironically, because the final 1966-1967 production, *Galileo,* showed the company assured and strengthen-

ing). The theater was to be rented for a straight commercial production during the summer. The fall (1967) season would open
with a non-Repertory Theater production, a revival of Lillian Hellman's very right-wing *The Little Foxes,* to be produced by the right-
wing Broadway producer Saint Subber and directed by Mike Nichols. Although Lincoln Center tried to palm this off as a Repertory
Theater production, the fact was that the work would be done entirely by outsiders and that the new season would be nine weeks
shorter and one play fewer. It was back to the old guard.

Presumably, the "regular" season of the Repertory Theater of
Lincoln Center would begin after *The Little Foxes,* but obviously
there would have to be shorter runs of each play. Just what will
eventually develop at Lincoln Center remains to be seen. Perhaps,
as some of the people with it predict, the Vivian Beaumont will
eventually become a booking house. Whatever happens will have
enormous implications for noncommercial American theater and
the fate of the cultural centers proliferating across the country. It
does seem that official culture and vital theater are incompatible in
America at this time.

The Association of Producing Artists (APA) is opposite to the
Repertory Theater of Lincoln Center in almost every way. Where
Lincoln Center has directorship policies not dissimilar to those of
baseball clubs (lose a pennant, lose a job), APA has always had
Ellis Rabb as its artistic leader. This is because Mr. Rabb started
APA — is *himself* APA. There are other differences. Lincoln Center is part of a giant institution, funded to the teeth and housed in
an elaborate theater. APA began from beneath the bottom, scrap-
ing around off-Broadway and wherever somebody, somewhere,
would take them in.

You would think that under these circumstances Lincoln Center
would be right wing, doing conventional plays terribly professionally, while APA would be left wing, looking for the unusual and
producing it with amateur enthusiasm. Exactly the opposite is true.
Blau and Irving chose genuinely left-wing dramas at Lincoln Center and produced them with genuine left-wing ineptitude. APA developed its technique to a fair though by no means impressive extent, but restricted its programming to either acknowledged classics

or APA specials suited to Rabb's effete tastes. Because of this, the company was warmly accepted by New York's right-wing critics.

It was depressingly obvious, though, that had APA received the criticism it rated, it would never have had the chance to develop a fair repertory company (and repertory is the key word there — APA works on the true, rolling repertory system and it is this that has led to the development of its actors). However, APA had problems that grew with its success.

Choice of plays was the prime one. The weaknesses in players and direction quickly disappeared, although some lead players remain to be weeded out — there was too much flamboyance and floridity. Its taste in production style leaned toward physical movement rather than dramatic intensity. But the matter of play selection is more complex; it involves taste and judgment and is tricky in the correction.

In its seasons at the Phoenix Theater in New York (when the Phoenix Theater itself was allowed to die unnoticed) from 1963 through 1965, APA did George M. Cohan's worthless and crude *The Tavern,* a trivial pair of Molière comedies (*Impromptu at Versailles* and *Scapin*) and Gorki's turgid *The Lower Depths.* These were pure waste. It also produced an adaptation of *War and Peace* that, while generally effective, had only passing value. The company's *Man and Superman* was not at all well done, mostly because few of the actors were yet capable of Shaw. Giraudoux's *Judith,* a fascinating play marred by some real foolishness, was quite admirably produced. But the only entirely successful production over that two-year period was Pirandello's *Right You Are (If You Think You Are).*

Of these plays, only the Shaw, the Pirandello and perhaps the Giraudoux were really worth the effort. Even if the others had been altogether successful, their selection was much too conservative. APA's problem was that it was either selecting its plays haphazardly or was doing only works that it thought it could do well. Neither method is wise.

If you will notice, all but the Pirandello are right-wing plays. They have no adventure in them. APA is not dominated by behind-the-scenes financiers or a stultifying festival image. Why does it lack the drive and curiosity a young company should have? Why is it so middle-aged? APA's choices showed too little vitality, too little adventure for a repertory company, especially one making it on its own. Such a company is obliged to dare, to try the new or the overlooked.

Ironically, the Phoenix Theater that APA superseded had just such a repertoire and died unnoticed, one of the most unfortunate victims of the New York wing split.

Until 1964, the Phoenix waged a lonely fight to give New York the left-wing classic dramas — not the Tchaikovskyite war-horses but the unproduced, almost forgotten great works of the past. The producing history of the Phoenix reads like an encyclopedia of the left-wing theater literature: O'Casey's *The Plough and the Stars,* O'Neill's *The Great God Brown,* Goldsmith's *She Stoops to Conquer,* Eliot's *The Family Reunion,* Ibsen's *Peer Gynt,* Marlowe's *Doctor Faustus.* The Phoenix productions were not all of plays that I consider great, but they were important and artistic plays. Their regular reproduction is necessary to a thriving theater. Moreover, the Phoenix produced other sorts of left-wing plays; for example, modern art works that were not being commercially produced: Brecht (*The Good Woman of Setzuan*) and Ionesco (*The Chairs* and *the Lesson*) were presented long before they became fashionable. The Phoenix produced new, left-wing works too, such as Kopit's *Oh Dad,* and recognized the artistic possibilities of the musical form (*The Golden Apple, Once Upon a Mattress*). It also presented adventurous British plays such as James Saunders's *Next Time I'll Sing to You.*

But although it drew enough theatergoers during the big off-Broadway years to almost carry a large house on Second Avenue, the wing cleavage forced it into economic crisis; it moved to a smaller house on 74th Street and finally had to disband. Both wings overlooked the death, accepting the flimsy cover of APA "merging" with the Phoenix. Ironically, APA was to produce right-wing war-horses entirely contrary to the Phoenix's previous taste.

After its 1964-1965 season at the Phoenix, APA announced plans for a Broadway season the following year and just as quickly abandoned them. Mr. Rabb made a grand and passionate public announcement that the foundations had refused to support his company. In fact, Rabb made this announcement before the foundations had even *ruled* on his applications. APA *did* come to New York the following year, but not with a repertory season. It came with a disgracefully condescending put-on of New York theater audiences — a phoney-nostalgic, camp revival of the Kaufman-Hart comedy *You Can't Take It with You.*

The artistic director of a repertory company has every privilege of indulging his private whimsies, I suppose. But he hardly has the right when the company is presenting itself as seriously theatrical. There was no artistic reason for reviving this appallingly dated 1936 play except the weirdness of inverted Thirties taste.

Most irksome of all, the entire right-wing critic-audience plane was indeed put on and Rabb had his cake and et cetera. The production ran nearly a season, making enough money to assure Broadway of APA's repertory in 1966-1967.

By the time *You Can't Take It with You* opened, APA had become as smooth as most resident theaters, but perhaps the only one (except for Stratford, Connecticut) to be right wing. In Rosemary Harris it had one of the two or three first-class leading ladies in the country, perhaps even the best of them all. But it was without a heroic leading man and was not the sort of company to produce one. Still, the full extent of its right-wingedness was never properly appreciated until Rabb induced Helen Hayes to join the company for its 1965-1966 season. A deep breath is necessary to accept the simple reality of that fact.

Rabb's cynical box office motivation for hiring her was only surpassed by the dreadful blow that he struck not just to his own company's morale but to that of resident actors in general. Their dedication is based on an abandonment of the star system in favor of technique, experience and true ensemble work. While most resident companies justify that dedication, Rabb's interest in box office, combined with his vision of the world as one great camp, could not be more depressing, especially in view of his genuine and considerable talent.

There is hardly any sense, however, in begrudging the success APA had when it finally did move to Broadway, repertory and all, in 1966. Right wing as it is, it is probably in a much better position to indoctrinate New York Broadway audiences into the true theater excitement of the literature than a left-wing company. Like it or not, a Times Square location spells big-time theater to the right-wing audience. And perhaps the conservative selections will provide an easing into art that these theatergoers need. I allow that argument, although I disagree with it. Right-wing programming, even when it is classical enough (*The School for Scandal, The Wild Duck,* etc.), will *never* attract left-wing theatergoers, and APA will find it impossible to draw the intellectuals, the college students and all the lost theatergoers. Its announced programming for the 1967-1968 season did, however, suggest that Rabb hoped to inject *some* left-wing orientation into his play selection. Some of the plays selected were adventurous indeed: *Pantagleize* by Michel de Ghelderode, and Eugene Ionesco's *Exit the King,* as yet unproduced in America.

These, then — the Stratford Shakespearean Festival; the American Shakespeare Festival; the American Conservatory Theater; the Minnesota Theater Company; the New York Shakespeare Festival; the Repertory Theater of Lincoln Center; the Association of Producing Artists — these are the big-time resident theaters in America.

The smaller ones around the country — the ones that have really *made the movement* — the ones that have not received national publicity — can be roughly divided between those that are created by a community and those that are created by an artistic director.

There was no set pattern to their evolvement. In many cases, the directors who were brought in were more adventurous than those who organized their theaters. What does seem generally true is that longevity breeds conservatism, practicality and institutionalism — a natural enough development. Too, directors tend to stage nearly every production in their first few years and then become producers, hiring guest directors and growing more involved in administration. Some remain firmly in control of the choice of plays and the artistic direction of their companies. Others lose interest in the essential theater that drove them to a resident company in the first place.

The major director-founded resident theaters are the Arena Stage in Washington, Alley Theater in Houston, the Front Street Theater in Memphis and the Dallas Theater Center. Alley and Arena Stage are two of the great success stories. Run by Nina Vance and Zelda Fichandler respectively, they both began as shoestring, desperately artistic theaters and developed faithful audiences. They were among the first big Ford Foundation grantees and are now financially substantial. Arena has a splashy new theater and is completing another, to be strictly devoted to American plays. Alley is finishing its own new house.

Both Vance and Fichandler have become promoters, very smooth in handling American Subsidy and highly professional in the conduct of their companies. Productions at Alley and Arena are as professional as anything in New York. Their schedules vary slightly, perhaps because Washington is a more sophisticated city than Houston. Arena is still left oriented and decided to go semi-repertory in 1967. Alley inclines toward the right and will even schedule a dead-right work like *The Great Sebastians* to satisfy the subscribers (Miss Vance concedes that the play is "banal" — a dreadful concession which implies that there is no good play capable of exciting her audience).

At the Front Street Theater in Memphis, George Touliatos has become fearfully cynical without quite realizing it. A bright and educated man who knows his left-wing theater as well as any director, Touliatos insists that his audiences are not ready for art and must be "educated." In the meanwhile he provides a steady diet of right-wing theater, ranging from outright junk (second-rate productions of second-rate Broadway musicals) to shakily produced box office reliables like *A Streetcar Named Desire*. Touliatos was never able to develop a genuinely professional company, but given the absurd range of productions this could have been predictable.

The Dallas Theater Center is not really professional. I don't mean that in the sense of performance. While Paul Baker, its director, is antagonistic to the Equity system and insists on hiring most of his company from the drama department he heads at Trinity University, still that company is quite good, very well drilled in acting fundamentals. However his theater is unprofessional in *attitude* and displays the worst traits of academic orientation (at least in the quasi-Kabuki, unbearable *Journey to Jefferson* that I saw there). The Dallas Theater Center reflects textbook theories rather than theater vitality and has the scent of the classroom.

The younger director-created theaters — the Hartford Stage
Company, the Actors Theater of Louisville, the Theater Group in
Los Angeles — are much more vital and left wing in play selection
and staging style. Jacques Cartier has disproved for me the notion
that audience taste must be nurtured slowly. His Hartford Stage
Company presents such left-wing plays as *The Balcony, Waiting
for Godot, Endgame* and Pirandello's *Enrico IV* without any audience flinch, indeed without any loss of enthusiasm. Unfortunately,
his board was frightened by a drop in attendance (from 92 to 82
percent of capacity), in 1967 and successfully pressured him to
schedule "better-known" plays. So the right-wing pressure works.

But, Cartier's consuming interest is left wing and his productions
crackle with invention, while being underlayed by a substantial
base of actor discipline. The Hartford Stage Company is one of the
most impressive, solid resident theaters in the country.

Richard Block created his Actors Theater of Louisville much as
Cartier created the Hartford Stage Company. Block, like Cartier, is
left oriented, but unlike him is afraid that his audiences are "not
ready" for "extreme" plays. This despite his theater's financial success with *Waiting for Godot*. The Louisville Theater provides a
steady diet of right-wing resident theater staples ranging from *All
My Sons* to *Miss Julie* to *Charley's Aunt*.

Theater Group was another director-created theater, but it did
not have a resident company. Gordon Davidson draws his casts
from the many serious actors in the television-movie beehive of
Los Angeles, giving them the chance to do such left-wing works as
Sartre's *The Flies,* James Saunder's *Next Time I'll Sing to You,*
Leonard Bernstein's *Candide* and Pinter's *The Birthday Party*
(those, incidentally, were all scheduled in one season — one of the
most attractive left-wing programs I have ever seen).

Unfortunately, the talented Mr. Davidson was swallowed up by
the massive Center Theater Group that capitalized on his theater's
reputation while denying him the directorship. Elliot Martin, a
right-wing Broadway producer, was given the overall control of the
Ahmanson Theater and Mark Taper Forum because such right-
wing enterprises conceive of *big-time* theater as Broadway's. In
fact, Broadway's even *bigger-time* Robert Whitehead stood anony-
mously behind *Martin*. Davidson was allowed the directorship of

the Forum — the smaller of the two houses — and was denied artistic autonomy. I warn you — watch out for your independence; watch out for the money interests; watch out for those cultural centers. They will extinguish the brightest artistic fires.

Among the resident theaters that were created by *communities* you will find some of the brightest, most well-balanced, best-educated young directors in America. But their artistic freedom depends upon the intelligence of their boards and that intelligence is highly suspect. In some cases the boards seem sensible, contributing financial support under an artistic hands-off policy. But the possibility of interference is always there and sooner or later financial crises are laid at the feet of the artistic director (why not try *just one* Broadway comedy?).

The most reasonable boards seem to be those of Baltimore's Center Stage, St. Louis's Loretto-Hilton Theater, Philadelphia's Theater of the Living Arts, Cincinnati's Playhouse in the Park and Theater Atlanta. These theaters all have serious artistic directors: Douglas Seale in Baltimore, Michael Flanagan in St. Louis, Brooks Jones in Cincinnati and Jay Broad in Atlanta.

In a ridiculous series of circumstances, the board at Philadelphia's Theater of the Living Arts lost such a reputation in early 1967. In fact, it had been a better board than most, and although its contract with artistic director André Gregory gave it a veto power over any one of the suggested plays except one original American work a season (Shocked? It isn't unusual), the power was *never used*. Certainly, the board did not give Gregory an easy time of it and many of his left-wing ideas led to acrimonious meetings. But it was Gregory's great originality that made the Philadelphia theater unique and it was his flamboyant productions of such plays as Anouilh's *Poor Bitos* and Rochelle Owens's *Beclch* that gave his company its special identity — something that every resident theater, ideally, should have.

When Gregory quit he complained loudly of "artistic interference," engendering predictable outside sympathy, but his resignation was really due to the release of his executive director for reasons unrelated to artistic matters. It is bad enough that so many resident theater boards of trustees force out independent-minded directors for the sake of commercial programming. We need not

look for it where it did not happen. It was a pity, for both the
Theater of the Living Arts and for Gregory, that he resigned. This
was not a "bad" board and did not deserve a reputation as one.
Even more pitifully Gregory moved on to one of the National
Council's "Project Discovery" theaters, taking the massive grant
and conceding government involvement and school-system orientation.

As for the other companies with relatively reasonable boards,
and led by employee-directors, they are meeting with variable audience responses.

In general, the smaller theaters in the more Northern cities do
well enough, while those in the plush new theaters struggle. Theater
Atlanta and the Loretto-Hilton Center for the Performing Arts
have two of the handsomest houses in the country, but they were
both playing to less than half of capacity during their first seasons
(1966–1967). Although their programming is not all that could be
desired, it is serious and well meant. And while they have obvious
difficulties getting trained actors (because of low salaries and the
unattractiveness of the South), their productions are smooth
enough.

But when a theater is artificially inseminated into an unprepared
community, audiences are bound to be slow in accepting it. There
must be time for acclimatization, for familiarity. If the boards of
trustees are willing to stick through the early, difficult years, these
theaters may very well take root. If there is, instead, a demand for
instant success (as there was with the Repertory Theater of Lincoln
Center), the projects will be doomed to revolving-door-director policies and inevitable failure.

Other of the board-controlled theaters are representative of the
worst right-wing elements in resident theater. The Seattle Repertory Theater is dominated by extratheater powers and hires directors who are malleable (first Stuart Vaughan and later Allen
Fletcher). The Pittsburgh Playhouse is dominated by the worst
kind of uninformed, uneducated, television-bred mind, and in all of
American resident theater is matched in its ruling mentality only by
Oklahoma City's Mummers Theater.

The Repertory Theater of New Orleans is one of the most absurd examples of theater-created-by-nontheater-people. It is the ultimate product of American Subsidy and the right wing. The New Orleans venture was the brainchild of the National Council on the Arts, and was one of the first Project Discovery units, loaded to the teeth with federal funds (both National Council and Health, Education and Welfare), and specifically geared for school-system productions. So unattractive was the proposition of playing endless school matinees, and of *having those productions approved by school boards,* that New Orleans found itself being rejected even by directors desperately in need of money (Rabb and Ball among them). The sad fact is that many resident theaters are forced by the need of arts council funds to accept some kind of school-production deal. They then cynically prepare a couple of Shakespeare comedies for touring (Shakespeare is the only playwright whom the boards of education will unequivocally approve). As for New Orleans, Stuart Vaughan, lately departed from Seattle, accepted the offer and organized the "theater" there.

The resident theaters, then, vary greatly in makeup, purpose, orientation and wing alignment. Of them, only St. Louis, Atlanta and Seattle play in true repertory. Of their directors, the wing range is wide (from the true left of Gregory, Jones, Hancock and Cartier to the right of Fletcher and Vaughan). Some have led their communities' taste, some have been led by them; most are financially secure but a few are in trouble; all hang in with American Subsidy. There is no way of knowing what will happen to them, but one thing is sure: they exist today where they didn't before and they are finally giving their public a real kind of theater with at least some left-wing influence, as opposed to the steady and exclusive diet of second-class right-wing Broadway touring companies that had existed in the past.

But like the rest of us, they have little power over the conditions of their lives. Their theaters are getting outside of control and the subsidy situation is something they have been lured into accepting. It may be easy to castigate them for allowing themselves to be taken in by it but, honestly, would it be worth giving up all of those theaters in all of those cities doing all of those plays with all of those actors?

Well it *wouldn't* be worth it, but the way things are going these theaters may very well become decreasingly valuable as they become increasingly institutionalized. Conceived as they are in a strange, detrimental conflict (rather than interplay) of wings, they could very well develop a remarkable case of senility in their infancy.

CHAPTER SIX

Something's Coming, Something Good

THE healthiest example of wing interaction in today's American theater, ironically, is on part of the Broadway stage. There, drama is being strangled by the right wing; there, comedies are tailored for, and supported by, archaic taste; yet there the American musical theater is roaring along, propelled by the confidence and the experience of the professionals and the excitement and innovation of the newcomers.

Theatrical validity is the result of this interaction, and because of it the musical is far more profitable and far less risky a proposition than the drama or the comedy. Producers are eager to present them and backers are eager to put money into them. The ticket-buying public, whatever its motives and whatever its tastes, is caught up in their vitality. It is convinced that it will *enjoy* a musical — *have a good time* at one — and it does. The musical theater is fine, fine theater.

It is joyous in art's greatest sense — jumping, beating, moving. It may not even be aware of its own artistic validity, but perhaps that is just as well. The self-conscious artist is not as free as the active, occupied, *functioning* one.

Those of us who are eager for the new will resent the old, but the standard Broadway right-wing musical needs no artistic defense. It can be irritating in its adherence to old formulas — anything right wing is necessarily unoriginal — but it is polishing earlier left-wing innovations. It may use music that remains in the style of the show tune, without any musical depth. It may be a collection of opening numbers, production numbers, scene-change excuses, Lucite brightness and manufactured, cornball jokes. It may present a ridiculous story as an imitation play with an absurd minimum of detail or characterization. Its moral and intellectual premises may be naïve, its conception and delivery the result of staging habits fifteen years old. And the vast majority of its examples may be noisy bores. But when well done it is grand fun, pure in form and produced with the sureness of a knowing hand.

The right-wing musical is either the musical comedy or the neo-operetta. It is the musical that We All Know and Love. It has overtures and dance music and choruses and song and dance numbers and ballads and comic songs. And it is just lovely. Today it is on a plateau, losing drive as the left wing moves in. The composers who carried it through the peak years — Rodgers and Loewe and Loesser and Rome — are beginning to fade as Berlin and Porter faded before them; their successors are only imitators. This is a pity. So long as the right-wing musical remains there is no reason why its music should not be written by first-class show-tune composers. By rights, people like Burton Lane, Harold Arlen and Hugh Martin should be taking up the slack. But discouraged as they are by the lack of librettists and, especially, lyricists in their own style, they have dropped out. (Lane's alienation is a particular shame; his scores for *Finian* and *On a Clear Day* are among the finest in the right-wing canon.) In their place have come composers who should still be working the Catskills. Charles Strouse, Bob Merrill and Jerry Herman are trying to sound like a Broadway that they, like the rest of us, loved through the strong years. Instead of working out of a new idiom of their own, they are mimicking the old one, and while they are serving to carry the right-wing musical between stages, they are also dragging it into unnecessary repetition. Surrounding them are the variety of neophyte tunesmiths who manage to have their work produced out of sheer investor enthusiasm for musicals.

The left wing is bringing changes that go directly to the structural-artistic core of the musical theater form. Today's right wing, as it developed through the years, uses a slim story that pretends to be a play. Fitted into it are about fifteen songs — ten of them, say, in the long (about an hour and ten minutes) first act and perhaps five in the short (forty minutes) second — along with three or four reprises. The songs are songs; that is, the action stops to make way for them and they are sung straight through. Their mode is that of show music and even the vocal style is "Broadway" (Alfred Drake, John Raitt, Jack Cassidy). Choreography, too, uses a 45th Street style of its own: fast, spread-eagled and gaudy. It comes at specific, cued points and does not use dance in the sense that ballet does — as a theater expression — but as "the number." This is theater as a vaudeville construction, using various elements (or acts) to create varying effects. The romantic ballad produces warmth, the comic song laughter, the fast production number excitement, the slow production number expansiveness, the act ender exhilaration. Similarly, each of these represents a different kind of stage animal: the solo singer, the pageant, the burlesque sketch, the song-and-dance. The book is supposed to tie them together.

Today's left-influenced interwing musical began life late in the Thirties with the introduction of trained composers and the movement of serious choreographers from ballet to Broadway. Even Brecht had his effect. His use of multiple stage elements in a unified theater piece and his realization that theater is created not at the typewriter but in the theater affected the composing of his collaborator Kurt Weill. Weill, in turn, moved from the perfect bitterness of his cabaret songs toward full-theater composing. Out of their theater-opera *Mahagonny* and ballet-drama *The Seven Deadly Sins,* Weill brought Brecht's theories to the American musical. He was one of the (if not *the*) first of composers to apply serious musical technique to the American stage.

Soon afterward (1943), Leonard Bernstein and Jerome Robbins drew *On the Town* from the ballet *Fancy Free* and the movement of genuine composers and choreographers into Broadway theater began. Songs would stop being just songs (something not unpainful to those of us who thrived on show tunes). Dance would become part of a totality, leaving the restrictive realm of the rousing chorus job near the end of act one.

As for the "book," it would stray from the shorthand play that had to be justifiable without music. It would begin to be something else — something new — something indigenous to the whole. Just what that will be can not yet be determined, but it will have to be a dialogue equivalent for music and dance — something that can braid with them.

The interwing musical uses music and dance in their deepest artistic senses. Music can produce incomparable emotional effects. Watch a youngster listening to rock and roll on his transistor radio, or an earphoned student enraptured at a music library. You have probably yourself felt the real, near-physical effect of music, whether it be the purity of Mozart or the depth of Brahms. This extraordinary effect has of course been utilized in the theater (every good musical, right or left wing, capitalizes upon it), but its possibilities have been only barely explored.

The quality of dance, too, is unique. It can express a literal message — tell a story — but it is basically movement to music. It is abstract. It is visual rhythm; grace controlled. Today's left wing is beginning to use dance as dance, feeling its special strength and beauty. Story must find a way for itself. With the musical theater using these forms in combination with all stage elements (light, costume, scenery, entertainment, ritual, pageant), extraordinary things can be done. They are beginning.

From the greater historical perspective — that is, looking over, say, a four-hundred-year span — the most significant theatrical development of the twentieth century will have been the evolution of the American musical. An entirely new stage breed and one which could not have even been dreamed of fifty years ago, it is a mask of its own to stand beside those of comedy and tragedy. Just imagine. A theater of music, of dance, of story — all in one production.

It is not without antecedents. Following a traceable line of development, from grand and comic opera to the operettas of Strauss and Offenbach, the classic satire of Gilbert and Sullivan, the Viennese picture postcards of Lehár and the beginnings of Rudolf Friml and Victor Herbert, it assumed an identity of its own in the late Twenties and early Thirties: George Gershwin, Vincent Youmans, Jerome Kern, Dietz and Schwartz, Irving Berlin, Cole Porter and Rodgers and Hart. Taking the yodeling heroes of operetta and putting them into the sailor suits of brash America, they cut the string sections in half and then in half again, making a sound of brass, drum brushes and show business. A singular theater animal capitalized on the birth of the American popular song to create the *show tune,* and a dam collapsed to let through an outpouring of songs that will probably never again be matched.

The validity of musical theater was so apparent so quickly that it never had much of a chance to remain left wing. It was theater as theater — the show — pure stage life — brightness and light and movement and excitement and plain entertainment. As quickly as it was invented, it was accepted.

By the Thirties, the Broadway musical had become a theater fixture, familiar enough for any theatergoer as he walked into the Shubert or the Majestic or the Imperial. And with war's end, these theaters were fulfilling his greatest expectations.

He expected to find a great, crimson, baroque house buzzing with dressed-up theatergoers; he expected to chatter down a crowded, carpeted aisle into a plush seat where he would scan a long list of musical numbers in his *Playbill;* he expected an orchestra to be gradually filling the pit before a heavy golden curtain; he expected the lights to go all the way out — black — and then a bright spotlight to hit a conductor whose baton was tensed in the air for a downbeat; he expected blaring, staccato trumpets to begin an overture with the show's fastest song before slowing into the brush-stroke (and muted-trumpet) ballad — "Lovely to Look at," "Bali Ha'i," "On the Street Where You Live" — while the curtain lifted to reveal a colorful scrim with a bold design having something, surely, to do with the story. Then, with the overture ended on a booming drum roll and a fat major chord, the lights behind the scrim would go up and the design would disappear to reveal a bright set, the chorus ready (you know it) to step out for the *opening number.* The rest would follow, as sure as the quiz in the program (How many of these current shows have you seen?). Comedy, a driving chorus, vaudeville, the ballad, the dance in the park, an inane plot. Ethel Merman wondering whether she will ever be pretty enough for Ray Middleton. Betty Garrett complaining about the great big crack in the back of her sacroiliac. Shirley Booth, a body-length grin, talking about love as a kick right in the pants. A revue in scarlet and patent leather being terribly smart-set while Billy De Wolfe does a knitting skit in drag. John Raitt in his pajama bottoms and Janis Paige in the tops.

> No death, like you get in *Macbeth*
> No ordeal, like the end of *Camille*
> This good-bye sends you out with a sigh
> The world is a stage, the stage is a world
> Of entertainment

Who could resist it? It reached everyone, although leftists masked their glee with condescension ("I love show music"). It *should* have reached everyone — it was exhilarating theater. And it was presented with increasing proficiency. The tools were being honed.

The right wing did the honing so well that the form came to exemplify Broadway professionalism. In fact, it became *known* as "the Broadway musical." Nobody did musicals but Broadway. Nobody *knew* musicals but Broadway. Composers knew their love songs, their chorus songs, their comedy songs. Orchestrators knew their overtures, their continuity, their bridges, their underscoring and, most of all, the Broadway *sound*. Designers had the scenic formulas ritualized, from the traveler curtains (moving one way as the chorus moves the other) to the wagons (those small sets that roll out from the wings with the hero standing at his desk making a telephone call). And they could churn out what all of us were eager to see and then memorize while wearing out original-cast recordings. As for performers, there seemed an endless line of toothy baritones, anonymous ingenues and superstar females.

But during the twelve postwar years it thrived without change. Having already reached its maximum development as the George Abbott musical comedy and the Richard Rodgers neo-operetta, it had gone to the limit of its capacities. So the repetition began as it moved ever more deeply into the right wing.

As part of that movement, its fun, its vigor, its popularity increased. *Call Me Mister, High Button Shoes, A Tree Grows in Brooklyn, Finian's Rainbow, Paint Your Wagon, Fanny, House of Flowers*. Musical after musical, and weren't they terrific?

The excitement of musical theater is in its vitality. It reaches audiences, as any valid theater must. And in its strictness of form lies its artistic identity. The musical is often used for commercial purposes. It often stoops to cheap appeal. But as a genre it is whole, it is real, and its show business quality is rooted in the oldest theater forms. Now that a left wing of real influence has developed for it, it is moving toward greater artistic expression, but that must not derogate the earlier musicals or the good ones in the present right wing. Their jazzy, juicy, Broadway-show musicality remains and without that kind of sound they would be nothing (ask a nontheater composer to write for the stage and you'll see what I mean).

To talk of postwar right-wing musical theater, one must begin with Rodgers and Hammerstein. While their first collaboration *Oklahoma!* has been mistakenly given credit for revolutionizing the musical theater, it did accept into the right wing several elements that had been innovated immediately prior to it: the ballet (as used in *Lady in the Dark, Pal Joey* and *On Your Toes*), the relevant lyric and the presumably integrated book.

The plays that Hammerstein wrote for the collaboration were embarrassing and childish, but considering the ludicrous boy-meets-girl books of the period, his were at least attempting to do more than kill time between songs and dances. If he labored under the delusion that he was writing social drama, perhaps it doesn't matter. What does matter is that he and Rodgers brought the musical out of the trivial and into the (attempted) significant. It was an important step. It was the taking of the musical seriously — by its creators. And that step must be taken before anyone else can take it seriously.

Rodger's work with Hammerstein marked his decline as a composer. It has been said that he stopped writing music when Lorenz Hart died and in a sense this is true. Hart was a poet, even while his frame of reference was largely restricted to a personal loneliness. His word sensitivity and metric adventurousness pushed Rodgers into composing that was clever in the best sense. Too, while Rodgers was already terribly successful and, worse, esteemed, he was not yet writing to formula. Blessed, really blessed, with a talent for melody, he was also a trained musician. He had harmonic ideas that were translated, through melody, into music that not even

Gershwin could shame. A song like "Little Girl Blue" (*Jumbo,* 1935) sounds simple enough, pretty enough, but it is ingeniously built, inverting its structure along a strangely bittersweet and remarkably long melodic line. Rodgers, like Gershwin, took the popular song seriously and foolish is the snob who rejects it. As written by real composers, such songs are not only respectable as music but require a talent every bit as noteworthy as that of the composer in more ambitious forms.

While Hart was going to pieces early in the Forties, Rodgers was reaching his peak years, having already tried his hand at extensive composing (*Slaughter on Tenth Avenue*) and eager to move into new musical areas. Except for some parts of *Carousel,* he was never to have the chance. Whether it was Hammerstein's comfiness and pseudoseriousness or Rodgers's overwhelming interest in profits, this great talent was to be stifled. Having once been somewhat of a left-winger, he would move ever rightward, loafing on technique while abandoning invention, finally becoming an extremist. As might have been expected, it was during those later years that he would be deified — a deification that he both accepted and was intimidated by — and, as usual, the years of veneration came when they were least deserved. The pity was that his great ability and natural talent were still there, unused.

The Rodgers and Hammerstein works were called "musical plays" but though plays-with-music, they were neither plays nor musical. There was never any true wedding of the musical and dramatic elements and so each production became a play-that-was-not-a-play decorated with musical numbers. Hammerstein would write what he considered to be a drama, although a musical production just never leaves time enough, between the songs and the dances, for a full-length play. (Hammerstein never really understood the qualitative difference between the drama and the musical anyhow).

And perhaps only their *The King and I* was intrinsically musical. It had a musical subject matter, a musical conception. Its setting was exotic, having a sound and a flavor of its own. There was a musicality to the Siamese accents, the Siamese movements — a special and particular kind of dance associated with the culture — a lushness of color and design in its nature.

But in the other works, Hammerstein's ideas were without musical quality — simpleminded stories making simpleminded points. *Oklahoma!* was seriously concerned with whether Curley would get to take Laurey to the box social. Its values were the goodness of farmland America and the badness of people (like Jud) who hang girlie pictures in their rooms.

Carousel was again set in a *Life* magazine America, the scene this time shifted to a New England that was as spurious as the Southwest of *Oklahoma!* Clambakes were substituted for picnics, but the values remained the same while Hammerstein seriously considered the possibilities of Billy Bigelow redeeming himself in a Thornton Wilder heaven of sequin stars and homey God figures.

Satisfied, after two such deep works, that he could step out on his own, Hammerstein wrote his first original book for Rodgers — *Allegro* — and with culture as available to the naïve as it is to the sophisticated, he translated the Greek theater's use of The Chorus into *Broadway's* use of singing and dancing choruses. So the singers reflected upon the thoughts of a hero who clearly had no thoughts of his own. Again, by the way, villains were identified with sexual interests; typical of the Victorian values in which Hammerstein's superficial liberalism was mired.

It is amusing that *Allegro* was (and still is) considered radical. It had some obvious novelties — no scenery — and it was determinedly artistic; but its structure and certainly its music were conventional. Though Rodgers's songs seemed longer than usual, it was because of repetition rather than development.

With *South Pacific,* Hammerstein joined the breast-beating hypocrisy that marked American racial thinking (when the password was "tolerance"). Somehow or other, the liberal of that time always managed to promote interracial romance while avoiding intermarriage (much later, Rodgers repeated this separate-but-equal line in *No Strings*). And the attitude was continued in *The King and I,* with another "inconceivable" romance and its obnoxious treatment of the Siamese as adorable little savages fortunate to have the Westernizing influence of the English. From that point, Rodgers and Hammerstein streaked rightward, creating increasingly cynical money makers and reaching their nadir with their final work *The Sound of Music,* with its paraphrased *King and I* plot, its avalanche of sugar and its singing *nuns,* for God's sake.

180] *A Theater Divided*

If Hammerstein's books were soggy, cliché-ridden, unadventurous melodramas, his lyrics were their equal. Reflecting his foursquare morality and greeting-card sentimentality, they marched evenly along to the even-tempoed thoughts that matched Rodgers's increasingly even-tempoed scores. By the time Hammerstein sank into solfège songs ("Do, a deer, a female deer") and phoney inspirationals ("Climb every mountain/Ford every stream") he had hit a molasses bottom.

Yet, there is no denying that Rodgers turned out a great many good songs during this lucrative collaboration. "All 'er Nothin'," "Out of My Dreams," "When I Marry Mr. Snow," and "The Gentleman Is a Dope" are riches in the theater-music tradition. Some of his sweet songs, like "Edelweiss" from *The Sound of Music,* are just lovely. Despite all the sickening, sexless love songs, from "People Will Say We're in Love" to "Some Enchanted Evening," Rodgers managed some nice things.

The Rodgers and Hammerstein living samplers were what the Sunday supplements were calling Musical Theater Greatness. But while their seriousness was middlebrow, it was not sham. The team believed it. They were convincing the public that a musical could be serious, and perhaps it is just as well that it was they who did the convincing. A little elevation mixed with a lot of pap was needed and the only way it would work was if the creators could swallow it themselves without throwing up. They were perfect for nudging the musical theater leftward.

This is especially true of *Carousel.* It was in this musical that Rodgers worked with pure music, and even development, as opposed to the standard thirty-two-bar song. The most obvious example was the "Soliloquy," which ran more than eight minutes. The action paused for it, in the standard way, but it was a dialogue song and not a set poem. The most important example, however, was the interweaving "If I Loved You," and the plotted structure of "When I Marry Mr. Snow." "If I Loved You" was sung straight through but it was also split into sections, interspersed with dialogue and action. "Mr. Snow" was a combination of prose and poetry, a story song sung by different people, as much dialogue as it was lyric. So even if "June Is Bustin' Out All Over" *was* an inversion of "Everything's Up-to-date in Kansas City," there was some real composing going on.

Rodgers and Hammerstein were never to progress beyond it, and it became increasingly difficult to separate Rodger's work from that of his regular orchestrator Robert Russell Bennett. Patterns became obvious, song motifs stock. And invention ended. As if to make the decline ironic, Rodgers would occasionally remind you of what might have been (as with his freshly harmonic "My Favorite Things" from *The Sound of Music*). But by and large his music became repetitious and Bennett's old-fashioned arrangements not only stressed this but even prompted the suspicion that Rodgers was loafing, writing only lead sheets (the notation of only the melodic line, leaving the orchestrator to fill in the harmonies).

Frank Loesser's career intersected Rodgers's. While Rodgers came to Broadway with a pocketful of technical skills and a genius for melody, Loesser was untrained. Within ten years after his first musical (*Where's Charley?* 1948), he would be a self-educated composer, a superior lyricist and eager for new musical forms while Rodgers would be an outright cynic, manufacturing hummable pseudomusic.

Loesser personifies the right-wing Broadway musical. When you think of the typical Broadway musical, you think of *Guys and Dolls*. It is perfect type. Loesser was born for the show tune. Whenever a Loesser production needs a filler in Philadelphia, he can knock off the perfect song effortlessly (if all wrong for what he was really after). As an example, the Broadway opera that he sought in *The Most Happy Fella* was pushed right out of its own style by "Big D," although the song was wonderful. Loesser can write a "Big D" without licking a pencil. It is what he wants to escape and cannot. It is his métier.

Loesser's career is curious. In the twenty years that followed *Where's Charley?* he was to write only five musicals, three of them commercially successful (*Guys and Dolls, The Most Happy Fella, How to Succeed in Business Without Really Trying*), one of them a Broadway failure (*Greenwillow*) and one an out-of-town debacle (*Pleasures and Palaces*).

The most impressive thing about him is that while he might have had an extremely lucrative career grinding out the kind of score he is so adept at, he tries something new with each production. Unfortunately, he tends to choose right-wing coworkers (George Abbott, Abe Burrows, Michael Kidd, Bob Fosse). If Loesser *were* to work with Jerome Robbins, or somebody who had absorbed Robbins's lessons, he would have undoubtedly moved into the flowing left wing that is now influencing Broadway.

As it stands, the Loesser history is ambivalent. Having shown musical promise beyond Broadway facility as early as *Where's Charley?* with more-than-simple songs such as "Make a Miracle" and "That Woman in the Picture," he moved into newer musical ideas in *Guys and Dolls* ("Fugue for Tin Horns," "My Time of Day"). The Loesser who could snap off a "Once in Love with Amy" was still there to toss in "A Bushel and a Peck," but the more ambitious composer was there too. He then decided to go All-Out-for-Art with *The Most Happy Fella,* composing more than thirty songs, including duets, trios and quartets, in clearly operatic modes.

Like Gershwin and *Porgy and Bess,* Loesser did not understand that the Broadway musical was not opera, but theater. It seemed to him, in 1954, that the only way for the Broadway musical to be artistic was for it to imitate Puccini. How ironic that this most Broadway of composers should not see the gold in his own vein.

But while it is easy to say that he should stick with what he does best, what does "best" mean? He wrote his loveliest music for *Greenwillow,* and his richest for *The Most Happy Fella.* The music for the film *Hans Christian Andersen* is charming. On the other hand, the *Guys and Dolls* score was absolutely right for the gaudy Times Square milieu of Damon Runyon. Ironically, his greatest success was with his most facile score — *How to Succeed* — and I suppose it was perfectly natural for this mediocre right-wing musical to win the right-wing prizes (Pulitzer, Drama Critics, etc.).

It is easy to describe the Rodgers and Hammerstein works as "theirs" because Hammerstein wrote the books and the team produced its own work. In the case of Loesser, and more so with less famous composers, the eventual work is not "his." Whose is it?

Talk all you will about ensemble creativity, a theater work must be a single person's vision. A musical is so complex, tying together so many theater elements, that none of the single contributors is in any position to take credit for the end result. Look at what occurs during almost any ten minutes of even a bad Broadway musical. A story is progressing and actors are reading lines. The orchestra is underplaying the conversation. The scenery is beginning to revolve behind the action. Players are approaching from the wings and perhaps upstage. The lights are restlessly changing (the average Broadway musical has more than a hundred light cues). The stage manager is in the wings, following the script and cueing the three-man team at the lightboards (they cannot even see the show from their positions beneath the stage). In the flies the dozens of flats are arranged in bewildering order and the flymen are tugging at the pulley ropes with languid efficiency.

There has to be a single man to control this sprawling assortment of people and factors — somebody who assorts, arranges and combines them. It could be the director, and the musical theater would seem to be a director's theater, if anybody's. It must be one person who guides an original script into an original score and assembles them into a working stage organism. Since it is the director who transfers them from paper to the stage, he who decides how it all should look and proceeds to make it look that way, he who gives the whole thing life, the director can be God, as far as the musical theater is concerned. The show's identity could flow from him. If he is not himself the choreographer, he can outline the dances and production numbers. He can supervise the musical staging — the control of people as they sing their songs. He can shape the mood and atmosphere. Oversee the musical, dance and dramatic rehearsals. And then draw all these elements together.

But this is not the way right-wing musicals are created. The advertised system is *group creation,* but in fact the separate components are created in isolation and the blending of them is a period fraught with conflict, misunderstanding and ego. The composer-lyricist-librettist team begins with what it thinks is a complete production, on paper. The producer then injects his ideas, the choreographer *his,* the director *his.* Each has a separate concept of the final version and each, naturally, want *his* contribution to be the ultimate one. The book writer resents choreographic intrusions on his plot, the composer wants his score sung *as written,* and so the friction grows.

Ideally, one man should do everything and rehearsals should be held centrally. The director should be a salad chef, blending the complex assortment of makings. His responsibilities are formidable.

The major directors of right-wing musicals are George Abbott, Abe Burrows, Bob Fosse, Michael Kidd and occasionally Joseph Anthony and Garson Kanin. Mr. Abbott was Mr. Right-wing Musical from 1948 (at the latest), when he directed both *Where's Charley?* and *Look Ma, I'm Dancin',* until 1961 and *A Funny Thing Happened on the Way to the Forum.* His sense of plot outline, song cue, production number, vaudeville comedy and show business typified these razzy productions. After 1961 he lost touch with the new times and theater developments passed him by.

But there was a time when his success with conventional musicals was so complete that he almost personally kept the left wing from coming into its own. In the fifteen-year period beginning in 1947, he staged eighteen musicals, almost every one a wonderful example of the *Broadway show. High Button Shoes, Call Me Madam, A Tree Grows in Brooklyn, Wonderful Town, Fiorello, Tenderloin.* Then, almost without its being noticed, they began to fall deeper into their ruts. The books that Abbott either cowrote or doctored grew hackneyed; the songs, dances, rhythms he enjoyed became dated. The sandwiched production numbers seemed increasingly ludicrous.

For *Where's Charley?* he had the Brazilian aunt tell a story about her youth to cue a big South American dance number to end act one. All right, that's 1948. Six years later he wrote a night club scene into *The Pajama Game* so that, plot aside, there could be a dance number ("Hernando's Hideaway"). For *Damn Yankees* in 1955, he thought up a fan club for the show's baseball player hero so that it could present an entertainment ("Who's Got the Pain?"). And as late as 1965, he was still dreaming up irrelevant union shows as excuses for production numbers (*Flora, the Red Menace*). This kind of construction, so crude, so obvious, does no justice to the smoothness of structure that the modern right-wing musical has achieved. But in terms of the overall right-wing feeling, it is Abbott himself who developed it. And Abbott, more than anyone else, who is responsible for the booming health of these musicals; and Abbott who passed completely out of the modern musical picture. Sadly, he stayed on to embarrass his reputation.

In the meanwhile, he managed — like any sensible executive — to introduce his successor. Could he possibly have realized that Jerome Robbins would completely supersede the kind of theater he had developed? Robbins was to become the spearhead of the new, left-wing musical theater and by 1966 would be the recipient of a $300,000 grant from the National Council on the Arts to establish a workshop for propagating that theater (the grant was an exceptional example of intelligent behavior on the part of a governmental-cultural body, though perhaps not astonishing considering Roger Stevens's past associations with both Broadway and Robbins).

While Robbins was training under Abbott in *High Button Shoes* and *The Pajama Game* the other new-generation directors were developing too, particularly Michael Kidd and Bob Fosse. Although they, like Robbins, were choreographer-directors (which was obviously the combination of the future), they were too restricted in their outlook to understand what Robbins knew. When Kidd added directing to choreography he insisted on keeping drama and dance apart. His choreographic habits were inbred (everybody dash cross-stage, then dash back; imitations of other activities: lasso dances, construction worker dances, and so on). More interesting things should have come of Fosse, but for all his experience under Robbins he displayed an incredible unawareness of musical theater trends. While the left wing was moving into serious ballet, making dance a part of a total theater piece, he remained with the separate-number concept. Even when given a chance for maximum dancing, he could only think in terms of "numbers," and though more than half of *Sweet Charity* was dance, it could never have been considered dance theater.

Also, Fosse had no perspective on his own work and was unable to notice the rut into which *he* had fallen. The tipped derbies, the elbows tucked in at the sides, the cute little steps, the tight little pipestem groups. It is a shame because Fosse is a talented choreographer and there are too few around for left-wing needs. But so long as he thinks in terms of "a dance" instead of "dance" — and so long as he expects choreography to begin and end with the story at a standstill, he will be unable to unify musical movement with musical-theatrical conception.

The most successful of the modern right-wing musical directors is Abe Burrows, who is Abbott's successor in the line. Burrows works in Formica. No matter what the material, he will slick it over so that everything looks as shiny bright as Broadway can possibly be (and that is pretty shiny bright). The shine can be great, but too often it will not cover up what is basically fake theater. It can also prostitute the well meant. Frank Loesser has been quoted as saying, "I wrote *How to Succeed in Business Without Really Trying.* Burrows wanted to direct *How to Succeed.*"

A Burrows show is a manufactured commodity that *seems* entertaining but frequently isn't. Nevertheless a great amount of craft is necessary to produce that sheen and it is not to be scorned. Smoothness in itself *is* admirable, and it is only when there is nothing *but* smoothness that the idea of theater is insulted.

The Burrows sheen is representative of the technique which the right-wing musical has perfected. When matched with talent and inspiration, it can prompt wonderful theater. Perhaps never more wonderful than *My Fair Lady,* which is unquestionably the finest right-wing musical in Broadway history. Has there ever been a moment of elation in any musical to match that of "The Rain in Spain"? A combination of sophistication and sentiment equal to "Why Can't a Woman Be More like a Man?"?

Well, whose work was *My Fair Lady* anyhow? To be sure, much of it was Alan Jay Lerner's. Lerner is not a great lyricist. Within the present, abysmal crop of lyricists, however, he is a master craftsman and certainly a diligent worker. With little originality and still less art, he manages to make his work meticulous. In this musical, his concentration upon *Pygmalion* was a fine example of research and care. His book even more so — it was as nearly self-sufficient a play as any musical's script will probably ever be (though with considerable thanks to Shaw).

The production was pure right-wing cabinet-making, fitting Hanya Holm's dances here, the Lerner-Loewe songs there. The look that Cecil Beaton gave it was elegant as only Beaton can be.

Moss Hart's direction, in no way musical itself, had not a hair out of place, not a bubble in the pomade. As for the Frederick Loewe score, it was as good as any ever composed for the right-wing American stage. Given the purpose of each song, a better one could not have been written, or so it would seem. It was the definitive neo-operetta score for the definitive neo-operetta.

Jean Dalrymple has been one of the few people to realize the lasting theater quality of such right-wing musicals and has regularly produced revival seasons at the City Center. Unfortunately, Miss Dalrymple's choices are consistently right wing (*West Side Story* was the only exception) and she prefers the repetition of box office favorites to the reproduction of less commercial, more innovative works. Again and again, the City Center presents *South Pacific, Carousel, Brigadoon, Oklahoma!, Guys and Dolls, The Sound of Music.* It has not yet dared *House of Flowers* or anything less commercially guaranteed.

But the City Center productions do point up another fact about our musical theater in regard to classicism, the fact being that the "old, great shows" really aren't classics. They date. Because of an inclination for fidelity, a trust in musical theater's artistry and a lack of funds, the City Center revivals rely on original orchestrations, original choreography, original books, even original sets. Should they? If the original works *were* classic, faith certainly should be kept, with no worry over dating. And if not? Then do them as nostalgia, or with *some* attitude, but not as if nobody was supposed to notice the staleness.

As for updating them, which is the policy of the Music Theater of Lincoln Center, I think this is both mistreatment of genuine theater works and misguided as a practical policy. *Annie Get Your Gun* is Forties theater, whether the orchestrations and sets are new or not, and a modern overlay will sit very uneasily on a structure built for another set of tastes. There is no sense ignoring good right-wing musicals that *have* dated, and I am not suggesting that. But there is also no sense in insisting, for example, that *Finian's Rainbow* is classic theater when its book is embarrassingly littered with Thirties-Forties left-wing messages (the hero is a union organizer, the point is a combination of racial reform and redistribution of wealth, there are even capitalists in top hats and morning suits).

In appreciating the artistic validity of the musical theater one must not fall into the trap of considering every favorite "great." Greatness — continuing validity — is a rare quality and the label should not be carelessly applied.

It would be impossible to designate a birthdate for the modern interwing musical. Some of its components can be found in the operettas of Gilbert and Sullivan (particularly *Patience*). Its essential theory — the combination of theater arts into a total stage creation — is Richard Wagner's. Wagner was unable to fuse them into the music drama he dreamed of, although he managed to enlarge the role of orchestral music and extend the aria into lengthy vocal-orchestral combinations, much as the musicals are doing today. But for all his awareness of theater, his operas are notorious for their lack of it, and he made no use of movement — dance or otherwise. Like many theorists, Wagner lost control of his ideas when actually producing work. But his vision remains at the heart of today's interwing musical theater.

Between then and today, that musical theater has been shaped by many influences leading to its present state of development. It was always bi-winged and its history is evolutionary. One of the earliest attempts at serious musical theater was *Porgy and Bess,* but in composing it Gershwin mistakenly assumed that Broadway musical theater was not art, and that opera was. Gershwin broadly imitated operatic forms (arias; duets, trios and quartets; recitative, etc.). DuBose Heyward provided a libretto that may be excused its caricature treatment of Negroes on the grounds of naïveté, but cannot be forgiven its melodramatic and cardboard story. Too, *Porgy and Bess* was entirely without musical staging and had minimal dance. It managed to lose the best elements of Broadway theater while acquiring the worst of opera's.

The obvious tragedy is that Gershwin never lived to see the development of the new musical styles that would have been so perfect for him. Between his determination to get a musical education and his brilliant, natural talent for melody and show style, he would have moved swiftly into multitheater musicals. Nevertheless, the *Porgy and Bess* score is magnificent, of course, and there is enough development and free form in it to suggest that Gershwin could have moved into modern musical theater techniques had he kept an eye on what Kurt Weill was doing. Six years after Gershwin died, his brother Ira realized this new musical direction and joined Weill and Maxwell Anderson in one of the earliest ventures into the new musical theater idea — a venture that was a forerunner of today's exciting developments.

Lady in the Dark (1941) provided a genuine example of theater-ahead-of-its-time. It was constructed in sections. Anderson's story of Liza Elliott, a fashion editor with a problem (she "couldn't make up her mind"), could not be taken seriously. But the analysis of her dreams through musical sequences, and the construction of those sequences, was a forecast of the methods that the musical was to discover.

Lady in the Dark had four such sequences — "Glamour Dream," "Wedding Dream," "Circus Dream" and "Childhood Dream." The grinding calliope "Circus Dream" was by far the most successful, although each of them worked in flowing dance-music-dialogue. It ran some sixteen minutes, as compared with the usual six or seven of the ordinary right-wing musical scene, and remains one of the best examples of ensemble musical theater. Ira Gershwin's substantially conversational lyrics may have had to deal with Anderson's child psychology (Can Liza decide between the magazine's Circus and Easter covers? Will she be "executive or enchantress"?), but they were story components.

The method showed up two years later in the lengthy opening sequence of *On the Town,* although the show never again used it. But this, Leonard Bernstein's first Broadway work, also served to introduce another and equally important side to the gestating left-wing musical theater: the dance as a functioning part.

On the Town had dance music that Bernstein himself had composed to blend dance art with theater art (it is extremely and unfortunately rare for a show's composer to write the dance music). And it introduced Robbins into a musical theater that he would subsequently revolutionize. In fact, it was Bernstein and Robbins who were responsible for the first musical to be deliberately conceived in the left-wing scheme. But before we get to *West Side Story,* perhaps that scheme might best be made specific.

The modern interwing musical is a theater work that combines the artistic values of music, dance and drama into a total blend in which these elements are inseparable. It uses them concurrently, rather than sequentially. While this does not mean that everybody is dancing, singing and talking at the same time, it comes close to it — as close as possible without creating confusion. The music is near continuous, weaving in and out of the action. The lyrics are generally dialogical. While there is dance as such, all movement is *dancelike* and no distinction can be made between "musical staging," "choreography" and "direction." The music uses the techniques of serious composing, as well as interesting modulations, surprise changes of key, odd time, dissonance, fresh harmonies — and applies them to the specific needs of the theater. The dance is ballet oriented and thematic, rather than being made up of the traditional, arbitrarily inserted numbers. The construction of the work, therefore, is mosaic, as opposed to the episodic nature of the right-wing musical. All of this is within a conception that is musically theatrical — that is, it is a musical idea, as opposed to a literary idea.

This left-wing musical theater is born in its environment; on the stage. How it will be possible to develop book writers for this all-out theater with the necessary combination of musical and stage sense is not my problem, but it is what this theater demands.

The most experienced writer in the form is Arthur Laurents, who wrote the scripts for three left-wing musicals (*West Side Story, Gypsy* and *Anyone Can Whistle*), and by rights he should know the most about it. Perhaps he does, but Laurents has always been absorbed with pop sociology-psychology and it has interfered with almost everything he has ever done.

Laurents's book for *West Side Story* was based on Robbins's conception of the work as a Spanish Harlem *Romeo and Juliet*. This somewhat sophomoric notion of translating the Montagues and Capulets into two warring gangs (the Jets and the Sharks) proved the production's weakest point. It was by no means helped by Laurents's social worker overtones and the entire production's homosexual undertones. With all those tight-Levi'd, T-shirted chorus boys fighting with each other, the show was a faggot's dream, hardly making the Maria-Tony romance passionate or even credible.

Robbins's conception was more valuable in terms of the show's identity as dance theater and its full-scale use of serious music. Bernstein provided the most theatrical, the most exciting, the most sophisticated and certainly the most difficult score for any musical up until that time (duo-pianists in tent revivals still struggle through it). To be sure, he had not been whistling his theater time away since *On the Town.* He composed some delightful songs for a Boris Karloff–Jean Arthur *Peter Pan,* and his one-act opera *Trouble in Tahiti* is a clever work that is as much musical theater as it is opera (Bernstein's own lyrics for it suggest that he should always do them). *Wonderful Town,* while basically a right-wing musical (George Abbott direction, Comden and Green lyrics), had some ingenious music, not the least of which were the comic "Wrong Note Rag" and the complex "Christopher Street." Finally, *Candide,* a mock operetta with a dazzling score, extraordinary lyrics (by Richard Wilbur, John La Touche, Dorothy Parker and Bernstein) and an impossibly heavy-handed book by Lillian Hellman. *Candide* must be classified as a left-wing musical, it was so different from traditional musical theater. But it was part of no movement. Its music, satirizing classic operetta, was not continuous, since it had to fit the light operatic mold, and its structure, also meaning (presuming, anyhow) to satirize operetta, was never intended to follow advanced Broadway thinking. In any case, it was an overproduced bore that would suddenly spring into hilarious and wonderful musical episodes, only to sink right back into de-Frenched Voltaire.

In the summer of 1966, the Theater Group at UCLA revived *Candide* and performed a near miracle with it. Director Gordon Davidson stripped Hellman's book of its heaviness, added some modern humor and restaged the work without the original truckloads of scenery, using simple grandstands for the chorus and striking designs for the physique. Bernstein restored some of the music deleted on Broadway and the work finally approached a stage worthiness that its score deserved.

But *West Side Story* was constructed to *move.* Robbins's theater ideas finally crystallized and he struck out to create a new kind of serious, artistic, but essentially theatrical musical. It had great significance for the modern left-wing movement in musical theater.

It made definite the trend toward choreographer-directors. This

combination had been tried before (Agnes de Mille choreographed
and directed *Allegro,* for instance), but direction and choreography had never before been blended into continuous musical staging. In the left-wing musical, it is the oneness of creative elements
that makes for totality. It is absurd to apply musical staging to only
the song parts of a musical. Take, for example, the "Tonight Ensemble" in *West Side Story.* The sequence is written for quintet and
is designed to be at once music, dance and drama — an all-theater
sequence. Bernstein's music, aside from its rhythmic and tonal
complexities, was written so that its three complete melodies could
be juxtaposed. Stephen Sondheim's lyric, of course, had to follow
the counterpoint, but more than that, it had to be designed so that
all three lines could be sung *against* each other. This meant that in
addition to the usual problems of meter, prosody and sense, he had
to take into account matters of language sounds. Examine a por-
tion of these triple lyrics:

Line 1	Line 2	Line 3
Tonight, tonight	All right	So I can count on you boy?
Won't be just any night		We're gonna have us a ball
Tonight there will be no morning star	I'll see you there about eight	Womb to tomb! Sperm to worm!

The lines are inane, I grant, but their structural complexity can
scarcely be equated with the writing of an ordinary song lyric. The
true poetry of Lorenz Hart was needed to write a lyric as lovely as
"My Funny Valentine" and Hart would have slit his throat before
writing "Sperm to worm!" But could he have followed Bernstein's
braiding musical patterns?

While "Tonight" is interweaving, the five singers are dance-
moving, generating a stage life out of the musical life (this is what
a program, in small print, attributes to the man who does the musical staging — one of a musical's most crucial credits). It is a tight
and especially stagey sequence, bringing the show to an emotional-
theatrical climax. It has every facet of musical theater working in
combination toward a full-stage purpose.

Outside of the Laurents book — outside of what was actually

being said and dramatized — most of *West Side Story* was exactly this way. Robbins kept the stage in motion nearly all of the time, and seldom allowed any movement to be nonchoreographic. Of course there were times when the dance had to pause and he was forced into conventional musical staging, usually when the songs and situations were ordinary ("I Feel Pretty," for example). But more frequently, the production worked as dance theater, whether in a full-scale production sequence such as "The Dance at the Gym" or in a comic trio such as "America."

As for Bernstein's music, it was formidably complex and thoroughly theatrical, applying musical depth to the needs of the stage and the work. Musical time like that of "Something's Coming," or harmonic structures like those of "Cool," can never be applied by a novice. They demand education and only a composer like Bernstein is capable of using them. Grant the strong influence of Copland and Stravinsky, but rather them than Irving Berlin. Moreover, Bernstein composed the *dance music* for *West Side Story,* and that is highly unusual on a Broadway that leaves the tunes and the credit to rinkydink pianists, while true musicians — orchestrators, dance music composers — fill in the details behind the scenes. The irony in Broadway dance music is that although it represents a lengthy and significant part of a musical's score its quality is generally restricted by the vanity of the credited "composer." In most cases, the credited composer insists that the dance music be based on his melodies. As a result, the dance music arranger — frequently the dance pianist — must build long dance music sequences on the limited base of hack melodies. And there is only so much one can do with that. Occasionally, the composer will be big enough to allow a dance music composer to create his own musical sequences and on such occasions the production benefits by fresh, truly dance-oriented music. But this is rare. Sometimes too, the dance music arranger will go ahead and insert his own music even though he is only credited as an arranger. By and large, though, the dance music for right-wing musicals is committed to rehashes of the soggy ballads and hack production numbers.

But the interwing musical is moving toward composers who are capable of writing real dance music. Even though such composition takes more time than many deadline-bound composers have, the left-wingers realize the importance of it and are taking that time. Stephen Sondheim composed most of the marvelous dance music for *Anyone Can Whistle,* and Bernstein's dance music for *West Side,* of course, was brilliant.

To underline the formidable technique behind the *West Side* score, note that Bernstein even worked (with Sid Ramin and Irwin Kostal) on the orchestrations, and that is something I can assure you is almost unknown on Broadway (the only other composer-orchestrator I can think of offhand was Kurt Weill). Bernstein had had his fingers burned when orchestrators simplified and misunderstood his scores for previous musicals and was not about to let it happen again. It is a long way from a piano arrangement to a full-blown orchestration, and an arranger can botch good music just as he can glamourize the hack.

The Robbins-Bernstein interaction on this production was an ideal example of the composer and choreographer-director team. They knew what they wanted to do, understood each other and were technically and artistically capable of executing their ideas. That they did not entirely succeed does not diminish the enormity of the step which they took for the interwing musical theater.

In the years since *West Side Story* opened (1957), there have been more and more examples of musicals moving straight along the line of absolute theater. Few fit exactly into a pattern and that is good, since original theater never comes out of schools. But all are marked by the seriousness of their composing, the all-inclusiveness of their conception, the interrelationship of their creative elements.

It is not surprising that the next example of the left-wing musical was again directed and choreographed by Robbins. This was *Gypsy* in 1959. But now Robbins had to prove the concept alone, without the tremendous artistic buttressing of a Bernstein score. While he again had Laurents and Sondheim to do the play- and lyric-writing, he was now using music by Jule Styne. And he was carrying Ethel Merman, a star accustomed to vehicles. How was Robbins to use the most modern, the most exciting theater tools while working with a prima donna on the one hand and on the other a Hollywood songwriter who had made good on Broadway with stock, brassy, right-wing scores (*High Button Shoes, Gentlemen Prefer Blondes*)?

Robbins evidently suspected greater talents in Styne, having worked with him before. But that he also conceived of a furiously artistic performance from the great but pure-soloist Merman must be chalked up to genius. Laurents wrote a script custom-tailored to her most intense, most personal characteristics. It shot her role through with everything that was *inside* of her. (Or, to put it another way, it made sure basically, that she really wouldn't have to *act,* but only intensify her own personality.) It grasped the gold in the Merman brass. And Robbins proved that a driving, artistic musical need not demand opera and ballet in their traditional forms. *Gypsy* was a full-blown, sophisticated work of theater art, capitalizing on the guts of Broadway.

Robbins also appreciated the musicianship in Styne — a musicianship of which the composer must have been unaware. Without Robbins' encouragement at that time, Styne would still have been writing "Let It Snow, Let It Snow, Let It Snow" or, at best, good, right-wing theater songs like "I Still Get Jealous." Instead he went on a tremendous creative kick that led him into a new kind of serious Broadway composing, blending energy with technique. Styne's only problem seems to be that he will fall into old show-tune habits unless there is some serious person nearby to stimulate him, and his post–*Funny Girl* work showed the problem to be still unsolved.

For *Gypsy,* Robbins moved toward the interweave musical from the opposite direction as he had for *West Side Story.* Working with Bernstein, he had come from the twin fine arts of music and dance. With Styne, he came from the right-wing musical, as translated into a fine art of its own. The result was not as interwoven as *West Side Story,* but it was more successful as theater. *Gypsy* was the Broadway musical brought to art by purity of form.

It was also sensational, capped off by concluding music that represented Styne's most ambitious composing up to that point. This was "Rose's Turn," which should have ended the show (instead, there was a sticky reunion of Gypsy and her mother, inconsistent with the production's bitter tone).

With "Rose's Turn," Styne was writing real music — real *theater* music composed only for the particular production (rather than as just a *song*). The form was at last free and extended and Styne was opening up, pushed by Robbins, as well as lyricist Sondheim, to go beyond formula construction. No longer restricted to sweet or bouncing melodies, he worked with dissonance and odd time. He altered meters in midstream and built his music to carry a flow of energy, moving into an ever-building intensity. The music caught Rose's fury, retching her unfulfillment, her bitterness, her deprivation of fame, her ruined dream of vicarious stage success. Sondheim's lyric — one of the finest he ever wrote — burned the acid deeply (and with practically never a need for a rhyme).

> I had a dream
> I dreamed it for you, June.
> It wasn't for me, Herbie.
> And if it wasn't for me
> Then where would you be, Miss Gypsy Rose Lee?
> Well, someone tell me when is it my turn!
> Don't I get a dream for myself?
> Startin' now it's gonna be my turn!
> Gangway, world, get off a' my runway!
> Time time, boys, I'm takin' the bows.
> And everything's come up Rose!
> Everything's coming up roses!
> Everything's coming up roses this time for me!
> For me! For me! For me! For me! For me! FOR ME!

To hear Merman bursting, again and again, "For me!"; to hear Styne's cutting, cragging, splitting lines, positively worthy (as well as derivative) of Shostakovich; to feel the wholeness of this musical conception, barreling into that final, screamed "FOR ME!"; and to experience it within the entirety of what Robbins had designed to precede it, to lead up to it and to conclude in it — *this* is exactly what the left-wing musical theater is all about.

Sondheim, having worked on *West Side Story* and *Gypsy,* was in a fine position to understand what Robbins was after and what the interwing musicals were. Although successful as a lyricist, he was a trained musician and was more interested in composing his own music than in writing lyrics for somebody else's. He had already written one unproduced musical (*Saturday Night*) and had provided incidental music for a couple of Laurents plays. It was a great stroke of luck for the American theater that he finally got the chance to compose *A Funny Thing Happened on the Way to the Forum.*

Forum was a strange Broadway episode. The Burt Shevelove–Larry Gelbart book is one of the handful of true interwing Broadway comedies. But while it made subtle parody of burlesque farce, correctly relating it to classical Greek comedy; and merged their cardboard characters (the bland ingenue, the stupid hero, the dirty old man, his battle-axe wife), it was received on Broadway as a broad, low girlie show. Its intricate, just-off-center mimicry and wild deadpan seemed to go unnoticed. As did Sondheim's score.

In fact, that score was terrific, matching the mad sense of the script with exactly the consistency that interwing musical theater demands. It had mock love music, mock heroic music, even mock vaudeville music, and all of it constructed upon the most educated of bases. Sondheim's music is only behind Bernstein's in wedding theater requirements with technique.

An incidental irony to this production is that while it was a left-influenced musical it was directed by George Abbott, the King of the Right. At least, it was *credited* to Abbott, apparently representing his freshest work in years. Yet, while the show seemed geared to Abbott's rushabout style of staging, it wasn't burlesque but mock burlesque and demanded a far more modern director. And Robbins had to be called in to stage a new opening sequence (the wonderful "Comedy Tonight") and liquify the dashing-about that was the basic spirit of the production. In fact, there was no choreography per se in *Forum,* but rather a continuous movement, not unlike a Marx Brothers movie. Such total choreography is pure left wing.

With this show, literally and figuratively, Robbins replaced Abbott as leader of the American musical theater. After it, Abbott could no longer resist the great revolution, falling back into a weak and flabby repetition of old, dusty musical theater (*Fade Out — Fade In, Flora, the Red Menace, Anya*). His time had passed.

Nevertheless, his school of direction continues, if as a relic, in the disciples who rewrite scripts for wisecracks, "tighten things up," keep everybody moving (for whatever reason) and juggle the songs, the dances, the snappy patter. These patchwork directors will continue to service the commercial demands for stock model, right-wing musicals.

A full season was skipped after 1962's *Forum* without any left-wing activity and then the movement ran into its first real setback. Up until that time, the new-style musicals had proved great financial as well as artistic successes. Blending left-wing adventure with right-wing technique, they boasted both originality and polish. They were reaching audiences. Set in the midst of the dated, the noisy, the talentless, the formula, they emerged as remarkable incidents of art appreciated (if not recognized) in its own time.

Then Sondheim's *Anyone Can Whistle* opened on April 4, 1964. And closed at the end of the week. It was that season's finest musical.

For this wonderful work, Sondheim moved deeply into serious musical-theatrical forms, emerging with a brilliant score, fully on a level with Bernstein's twin masterworks *Candide* and *West Side Story*. *Anyone Can Whistle* had two musical-balletic-dramatic sequences that ran for well over fifteen minutes each, in themselves the most imaginative, ambitious and successful scenes to be written for the musical stage *to date*. (Ultimately, the short song *must* be abandoned for long-lined, free-weaving musical structure.) The remainder of the *Anyone Can Whistle* score, with only several straight-song exceptions, blended into the wild fun that was looped into Laurents's book.

To be perfectly honest, there was a great deal in that book that was embarrassingly childish about nonconformity, and a ban-the-bomb message climbed in and out of Central Park West. But there was so much that was healthily antipsychiatric, so much that was spirited and bright, so much that was wildly comic about a hundred things that seldom reach the stage, that I see no sense in complaining about it.

Laurents's fun ranged from night club show business to commercial religious shrines, and if you knew your ballet, your music, your things-in-general, there were wisecracks, parodies and burlesques at every twist of the speeding production. Imagine, for example, a girl who abandons her sexual inhibitions only when speaking in French and dressed in red (her appearance is heralded by an orchestral burst of "The Lady in Red"). Her "French," in fact, is the high school French of an American tourist (*"Vous aussi," "Qu'est-ce que c'est,"* and so on). Each time one of these phrases was

uttered, a thoroughly unnecessary translation appeared on a sus-
pended screen. This is left-wing humor — dry, intelligent, witty. It
has, at last, a brightness equal to the many, many people who have
deserted the theater because it had become too stupid for them.

Mixed into *Anyone Can Whistle* was a choreographic identity by
Herbert Ross that gave it some of the wittiest dances I have ever
seen. His fun with *Swan Lake* was here, *La Valse* there, Sondheim's musical satire working hand in glove with Ross's choreographic. And if you had your wits about you there would be sandwiched laughs on anything at all. Games flashed everywhere.

One right-wing critic called it "sick." *Variety,* reviewing it out of
town, called it "theater of the absurd" (a term it uses sweepingly
and damningly for everything it doesn't like — or understand).
Another New York critic complained that you couldn't whistle the
tunes. (A Prokofiev musical would fail on Broadway because
somebody said you couldn't whistle the music. It is a fine day when
whistleability, as judged by a whistler whose repertoire ranges from
"White Christmas" to "Some Enchanted Evening," is used as the
measure for music.)

During that same 1963-1964 season, *Hello, Dolly!* opened to
incisive right-wing reviews (a charmer, the best in decades, a bang-
up, knockout, sweetheart of a musical) and proceeded to be a great
disappointment to many who saw it. In fact, it was related to the
interwing musical, if at somewhat of a distance, and was just overpraised. It couldn't be *of* the new form because its music (whoever
wrote which songs) was restricted to the stock "number," was not
ambitious and got by mostly on the strength of Philip J. Lang's
superlative orchestrations.

But Gower Champion was working deeply in the new mold and
created a wholeness for the production. It was he who matched
high style in *idea* with high style in *performance,* making of it a car-
toony, primary-colored, one-dimensional kind of puppet show and
grasping the central orginality in Thornton Wilder's *The Match-
maker,* upon which it was based. (It was a trick in itself to wring
the preciosity out of Wilder.)

In a major sense of the interwing musical, *Dolly* was the creation
of a choreographer-director. Champion capitalized on the superdry
sarcasm of Carol Channing in much the same way that Robbins

had grasped Merman's flamboyance for *Gypsy*. Channing, like *Dolly*, never strayed from the style, never left its idea, never stopped to go from artifice to naturalism. Even more impressively, the production had every down-to-the-last-chorus-boy detail planned, timed, executed (so carefully that from one performance to the next, its total running time never varied more than two minutes. This is extraordinary, considering the complexity of a Broadway musical.) *Dolly* was the last word in professionalism. (Jerry Herman's next musical, incidentally — 1966's *Mame* — was a camp *Dolly*, a shameless and effete copy that confused style obsession with style itself. And an oddity since *Dolly* itself was often a camp).

If *Anyone Can Whistle* brought adult wit to the interwing musical and *Hello, Dolly!* brought style, it remained for *Fiddler on the Roof* to step into art. And it was fitting for it to be Robbins who took it there. Never has there been a production that carried the full artistic force of the musical theater so successfully.

Robbins built *Fiddler* around the theme of tradition — how it makes a people and how it forces changes. In this case the pattern followed the need for and the heartbreak of those traditions. Small traditions, of matchmaking, of male-female segregation, and large ones — of intermarriage, political systems, homelands.

From the moment that *Fiddler on the Roof* began, it moved musically. It was just a Chagallesque fiddler, perched on Tevye's cottage, but that image was the start of the production's motion, even in the slight movement of a bow. It was a *picture* of dance. And out of it came Tevye, beginning his chant, his vocalized idea, his dance movement. From this, with exquisite control and the growth of a sense of community, emerged the long "Tradition" sequence that laid the foundation for the entire work. And throughout, musical motion mixed with musical sound and musical construction. It was not opera. It was not ballet. It was not a musical comedy. It was what the new musical theater — and its art — *is*.

Again, Robbins had pushed a composer beyond himself. Jerry Bock had been moving leftward from his original orientation as a stopgap, right-wing composer. After writing some good, though not very theatrical, songs ("Too Close for Comfort," for example) for the Sammy Davis vehicle *Mr. Wonderful*, Bock provided a hack score for a horrendous musical tragedy called — to his regret, I hope — *The Body Beautiful.*

That was followed by the pleasant, though overrated, *Fiorello,* which was straight right wing, directed by a still-in-his-element George Abbott. Bock's music was now clearly theatrical. His next score moved away from songs for their own sake and toward music geared specifically to a show's need: *Tenderloin* was a very funny and unappreciated musical that managed to be both nostalgic and sarcastic about the 1890s New York of reformers. Helped by the clever, mock-sentimental orchestrations of Irwin Kostal, Bock turned in straight songs, it's true, but good, pointed ones. Interested now in thematic ideas rather than just-another-musical, he next went Hungarian with the extremely subdued and warmly sentimental *She Loves Me,* composing a long and long-lined score that moved even more deeply into composing for a production's needs rather than grinding out show tunes. And his music demanded even more conversational and character work from his journeyman lyricist Sheldon Harnick. The lyrics were growing complicated. They were blending into the body of the work.

Then, the *Fiddler* score, which may not have been what real musical technique might have made it, but which applied Jewish harmonies and rhythms to Bock's melodic bent. Too, it had strong examples of the extended musical sequence ("Tradition" and "Tevye's Dream"). And most essentially, it never, never broke stride with Robbins's idea. As a result, the production's overall dance, its overall music, its overall *sense* never ended, was never interrupted. Here is an example: Muttel the tailor is in his shop, trying on the purple satin coat and the high black hat in which he will be married. The shop slides away and the wedding scene draws in, the traditional canopy brought over the groom, who has remained motionless. The lighting has now changed to an abstract suggestion of a *shul,* and the bride, the parents and the wedding guests are organized into a formal group. The rabbi performs the ceremony in mime and then brings the wine glass to the floor in a sweeping, slow motion that is both dance and action. It is stamped upon and broken and the formality erupts into a wedding celebration which continues for more than ten minutes of song, dance and dialogue. Into this move the Russian police, instigating a pogrom, disrupting the wedding and smashing the gifts, the tables and, in effect, the East European wedding tradition. The mood of joy shattered by cruelty, Tevye walks downstage and raises his arms to heaven with the unspoken question "Why?" as the curtain drops on act one. The entire sequence runs to nearly twenty minutes, it never stops moving, musically, and it is extraordinary.

Fiddler on the Roof was a complete, beating organism worthy of being called art. The great theatrical conception toward which the musical theater had begun moving with *West Side Story* was close to consummation.

Fiddler opened in September of 1964, and for the next few years there were to be only partly left-wing musicals (*Cabaret, The Apple Tree, I Do, I Do*).

In writing *The Apple Tree* (fall 1966), Bock and Harnick were obviously confused and still in need of Robbins's strong leadership for musical theater structure. Without him, and with the inexperienced (in musicals) Mike Nichols as director, they foundered between left- and right-wing influences without the necessary counterbalance. The production was divided into three sequences, three separate one-act works. The first (based on Mark Twain's *Eve's Diary*) and last (based on Jules Feiffer's *Passionella*) were in the right-wing style, injecting songs and dances between episodes in a play-story. But the middle (based on Frank R. Stockton's "The Lady or the Tiger?") was a continuous fabric of theater elements applied to a massive mockery of old show styles — pageantry, exotica, even torch singing. Bock now had the freedom from "song" limitations to play openly in loose form, and while his score for the entire production was quite good and regularly knowing, in *Tiger* it opened up and flowed. Even Harnick, whose humor usually runs to the obvious, picked up the left-wing tone ("I've got what you want/I've got what you need/I know how much you want it/Yeah-yeah, Sanjar").

Because of the disparity of material, the separateness of creative contributors, the mixture of styles and an incoherence of structure, *The Apple Tree* didn't work, but its *Tiger* sequence did indeed show the continuing strength of left-wing musical influences. Unfortunately, it was difficult to ascribe credit for it. According to the program, Nichols was responsible for the staging, Lee Theodore for the choreography and Herbert Ross for "additional musical staging." Now who did what? Especially for *Tiger,* which was *all* musical staging, never really stopping to be "play" here, "dance" there, "song" elsewhere. Frankly, I thought Ross because from experience I considered him the only one capable of it, but how could anyone know? Broadway theater programs are regularly misleading and unreliable, whether it be in credits for direction, choreography or even music and lyrics. There are substitutions and additions that are never acknowledged to the public — a fraudulence or intentional vagueness that would never be considered by any businessman. It is unethical and should be corrected.

But there was a *dramatic* production in 1966 that demonstrated *all* the traits of left-wing musical theater. This was *Marat/Sade,* the Peter Weiss play that the Royal Shakespeare Company produced on Broadway to an extraordinary box office success (it was one of the rare plays able to bring the alienated left-wing audiences out of the woodwork). As staged by Peter Brook, this production moved to a more controlled, more metric and more musical lifebeat than any musical in years. Weiss meant to match the all-out antirational, theater techniques of the theater of cruelty of Antonin Artaud with the antitheater, rational purposes of Bertolt Brecht. The matching paralleled the play's protagonists: the Marquis de Sade, an antirational naturalist, and Jean-Paul Marat, a dedicated (if fanatic) reformer. The result was a hair-raising intellectual tirade, the likes of which had never been seen on the New York stage — certainly not on the postwar New York stage of realistic, plodding, right-wing drama.

The sniveling, chain-rattling, clumping, retching inmates of the asylum maintained a steady and percussive rhythm. Their group shapes and movement were continuously controlled, choreographic in the deepest sense. Does the fact that Richard Peaslee's marvelously effective score ran only thirty-five minutes make this no musical? Does the fact that it was presented as a "play" make this no musical? Does the absence of an orchestra in the pit, an overture, singing and dancing choruses make this no musical?

Marat/Sade was the finest musical of the 1965-1966 season. It had a musical identity and a musical physique. I don't mean this in any abstract or theoretical sense. It was musical in a perfectly legit-

imate, perfectly obvious way. What is difficult about the idea is
only that we are accustomed to think of musicals as brassy song
and dance shows. And that is where a problem lies.

It does the theater no good to be parceled out into rigid classifi-
cations: this is a comedy, that a drama, the other a musical. The
theater must be open to imagination, closed to compartmentaliza-
tion and rigidity. There are strange and great things waiting to be
done on the stage, especially the musical stage, unexplored as its
possibilities are. There are new ways of thinking, new attitudes
surging through this country. The music industry is vivid with going, crashing music. Rock and roll, as genuine a music as there is,
has moved out of its basic, repetitious chords into new, fascinating
modulations, rhythms, harmonies and instrumental combinations.
The record industry has stimulated new sounds, new audio techniques, new effects, new music, new uses for instruments. With this
music have come dances that see young America going far more
deeply into the *idea* of dance than ever before. And becoming inventive about movement, body, improvisation. That is real dancing.

These inventions of today's heady America must be accepted
into the musical theater if it is to remain contemporary, along with
other kinds of dance and music that have become popular. It is also
absurd for the musical theater to be without the new-style com-
poser-arrangers who have rescued Hollywood from the prewar,
pseudo-Tchaikovsky composers. Henry Mancini, Burt Bacharach,
Quincy Jones, Neal Hefti, Johnny Mandel, André Previn and Elmer
Bernstein should have long since started working for the theater
(Bacharach, Mancini, Previn and Bernstein have begun). Too, the
musical theater has never made use of America's tremendously original jazz musicians. Miles Davis, Gerry Mulligan, Dave Brubeck
and Thelonious Monk have been unforgivably ignored by our theater. It is ludicrous for so talented and capable a jazz musician as
Eddie Sauter to be doing *orchestrations* for hack, right-wing Broadway composers.

While on the subject of orchestrations, their value should be
pointed out. There is more music in a musical — even a right-wing
musical — than mere songs. The score is virtually continuous.
Who composes all of that? And there is more to those songs than

melodies. They have harmonic depth and structure. Who writes that? The orchestrator, of course, and it is he, most frequently, who creates the bulk of the music for any musical (at least, the music as you finally hear it). Broadway's orchestrators are generally far better trained than the composers they make sound so good. And it is these orchestrators, along with vocal arrangers, dance music composers and musical directors, who are largely responsible for the music in the musical theater. Unfortunately, they are seldom credited. They should be. It takes genuine ability and technique to put a musical's music together and it is people like Don Walker, Sid Ramin, Irwin Kostal, Philip Lang, Ralph Burns and Eddie Sauter who provide it.

Although the basic technique of the new, all-theater musical has already been fairly well laid out, there are a number of problems that remain to be solved. The primary one is the *book*. The idea of the shorthand play has got to be superseded. Left-wing directors sense this but their librettists have been unable to do anything about it. If the book is not a play, then what is it to be? The answer has to lie in a musically indigenous literary equivalent to this new, all-out theater. The assumption that a narrative must connect musical sequences has to be forgotten. Certainly, *something* must connect all the interweaving music and dance, but a new form must be found.

The answer lies in invention. Shevelove and Gelbart came up with one possibility for *A Funny Thing Happened on the Way to the Forum,* using one-eyed slapstick. Laurents used flowing satire for *Anyone Can Whistle,* and was perhaps the first to adequately weave narrative with lyrics (in collaboration with Sondheim, of course).

Tom Jones and Harvey Schmidt, the young, very talented and inventive librettist-lyricist and composer, have been fighting this book problem since their first work. *The Fantasticks* mated a bittersweet fairy tale with bittersweet music, avoiding realism for the fanciful. Their *110 in the Shade* tried for more, but was handicapped by its straight-playwright N. Richard Nash, who insisted on keeping a straight-play book (an adaptation of his own *The Rainmaker*). Having control over the book for their next work *I*

Do! I Do!, they minimized dialogue and even eliminated it in many sections. In fact the first nine minutes had no dialogue at all, and song blended into song.

Yet, they were still "songs," using basic AABA patterns for the most part. Mr. Schmidt is not a trained composer. He can neither read nor write music and must actually have an annotator sitting beside him at the piano watching each chord, *each finger on the keyboard,* and then marking them down. This is not quite as shocking as it sounds, although it is shocking enough. Broadway composers have a tradition of academic ignorance and many of them, especially in the past, have been much worse piano players than Schmidt. Too, his musical instincts are not unsophisticated and his piano arrangements definitely state most of the harmonies that his orchestrator later fills out with instrumentation. His melodic instincts are true and *that* is something for which *no* amount of musical education can substitute. Moreover, Schmidt is eager to learn to read music and write his own dance music and orchestral arrangements. He ought to. The limitations that an inadequate musical education places on a composer are immeasurable. Knowing his harmony and theory he can implement ideas and realize the infinite possibilities of musical composition. The sheer musical ignorance of many of today's Broadway composers is appalling and accounts for most of the hack, *show tune* imitation that crops up in right-wing musicals.

Schmidt is not yet enough of a composer to write the fully textured, extensive music that Jones's ideas really demand, but the work these two are doing is moving directly toward solving the most difficult problem of the left-wing musical.

As for lyrics, they too remain problematic. Strangely, with the booming vitality of the musical theater, lyricists grew worse as composers developed. American musical theater has had some wonderful lyric writers, Lorenz Hart of course being the giant. Hart's extraordinary wit and his genuine poetry raised lyrics to the level of art and set the standard for cleverness and sensitivity. Unable to match him, his successors found themselves emulating him on the one hand and putting him down on the other, never really trying for anything truly creative on their own.

As a result, lyric writing crashed downhill, losing track of prosody needs, freshness of poetry, intelligence of thought, musical sense and rhyme schemes. With the composers growing ever more ambitious, the lyricists grew ever less capable of providing for them. They were quite willing to pad when extra beats posed problems. The words remained the same — lovey-dovey or heavily clever. Things became so bad that Comden and Green flourished as top lyricists, although their brand of satire was obsolete almost as soon as they became successful.

The modern lyricists can no longer think of a song as a separate job. He must see it as part of a musical theater whole. He must stop thinking in terms of rhyme and work in conversational modes. He must have an awareness of an entity of which his work must be a natural part. He is on ground almost as strange as that of the modern librettist and will have to forget about the traditional musical theater that probably first attracted him to his work. Now he must *invent* and perhaps only Sondheim, Loesser, Fred Ebb and Johnny Mercer are capable of it.

As American musicals grew increasingly popular in London, the English were bound to attempt some of their own. Most of these were fumbling attempts to imitate the New York style, crippled by an unfamiliarity with technique and an insistence upon duplication. One of the first British musicals to attempt anything new was *Oh What a Lovely War,* created and directed by the left-wing Joan Littlewood. It was brought to Broadway in the fall of 1964.

Miss Littlewood is a director who believes in spontaneity and improvisation and is willing to sacrifice preparation for their sake. This was not a method for coping with the complexities of a musical and her production showed it. But amateurism is inherent in the left wing.

There were more irritating aspects to *Oh What a Lovely War.*

The production was an attempt to recreate the milieu of the First World War in terms of its own absurdities and it was a victim of its material as well as its form. The style was generally Brechtian, presenting the lighthearted and platitudinous songs of 1916 England while the violent statistics of war were intermittently flashed on an upstage screen as a bloody counterpoint. The cast was costumed in black and white clown satins, a precious attempt at commedia dell'arte theatricality. The structure was slapdash, a string of sketches — usually in the British music hall style — using elementary irony, invariably heavy-handed and occasionally coarse.

The songs were played and sung straightforwardly (and sometimes quite badly) with virtually no musical technique to reinforce attitude. Dance and general movement were almost entirely ignored.

But most irritating was the show's bribing of both itself and its audience with the assurance that they were pacifistic and intelligent people gathered to celebrate their mutual sensitivity. This was cheap, self-serving humanism.

Because of its exaggerated anti-establishmentarianism and generalized pacifism, *Oh What a Lovely War* became and remains a favorite of the left-wingers who do not understand musical theater.

With Broadway's acceptance of a left wing, the musical theater was now capable of developing a far-left influence as well. In part, this was the result of the far left's discovery of the theater-of-the-show (it had previously thought of the theater as a platform for outsider messages, soul-searching and the self-styled avant-garde). With the invention of happenings, the extremists came back to pure theater and, inevitably, to music.

One of the centers of musical theater among the left-wing extremists is the Judson Poets Theater, which Al Carmines, a minister, runs in the Judson Memorial Church on Washington Square. Mr. Carmines, who composes (and often plays) the music for these weekend productions, has a big thing going for the old-time Broadway styles, and while his affection is largely precious it is rooted in a legitimate appreciation of the genre. As a result, most of the Judson musicals are combinations of camp, vaudeville, bizarre comedy and artsy slapstick.

One of the best known is *Home Movies,* by Rosalyn Drexler, a rare example of a Judson production being given an off-Broadway production. And it was typically Judson, loaded with ricky-tick Carmines music, faggot routines, and the general range of hippy humor. It is unfortunate that far leftists are incapable of subtlety and botch their own material by overdoing it, but this is the fault of inexperience. In the case of *Home Movies,* the genuinely sophisticated comic premises were vitiated by a general vulgarity of manner and every variety of self-conscious cuteness, from the harmlessly unfunny mockery of spirituals ("Nothin' — nothin' —

nothin' — nothin' — that's what the Lord has done for me") to simple pornography geared to a Bennington girl gone bohemian.

Another far-left musical was more successful in getting what it had on its mind onto a stage. *Dynamite Tonite,* a "comic opera for actors," was the most exciting work to be produced by the short-lived Actors Studio Theater. The Arnold Weinstein libretto was highly derivative of Central European antihero, antiwar theater. Set in "a bunker — under an unspecified battlefield in a more unspecified war in a less specified time," it brought to mind Berg's *Wozzeck,* Hašek's *The Good Soldier Schweik* and any number of Brecht-Weill collaborations. But though its unoriginality would seem to disqualify it as far-left theater, *Dynamite Tonite* most certainly was leftist because of its moral and artistic attitude. It bristled with mockery of misplaced values ("My dog was raped and my sister's education disrupted"), lightheartedness to emphasize horror ("One little bomb and boom you go") and simple truths ("I only hate you when I call you captain"). It also ran to irrelevant modern comic references ("Give me liberty or Republic Pictures"). But Weinstein's fresh attitude largely made up for his unevenness. Similarly, Mr. Bolcom's score ran from the music hall rhythms and tinny orchestrations of Weill to parodies of grand opera and catchy, sarcastic vaudeville. He drew heavily on the Stravinsky of *Story of a Soldier,* the Milhaud of *The Creation of the World,* the Weill of *Johnny Johnson.* But as strong as these influences were, his score was vastly musical, deep and theatrical — very impressive. *Dynamite Tonite* was exciting and bitterly entertaining.

Dynamite Tonite was reproduced in the fall of 1966 by the Yale School of Drama and this time emerged as a still better work. Weinstein's libretto had obviously been tampered with and Bolcom's score musically reduced as a result of the pre-opening pressures of the commercial off-Broadway production. At Yale, *Dynamite* proved to be funnier and less derivative, truly an opera for actors and bright in the best, most knowing sense. This production returned to off-Broadway for another try early in 1967 and was predictably misunderstood and rejected once more.

Extremist *right-wing* musicals are, need I say, at precisely the opposite end of things. There it is the execution rather than the intention that is admirable. There is probably no better example than *Do I Hear a Waltz?*, which opened on Broadway in the spring of 1965.

By that time, Richard Rodgers had abandoned all pretense of dedication. The producer of his own work, with financial interests running from the publication of scores to the production of original cast recordings, Mr. Rodgers had become a theater businessman first and a composer only incidentally. He was not betraying a theater that he had once helped bring to the point of greatness. He could only concern himself with hiring the professionals to help him manufacture slick imitations of theater.

He paid Arthur Laurents to draw a book from his early success *The Time of the Cuckoo,* and Laurents proceeded to hack it into shapelessness, bought and paid for. He rented Stephen Sondheim to write lyrics (the gooiest "magical, mystical miracle" lyrics Sondheim ever wrote). Sondheim had his own pressures, it is true — Hammerstein had practically godfathered him into the theater and Laurents was an old, respected friend — but even that could not excuse the sellout. Ralph Burns, an extremely talented but cynical arranger, gave Rodgers the orchestrations necessary to make everything sound like *The Sound of South Pacific and I*. Laurents, concededly, was eager enough to do it.

The result was a production without the faintest interest in itself; without enthusiasm in performance, in manner or even, I suspect, in creation; a prostitution of Laurents, Sondheim and the idea of musical theater; an exposure of Rodgers as a needlessly money-hungry man whose stature was stunted, whose ability was stifled and whose legacy was the degradation of the musical theater he was still being credited with fathering.

Such far right-wing extremism is rare on a Broadway that, for all its reputation for cynicism, usually presents work that has been sincerely created. It is a commercialism that can be found most blatantly in the Music Theater of Lincoln Center (of which Rodgers was the first president).

There, Lincoln Center is presenting operettas of twenty and thirty years ago, cast with big-name (and often talent-dry) drawing cards. To be sure, this theater was created with profit in mind. It is the only component of Lincoln Center that is not subsidized and is meant to be not merely self-supporting but actually profit-making.

Rodgers could not have been better chosen for the job. Selecting such gaudy operettas as *The Merry Widow, Show Boat* and *Kismet,* he shamelessly alternated them with revivals of *his own* neo-operettas. When possible, he booked productions that had already been mounted in other parts of the country (by the Los Angeles Civic Light Opera, for example) so that budgets could be even tighter. He turned down every suggestion to revive musicals that had been original, unfairly short-lived, ahead of their time or in any way left wing. He spent lavish sums on vulgar sets and costumes, meant not to fulfill the needs of a musical production but to fill the eyes of a tourist. In every sense, the revivals were overdressed, overpadded, overage and frigid prostitutes in a middle-class theatrical brothel.

It is almost unbearably ironic that the tremendously vital musical theater of Broadway — both left and right wings — is being entombed in the name of the "recognition of an American art form" in this marble mausoleum. And even more ironic that the Music Theater of Lincoln Center is incomparably more commercialized than Broadway ever was. But American culture and Broadway will survive it. More significantly, the musical theater will go on to fulfill the great stage adventure that is already so well begun.

CHAPTER SEVEN

A Million Laffs

IF Broadway's musical has developed into a third mask for the theater, its postwar comedy is stewing in the reactionary juices of the modern American stage. Nowhere is the right wing more destructively dominant than in the comedy, which remains restricted in style, structure and sense of humor to an English formula established in the Twenties and Thirties by such playwrights as W. Somerset Maugham and Arthur Wing Pinero.

This formula is the situation comedy with overtones of farce, undertones of social comment and a single set. It is populated by as few characters as possible (usually five or six), sprinkled with one-liners and wisecracks, furiously "realistic" — as only the Broadway phoney can be — and directed for maximum speed and polish. Its dramatic structure is right wing: it uses plotting, revelation and climax; and its set of values is conservative. Sexually, these comedies depend upon promiscuity and sophistication ("sophistication" as a *Life* magazine picture of New York's East Side), but they are rooted in puritanism. For example, the girl who had apparently been sleeping all over town turns out to be a virgin. Or she marries the man who had been giving us locker room chuckles about his conquest for the first two acts.

There is no sense in condemning such comedy out of hand. The bedroom has always been funny. As well it should be — the sex game is taken so seriously in America that the playing of it is bound to be comic.

But the reliance upon situation comedy, and more crucially the couching of that comedy in nonsense stories created only to carry period humor, has kept Broadway's comic theater away from the tastes and attitudes of the modern left wing. Today, there is negligible left-wing comic influence — on Broadway, in the resident companies, anywhere in American theater. The wide range of comic references, parodies and complex games that amuses contemporary, literate America is entirely absent from the stage. The interests, values and levels of thought that now occupy the adult mind must be satisfied elsewhere.

Ironically, modern intellectual America is on a great laughing jag. In coupling education with brightness, it is finding fresh, mad air in a gale of laughter blown by a new awareness, a new insight into its own identity: the silliness in mass magazines and popular music, in smugness, hypocrisy, phoniness and reform; the weirdness of art fads and inflated reputations; the thousand foolishnesses in everyday living. All of this is seen for the healthy laugh it is worth and the left wing is not only laughing but finding new ways to do so. In films, in novels, in art.

Not, however, in the theater. It leaves that to the vulgar and moronic hackery that the right wing is doomed to without left-wing influence. And laughs its laughs in the living room, in the movie theater, in literature. The wacky abstract humor; the juggling of the language for mockery, for purposeful absurdity; the savage attacks upon long-accepted values in religion, justice, government — these are all absent from the stage, resting in the exiled left wing.

There is some explanation for this refusal to apply such humor to the stage. Today's America is so controlled by right-wing-value protectors that the ideas implicit in left-wing humor will be viciously attacked by the forces of well adjustment. A perfect example was the tragedy of comedian Lenny Bruce, who was hounded to death by a society that would not put up with his assaults upon its holy beliefs.

Bruce was hardly an intellectual. His points of view were borrowed from left-wing circles (impatience with hypocritical race liberals; contempt for big-time religion; disgust with reflexive sentimentality; hatred for white-collar self-satisfaction and middle-class values).

But his sense of humor (as well as his innocent enthusiasm) was wonderful and he became the darling of the literati early in the

1960s. Soon, though, the police, the courts and other Protectors of Our Way of Life began to keep Bruce out of work on charges of narcotics possession and obscenity. The possession of narcotics may be criminal but it is baffling to me how imprisonment can help an addict.

The obscenity business was far more offensive to an America whose vocabulary is dominated by the word *fuck*. Bruce seldom used coarse language. He relied on jazz jargon until the final, frantic stages of his career. And then he generally applied it in mimicry. Still, his act was incomparably "cleaner" than the ordinary night club comedian's.

Nevertheless, night club owners grew leery of police raids and Bruce's income dropped from $100,000 in 1960 to $2000 six years later. On August 3, 1966, he was found dead of an overdose of morphine. A friend attributed the death to "an overdose of police," but it was really an overdose of America — the *morally and intellectually* right wing that had no understanding, no sense, no appreciation of left-wing values. The Bruce case is a perfect example of the right wing's refusal to allow the very existence of the left wing.

This is the sterile, murderous soil in which American culture is attempting to grow. Adorned with neatly trimmed, heavily landscaped Christmas greenery on the surface, it aborts any individuality, any attack on its fraudulent underpinnings. Part of that fiberglass cultural landscape is our orthodox theater. And that theater, so much the product and the reflection of fundamentalist American right-wing values, cannot allow or understand the philosophical bases of the left wing.

On a more simple level, the producers and audiences just will not get the jokes. To "get" a joke, the listener must be working from the same sensibility as the humorist. When the humorist is left wing and the listener right, comprehension is impossible.

The Broadway plays that are called comedies reflect reactionary tastes in content and in style. It is these plays that the left wing resents and identifies as comedy itself. Instead of understanding that the idea of comedy remains honorable, it rejects the entire genre. Consequently, left-wing playwrights refuse to write plays designed primarily to be funny.

Yet there is comedy in left-wing theater. Unlike the careful so-
lemnity of right-wing drama (from *Tea and Sympathy* to *After the
Fall*), the *modern* drama is not without humor. "Comic relief" is a
cliché because it is usually necessary for balance and contrast. Absolute seriousness is doomed to overweight and pomposity. Moreover, it is just *easier* and often more effective to make a point
through comedy than through didacticism. The most complicated
of attitudes can be implied through irony or parody. The plays of
Samuel Beckett, certainly the deepest of our time, are shot through
with comedy. Harold Pinter will write comic business for the sheer
sake of fun. Ionesco can almost be classified as a comic playwright
because so much of his work is just plain funny.

In fact, mid-twentieth-century art may eventually be categorized
as tragicomic, with Joyce's *Ulysses* the lodestar. Our characteristic
tone of voice has come to be the obliquely bitter, high spirits carrying frustrated idealism over our heads like a mocking banner in the
wind.

But the American comic stage is bereft of left-wing influence.
The American comedy, in fact, and sadly, is the Broadway comedy
— *Anniversary Waltz* and *Never Too Late* and *Barefoot in the
Park* and *Mary, Mary,* which, while no better or worse than most
has come to typify the Commercial Comedy to theater intellec-
tuals.

Since the right-wing comedy *is* American comedy, it is necessary
to discuss a few of them. I won't cite too many since we know the
type (and, heaven help us, have even enjoyed some of them). But,
as a reasonable enough example, I think, let's look at George Axelrod's *The Seven Year Itch.*

This 1952 play is about a middle-aged man whose wife is away
for the summer. Discovering that a young girl is subleasing the
apartment upstairs, he daydreams a seduction of her by an absurdly suave version of himself and subsequently realizes the
dream. He then returns to his wife.

The style of the play is smooth, sophisticated and *Broadway.* Its
writing is professional and its structure simple and stageable. The
script is littered with *very New York* name-droppings ("Gramercy
Park brownstones," "Brooks Brothers," "Schrafft's"). The humor
is largely based on the discrepancy between a man's image of him-

self and the reality. The hero is a right-wing husband who harbors delusions of savoir faire but is really confused, helpless and near impotent. He is a very domesticated creature who is happiest when controlled by an efficient, home-making and hypercompetent wife. In short, the slick magazine idea of the American man as a puppy in his wife's kennel.

In the end, right-wing morality triumphs, but not before the infidelity is achieved and enjoyed. So the subjugated male is allowed to have his cake while eating the pitiless and degrading right-wing moral code.

The Seven Year Itch is not unamusing. Mr. Axelrod capitalized upon the middle-ager's fear of lost youth and his continuing interest in beautiful girls. There are certain pieces of cultural information that the audience should possess to understand some of the jokes, though that information is of a definitely middlebrow nature (the lyrics to several Cole Porter and Rodgers and Hart songs, for example). Largely, the play is a slim piece of manufactured theater and is harmless enough as entertainment.

The problem is that it was as successful as a Broadway comedy ever gets. And for this to represent the top level of American comic theater is something short of comforting.

However, the *success* of *The Seven Year Itch* does not mean that it is the foremost kind of right-wing comedy. In fact, the successful right-wing Broadway comedy is seldom the finest example of its genre. It is the middling, cute-at-best comedy that runs for two or three years and not the especially funny play. The great successes are plays like *Voice of the Turtle, Born Yesterday, Mary, Mary* and *Barefoot in the Park*. While the funniest, like Ronald Alexander's *Nobody Loves an Albatross,* will barely eke out a (1963-1964) season's run.

Nobody Loves an Albatross pretended to attack the television industry as a cutthroat, ill-mannered, unethical and penny-witted hive of connivers and cheats. The pretense was only a cover for a barrage of repartee, flying jokes and wild nonsense that had Mr. Alexander practically over the line and into the non sequitur comedy of the left wing. At one point, when the leading man called a brassy lady "an entire fag," Alexander went over that line. But he quickly pulled back, remaining within the comfortable guidelines of realistic right-wing comedy. As such, the play was undeniably funny. Too funny in its quickness and ingenuity to be successful.

On the other hand, a Neil Simon play like *Barefoot in the Park* manages just enough minor sophistication to appease self-styled urbanites while being broad enough to be understandable to the wide range of audiences. It is, like *Mary, Mary,* a perfect example of right-wing formula comedy. After all, it deals with newlyweds in still another East Side brownstone. Their characteristics are simple enough for pigeonholing (the boy is exasperated, the girl impulsive). The actors can play these basic roles within a roomy and economical single set and they can *spat* for three acts before kissing and making up.

If this is not enough to appeal to all audiences, it is carried by no simpler (or duller) a running joke than having out-of-breath characters perpetually climb the house's five floors. It is jerry-plotted to carry every joke its author and director could conceive.

It is *Barefoot in the Park* rather than *Nobody Loves an Albatross* that becomes a Broadway success. And as a result, there are dozens of open-and-close imitations each year. It is they, I think we forget, that make up the bulk of each season, and their sheer stupidity, fatness of thinking and vacuity of humor define the state of today's comic theater. Which do you recall? *A Rainy Day in Newark? The Best Laid Plans? Have I Got a Girl for You? Love and Kisses? Fair Game for Lovers? P.S. I Love You? The Family Way? The Paisley Convertible?* This is right-wing comedy.

Except for the Burt Shevelove-Larry Gelbart book for the musical *A Funny Thing Happened on the Way to the Forum,* the only left-wing comedy ever to open on Broadway was Murray Schisgal's *Luv.*

This was written in the surrealist style that marks most left-wing plays, a style which Mr. Schisgal had earlier displayed in his one-acters *The Typist* and *The Tiger. Luv,* really, was a repeat of *The Tiger,* which had been a mildly amusing comedy about a nonconformist would-be intellectual who winds up in a thoroughly conformative romance. The nonconformist follows a line of philosophical clichés: the State of Man. He is Lonely. In Need of Companionship. Annoyed by Conformity and the Blandness of Existence.

And the conformist follows a line, retaining all the clichés of a forgotten college education (this was a standard Elaine May character). When she begins repeating these clichés in an effort to pacify her would-be rapist, he only becomes more antagonized by her. But *The Tiger* did not handle the kidnapper's clichés well enough to make the parody clear and as a result the play was confusing.

Schisgal used precisely this scheme of humor through cliché for *Luv,* and though such humor is good and up-to-date it isn't a substantial enough theater device for a play scheme. *Luv* kidded the clichés of American romance, and having little to offer beyond its initial joke, it was stretched past its limitations.

Schisgal's mimicry of romantic slogans ("Give love a chance," "Where there is no trust, there can be no love") was extended well beyond the amusement threshold. His kidding of mass magazine marital advice, pop-sociology sex analyses and television females, while appropriate enough, never amounted to more than padding and redundancy. Nevertheless, the play was a rare example of comedy in the left-wing style: its point, sense of humor and stage structure were anti-establishment.

Unfortunately, its success cannot be taken as a basis for optimism. *Luv* managed to open on Broadway because it had an unusually progressive producer and because *The Typist* and *The Tiger* had established a success reputation for its author. It succeeded because of rave reviews by misunderstanding critics (not a single right-wing critic wrote about its basic point, the love cliché in America).

The only completely successful left-wing comedies I have seen were produced off-Broadway. These were Ann Jellicoe's *The Knack* and Burt Shevelove's *Too Much Johnson,* but before going into them I would like to point out that these are left-wing plays *that are plays*. That is, they are written as plotted, dramatic pieces. Left-wing comedy — like left-wing anything — should not be restricted to a single form. We tend to think of comedies as funny plays — stories with jokes and amusing situations — just as we tend to think of musicals as song and dance shows. This is a terribly restrictive attitude. Comedy can be anything — have any shape, any presentation, any look. It only need be funny.

As yet, this freedom has not been tested. Except for the rash of so-called improvisational theaters early in the Sixties, our comedies have remained close to traditional formats. These formats will have to be diversified before there can be any kind of vitality in left-wing comic theater. For after all, the stage can break loose from old forms for comedy just as it can for drama and musicals. When the noise, the running, the color and the imaginative happenings begin to occur (as in a movie like the Beatles' *A Hard Day's Night*), then there will be a left-wing comic form. For now, the examples are only at the beginnings of invention.

The Knack is about three boys and the girl whom two of them are trying to seduce. The most likely to succeed is Tolen, a ladies' man who claims to have mastered the art of seduction and, if he is to be believed, is in constant practice of that mastery. The least likely is Colin, a meek, awkward and gallopingly nervous school teacher. While Tolen is sexual in a crudely esoteric way ("There is little charm and no subtlety in the three-minute make"), Colin is a novice at casual (or any) erotica. Mediating between them is Tom, a very bright, very articulate boy with a sensitivity to shapes, movement, colors and size. He is an individual — sensitive but neither artsy-craftsy nor phoney. He is the buffer between Colin and Tolen.

Their victim-bait-test tube is Nancy, lately from the provinces and swept into the trap on her way to the YWCA. Whether she is really seeking a Tolen, whether she is really seeking a Colin, whether she is too willing a seducee or whether she is merely an innocent at the mercy of circumstance is one matter of the play. But there were more things on Miss Jellicoe's mind. For *The Knack* was as much about international politics as it was about interpersonal relationships, although the author rightly considered neither matter of greater importance than the other. Nor do I.

However, as Jellicoe uncannily noticed, they are very similar. While *The Knack* left its political relevancies satisfied with implication, there was one passage in which they surfaced. This was in the midst of the third act's sexual frenzy, after Nancy has shrieked, thirteen times, "I've been raped" (nothing of the sort has happened; she has only been wishfully shrieking).

TOM

Since you take this attitude, there seems no rational course other than to negotiate. Open negotiation.

TOLEN

Negotiate!

TOM

Negotiate.

TOLEN

Negotiate with a woman. Never.

TOM

Then what is your suggestion?

TOLEN

Authority.

COLIN

Oh?

TOLEN

Authority.

COLIN

Ah.

TOLEN

In all his dealings with women a man must act with promptness and authority — even, if need be, force.

TOM

Force?

TOLEN

Force.

TOM

I cannot agree to force and certainly not to brutality.

TOLEN

Never negotiate.

TOM

Calm, calmth.

This continues for another two pages of script, with Tom urging negotiation, parley and calm, Tolen insisting upon force, Nancy giving them three minutes before calling the police and Colin vacillating. Structurally, the scene is divided into four sections, each reflecting statements of attitude and swayings of commitment. I should think the parallel to postwar international relations is obvious. Nancy, of course, represents the small, neutral countries that were being courted by the Eastern and Western blocs. Tom represents reason: the United Nations, ideally speaking. Tolen stands for power and Colin for the reactor to that power. Depending upon your sympathies, either Tolen or Colin could represent the Communist bloc and the American bloc, attempting to divide the world into their areas of influence.

However, Jellicoe will not restrict herself to a temporal political situation. The behavior of nations is analogous to the behavior of individuals and humans have always attempted to get control of other human beings. The situation of Colin, Tolen, Tom and Nancy remains human and pitifully illogical. Force is force and is always terrible. Weakness is eternally ineffectual. Decency is inevitably trapped in the middle and is without even the victim's sympathy.

The idea is crystallized in an earlier speech by Tolen:

> One is born with an intuition as to how to get women. But this feeling can be developed with experience and confidence, in certain people, Colin, to some degree. A man can develop the knack. First you must realize that women are not individuals but types. No, not even types, just women. They want to surrender but they don't want the responsibility of surrendering. This is one reason why the man must dominate . . . For you must appreciate, Colin, that people like to be dominated. They like to be mastered. They ask to be relieved of the responsibility of deciding for themselves. It's a kindness toward people to relieve them of responsibility. In this world, Colin, there are the masters and the servants. Very few men are real men, Colin, are real masters. Almost all women are servants. They don't want to think for themselves. They want to be dominated.

This Machiavellian rationale for tyranny, placed in the mouth of a small-time, clothes-conscious Casanova, keeps the proportions of *The Knack* true. The play is not meant as allegory — its point is not politics. But neither is its point the cruelty and kindness endemic to seduction, since it is not a romance (though it is romantic). The play is about the treatment of people by people, and its reason for existing is the stage. There, its character is as left wing as its thinking, and its humor as modern and original as its surreal makeup.

The distinction between left- and right-wing comedies should be clear enough, even without comparisons. Like anything left wing, the theatrical comedy takes an *attitude* contrary to that prevailing and presents it in a *style* contrary to that prevailing. This in no way limits it to any "avant-garde" or currently modish technique. It can be *anything at all,* and this cannot be too strongly emphasized, for the worst possible theater influence is a school of thought or of playwrighting. Art must always be individual.

The left-wing comedy depends upon wide intelligence in its writing as well as in its comprehension. Sometimes this will take the form of various references, the understanding of which demands a certain amount of information on the part of the spectator. But such referential humor is not limited to the left wing and can be found in right-wing comedies written by playwrights with broad interests. A right-wing comedy like Samuel Taylor's *Beekman Place* might have a violinist named Bach-Nielsen for a musical joke just as a left-wing comedy like *Luv* might paraphrase the old Sensitive Person joke about a dog urinating on an artist's foot. To understand one joke you have to know who Nielsen is and to understand the other you have to know the old story.

However, there are differences in the *kinds* of humor to be found in one wing as opposed to the other. They are based on values, attitudes, outlooks. After all, what the right wing considers important the left wing considers trivial, and what the left wing considers important the right wing considers destructive. Such differences in humor are as obvious as the differences, say, between the styles of the left-wing comedian Jonathan Winters and the right-wing Bob Hope.

For example, in *The Seven Year Itch,* the restless husband is nervously awaiting the girl he hopes to seduce.

RICHARD

If anything happens, it happens. That's all. It's up to her. She looks kind of sophisticated. She must know what she's doing. I'm pretty sophisticated myself. At least I used to be. I've been married so damned long I don't remember.

Compare this with the closing scene in *The Knack,* which finds Nancy insisting that she has been raped while the three boys anxiously try to calm her down. Tom has managed to challenge Tolen's ego by complimenting Colin on his sexual progress:

TOM

Well done. Very good. You're getting on very nicely, Colin. Much better than the great Tolen.

TOLEN

That sexual incompetent.

COLIN

Eh?

NANCY

He's not incompetent. What's incompetent?

TOM

No good.

NANCY

No good? He's marvelous, he raped me.

TOLEN

You have not been raped.

NANCY

I have.

TOLEN

You have not been raped and you know it.

NANCY

He raped me.

TOLEN

You have not.

NANCY

I have.

TOLEN

And certainly not by —

NANCY
Rape.

TOLEN
Him. He wouldn't know one end of a woman from the other.

NANCY
Rape, rape.

As in the scene from *The Seven Year Itch,* this finds its humor in nervousness. But in the case of the right-wing comedy we are meant to laugh in identification — we are supposed to recognize our own dreams of seduction as well as our own incompetence in fulfilling them. In *The Knack* we laugh at the sheer absurdity of the situation. And with its idiocy backed by the lovely destruction of Tolen's poise it runs headlong into rhythms carefully introduced by the playwright. Just as the words are used, as poetry, to set a tempo, other sounds are percussively employed. A stage direction reads: "Tom begins to knock a nail into the wall about nine feet above floor level. His banging deliberately punctuates the dialogue."

With this ballet of words, sounds, stage activity and ideas growing to a peak, Jellicoe cuts everything short with the drama that is the play's inheritance. Tolen throws his cruelest, most defensive jibe at Colin:

TOLEN
You can't even catch her, Colin, can you? Never mind rape her.
I think you are quite incapable of making a woman, Colin. Look,
I'll show you.
COLIN
If you touch her — I'll kill you.

Now Tolen is defeated, and after a very long pause he releases Nancy, who goes to Colin. Tolen then sees another girl passing by, laughs and goes after her. Tom, who has just hung a chair on the wall for the pure look of it, looks at it, says, "Ah yes, beautiful. Ah yes." And the play ends. Good, isn't it?

The difference between *The Knack* and *The Seven Year Itch* is exactly the difference between left- and right-wing comedy. The Jellicoe play could not possibly be real. The things its characters say and the events that happen to them are *fancified* reality. The humor is in implication and allusion, controlled wildness and orchestrated noise. The point is subtle and multiple. It is written to be staged. That is, it is never meant to exist literarily but only as a theater event. As a result, the director cannot just translate the written dialogue to spoken dialogue. He must use the movement, the sound, the rhythm, the *stage life* of the play to return it to the living thing that it had originally been in the author's mind. *The Knack* exists as a script only because preservation demands that. It really has no business there and its entrapment on paper is much like an attempt to describe music with words. *The left-wing stage is not restricted to the literary.*

The right-wing stage, however, is. *The Seven Year Itch* reads comfortably because it was written to be read. When produced, its director need do nothing more than cast appropriate-looking personality actors and guide them about the stage. His lighting is dictated by the script's demands for "dream lighting" and the usual requirements of matinee comedy (bright and crisp, bright and crisp). His blocking is natural and obvious. As for the play itself, the humor is straightforward, using basic satire and simple situation.

While *The Seven Year Itch* was originally produced in 1952, there is little difference between it and the comedies opening on the Broadway of fifteen years later (except that it is better than most of them). In style, methodology, sense and value structure, it is in no way dated, since Broadway comedy is so archaic anyhow. *The Knack,* however, *could not possibly* have been written in another era. It is young while the Axelrod play is middle-aged. Its stage spirit and its intellectual identity are part of the post-war generation. It is *all new,* and only at the beginning of what left-wing comedy will inevitably become.

The impression may be given that only the left-wing comedies are worth anything and that whatever credit is being given the right is begrudged. To a degree, this is true. I have seen not even a handful of right-wing comedies that I would call of more than passing amusement (although in my youth I considered Broadway comedy representative of the most chic mentality imaginable).

But three points must be stressed. First, there are infinitely more right-wing comedies than left. Second, when a left-wing comedy is produced, it is partly the result of a left-right coalition, if only by the fact that it was *produced at all*. As a result, it benefits from professional staging, acting and production values and is not handicapped by the amateurism that is the left wing's bane. Third, almost every right-wing comedy is presented with all the aplomb of Broadway, and in itself this can make even a foolish enterprise palatable.

Now there is no point in fighting the existence of occasional entertainment value. A right-wing play like *The Odd Couple* is undeniably amusing, and as a matter of fact its first five minutes are almost unbearably hilarious. One could credit those five minutes to Mike Nichols's visual-oriented direction, but that would be a cop-out. The fact is, playwright Neil Simon assembled a barrage of marvelous poker-playing wisecracks. Too, Simon is a potential left-winger who stocks part of each play with deadpan, offbeat, nonsense humor. But his comedies are insistent upon plots — even though the stories are paper slim — and are generally wisecracky. All right, *The Odd Couple* was funny. And all right, some right-wing comedies are.

One trouble is that left-wing critics refuse to concede even this. It is not so consequential a trouble as the inability of right-wing producers and audiences to comprehend the left-wing sense of humor. Why should they? The successful right-wing comedy will run for years. But it is senseless for them to dismiss the left-wing audiences that would respond to up-to-date comedy. Dismissing them dismisses the future.

I would like to mention one more left-wing comedy before moving on to revues. I would like to mention it mostly because it is the only other one I can recall as having been produced within the regular, commercial milieu of New York.

Burt Shevelove's *Too Much Johnson* was an adaptation of the play by William Gillette, the turn-of-the-century American actor who wrote vehicles for himself. A typically broad farce, it depended upon merciless coincidence, philandering husbands and Cuban plantations to propel it through a setting created to display its star. Mr. Shevelove lifted it from the original script and set the entire thing just off center, imperceptibly changing the tone from the straightforward to the tongue-in-cheek, much as he and Larry Gelbart had done with *A Funny Thing Happened on the Way to the Forum*. It became an extraordinarily original kind of straight-faced farce, a put-on of the original.

Like most left-wing comedy, the humor in Shevelove's version of *Too Much Johnson* was not communicated through the meanings of words. The speakers of lines were not supposed to realize that what they said was funny. Taken literally, the comedy would have seemed stupid and heavy-handed, but it was the very stupidity, the very heavy-handedness that was so funny. Too, like *A Funny Thing,* the basis of the humor was the theater itself. Both mimicked a *kind* of theater, extending and exaggerating it without going as far as burlesque or parody. So, when the major character (Mr. Billings) appears with flashy teeth clamping a big cigar, swathed in a camel's hair coat, he need not be overplayed. The fun exists in his kind of old-style character. And when he says, "There is a way out of everything — you just have to hit it," the humor is not in the line but in the *kind of line it is*.

Too Much Johnson begins aboard a ship (which William and Jean Eckart designed to caricature old-time shipboard sets). There, Billings, his wife and his mother-in-law are sailing for the plantation that he has told them he owns. He doesn't own it, but has been using it as an excuse to regularly leave Yonkers for extended visits with a little French trick in New Jersey.

Also aboard ship is Mr. Faddish (nobody in the play has a first name — they are Mrs. Batterson, M. Battish, A Cuban or Another Cuban). Faddish's daughter has been promised to one of the play's dozen Mr. Johnsons. Other passengers are the little French trick's husband, who is searching for his wife's lover, and a crowd of nit-wits. From the shipboard confusion to an absurd denouement on the plantation, the tone is subdued-whirlwind. Billings is always skimming onstage, rubbing his hands in a breeze of confused schemery, talking about digging up bananas and plowing coffee. Then he will drop a straight, ridiculously heavy line ("If you mention his name again I'll kick a lung out of you").

The trickiness of tone and the cleverness of comic pattern were much too left wing for the New York of early 1964 and, unappreciated, the production closed in three weeks. More significantly,

Shevelove left for England, where he and Gelbart found the theatrical wing alignment far more conducive to originality (and where,
for a left-wing film comedy called *The Wrong Box,* they could
write a line like "I can't hear you. Please speak a little lower").

It was that newly healthy English theater of the Sixties that also
produced the tremendously original and hysterically left-wing comedy of *Beyond the Fringe* and its offspring The Establishment.
They represented a breakthrough into a new kind of stage humor,
away from plot, away from punch lines, and into the same kinds of
surrealism that had been developing in drama. (After all, why
should the language of comedy be different from that of drama?)
These companies were mistakenly considered topical/political.
Though their material was often drawn from political events, that
was not their most significant theatrical plane. The most important
thing, theatrically speaking, was their left-wing approach to the material.

At about the same time, a group of young, serious actors in Chicago started a movement toward improvisational theater. Beginning as The Compass Players and developing into The Second City,
they produced exercises, sketches and dramatic scenes that moved
directly out of left-wing ideas and stage methods. While the concerns were serious, the theater form was comic, and so the inevitable strength was in pathos (as in a lonely man becoming involved
with a coin-operated, mechanical "friend" in a subway station).
Though it advertised itself as "improvisational," this was only occasionally practiced. Generally, routines were invented, rehearsed,
developed and perfected until they were as planned as any other
theatrical production.

Can art be improvised? From a practical point of view, top-of-
the-head creation may benefit from spontaneity, but it is doomed to
be sloppy, disorganized and without the control that serious art
requires. If the artist does not know, when he begins, how the work
is to conclude, how can he plant the seeds of climax in the exposi-
tion? And how can he exercise a running manipulation of his audience? These were exactly the problems that hampered The Second
City when it tried genuine improvisation. Asking an audience for
"ideas" (a subject, a point, a character), it would wander until the
players nudged practiced routines into it. These would jut out as

the cheating they represented and the whole piece would rarely carry the effective weight of a tried and tested scene.

I see no performance value in improvisation. If it means anything to an audience to know that the actors are ad-libbing, it is a trivial meaningfulness — a novelty. If it represents a challenge to the performer's quickwittedness, a satisfied challenge does not mean a successful theater piece. In fact, such theater only makes a parlor game of the theater. It transfers attention from the art to the artist.

This does not lessen the value of improvisation as a workshop exercise in the training of actors. The actor must have an understanding of the creative process — he is not, after all, only a reproductive instrument. In working out of himself, he can learn through experience, the inner sources of behavior. However, I would hardly place improvisation high on a list of necessary acting tools (and certainly not as high as the Actors Studio does).

The concurrent popularity of *Beyond the Fringe,* The Establishment and The Second City was hardly coincidental. In all three cases, these companies were satisfying the hunger of young intellectuals for modern, adult comedy. They presented educated humor referring to a real world: the related absurdities of right-wing nuclear races and left-wing ban-the-bomb organizations (*Beyond the Fringe*); the foolishness of both the left-wing homosexuals and the right-wing antihomosexuals in the Lord Hume scandal (The Establishment); the silliness of both right-wing philistines and left-wing intellectuals (The Second City).

That is because they had developed a nondenominational point of view. This sometimes manifested itself as an objective, nonpartisan, unflinchingly cold-blooded attitude demanding sense. And sometimes as a naïve, immature, confused, inconsistent childishness. The right wing was rooted in subjectivity, partisanship and only one side of "sense" — *its* side. The left wing is not without its own convictions. "Commitment" became the byword of the postwar left wing. The left wing believed in reform, action and the possibility of implementing change, strangely like (although only superficially) the Thirties generation of Socialists (left wing then, right wing now). However, it is in these convictions that the left wing betrays its weaknesses. Committed to change things, as the left wing always is, it agitates without knowing how to change or what to provide in exchange. Forced by its own commitment into extremist positions, it finds itself, for example, defending Negro racism or Chinese Communist agression despite a basic revulsion for *any kind* of racism, *any kind* of aggression.

Although *Beyond the Fringe* was generally considered political satire, its political references were in fact, few and minor (certainly so when compared with its relative, the British television program *That Was the Week That Was*). It was basically a comic theater thing. Very funny but not merely humorous. Funny in the newest, maddest, educated-lunacy style. The comedy was for its own sake — to laugh and laugh and laugh.

One kind of such laughter was in a sequence that had a one-legged actor applying for the title role in a Tarzan movie. The actor is told, "You are deficient — mmm — in the leg division — mmm — to the tune of — mmm — one." Such humor can be said to have a point (demolishing artificial blinders about physical handicaps). It is what the right wing called "sick" during the cleansing blast of bright humor that swept the country a few years earlier. It existed, really, just to be funny.

An even better example of the new, for-its-own-sake comedy was in *Wait a Minim,* a generally dull entertainment that was brought from South Africa to London and then to New York (and which attempted, simultaneously, to be left-wing-disgusted-with-apartheid while being right-wing-pure-white in personnel). This was a pantomimed, slow-motion search by a candle-holding Elizabethan for a group of armored knights who marched in and out of the wings making steady clucking, knocking and zonking noises. At the same time, one, two and then three maidens sleepwalked their ways cross-stage to the same clucking, knocking, zonking orchestration. How can you explain the humor in the ticktocking noise and the spinning, marching, mechanical doll movement? It is the humor of nonsense.

Only slightly more pointed was a sketch in an Establishment edition of May 1963. This was a careful, name-by-name explanation of the South Vietnamese governmental hierarchy of that time, going from Ngo Dinh Diem to Ngo Dinh Nhu. It was only after dozens of complicated names and relationships were rattled off that a film clip of President Kennedy was shown in which he explained the same situation, in the same way. In this case, The Establishment let reality satirize itself. But although the company was more inclined to deal with political personalities and events than was *Beyond the Fringe,* it found the humor not so much in the events as in the continuing stupidity and pomposity of the human personality in a position of power.

The Second City followed its own interests — the silliness in the left wing of which it was a part. Its areas were literature, music, art, the theater, folk singers, protests, and so on, from the general point of view of the Jewish intellectual (it was a remarkable evening when a Second City sketch mocked an Irish-Catholic, Knights of Columbus, near-beer drinker). A typical Second City sequence would satirize the suburban Jew so eager to assimilate that he has Frank Lloyd Wright design a temple that calls its shamas a sexton and mounts the Chagall stained-glass windows in its *apse.*

But Second City understood the comedy of the implausibile as did its British correspondents. The wonderfully funny Anthony Holland would describe a Mahler concert in Vienna that had in its audience Sigmund Freud, Oskar Kokoschka, Edward Teller and Jean Harlow. His "Vic Venerio" would teach physical education at Margaret Sanger High School. Conventional midwesterners visiting their secretly homosexual son would notice a picture of his roommate and remark upon his good looks. The son replies, "Thank you."

Ironically, the best of the Second City people went on to great success on the right-wing stage. This was because they were performers rather than actors and right-wing theater is geared to that. Mike Nichols, Elaine May, Shelley Berman from The Compass; Barbara Harris, Zohra Lampert and Alan Arkin from Second City. But none of them could act — they were performers, most of them limited to one basic routine: mimickry. Lampert remained that way in productions that ranged from Brecht's *Mother Courage* to Miller's *After the Fall.* Arkin was unbearably funny in a comedy called *Enter Laughing,* but only because the role gave him full freedom to do a Bronx-Jewish basketball-playing James Monroe High School graduate — a perfect Second City type. Subsequently playing in *Luv,* he proved himself without even a rudimentary knowledge of acting. Yet because Lampert, Arkin and especially Harris were extraordinary *entertainers,* they could become tremendously effective in the kinds of right-wing productions that were geared to such "acting."

On the other hand, Nichols's sense of left-wing humor and his understanding of the new stage approaches made him one of the first inbred left-wing directors. The Compass Players were not restricted to improvisation but produced serious, left-wing drama too (including Brecht's *The Caucasian Chalk Circle*), and Nichols was aware of the theatrical lineage behind the leftward movement. When he finally began directing with *Barefoot in the Park,* he was not yet able to blend left-wing theory with right-wing practice. But as his work continued, he served a terribly important role in moving left-wing plays (*The Knack, Luv*) into the right-wing milieu, if only through the influence of his by then big-time name. Nichols has the knowledgeability, the taste and the inclination to do for left-wing comedy what Jerome Robbins has done for left-wing musicals. Whether or not he will prove as committed and as creative as Robbins remains to be seen.

So far, his work has been encouraging, though not yet exciting. He staged *Barefoot in the Park* in a good but conventional right-wing style. It is to be presumed that he was hedging on his first directorial bet and was not allowed (or did not feel free to take) the freedom for a full exploitation of his left-wing ideas. Certainly, the right-wing Neil Simon script did not inspire creative staging. After that great commercial success, he concentrated on the visual, the moving, the pure stage, as in the opening beer-spraying, potato-chip-flying sequence in *The Odd Couple.*

The left-wing directing of the comedy, then, follows the same trend as that of the musical and the drama. As in all modern theater, it demands creative work of the director. He must do more than transfer the work, like a decal, from the script to the stage. He must think in terms of a living theater piece. He must be aware of his own contributions. He must use any applicable theater elements. He must keep his stage moving, his people interacting, his theater piece dynamic. He must be aware of sound, touch, sensation; he must work with light, color, tempo. The humor must not be restricted to lines but must reach out from all directions. The production must *go*.

The nature of far right-wing comedy should be obvious enough. (The word "obvious" has been used, as I am sure you have long since realized, to disguise opinion as fact.) A far right-wing comedy is neither a comedy, a play nor a theater event. It is a plastic, manufactured commodity. Like the extremist right-wing musical, it is based on Broadway the marketplace, where the concern is not with theater but with customers, costs and marketing. It occurs in a regular Broadway theater and has regular Broadway-comedy sets (usually a New York apartment or a suburban home, furnished with the taste of a trading stamp catalogue). It has regular Broadway actors and a regular Broadway director. However, it is seldom written by a regular Broadway playwright and usually has a nonactor Big Name for a drawing card. A good example was *The Impossible Years,* which opened a healthy (depending upon your medical standards) run in the fall of 1965. It was written by two men credited with more than five hundred television scripts, an all too believable figure. Its leading player was Alan King, a comedian whose material-in-trade was the beleaguered suburban husband. Not surprisingly, he played a beleaguered suburban husband.

There is no point in wasting would-be critical barbs on this "play." However, a theater cannot be defined by what it should be, but by what it is, and, like it or not, the extremely right-wing comedy such as *The Impossible Years* makes up a sizable percentage of the Broadway theater's activity.

The Bob Fisher–Arthur Marx script was about a psychiatrist who disrupts his daughter's romance in the fear of Broadway's most poignant tragedy: the loss of her maidenhood. Since the aversion of that tragedy (the revelation that the young couple had already been married) was two hours away, there was plenty of time for special, star material. This ran to lines like "Doing sixty miles per hour in a drive-in theater," and "Take a breather on Linda and you wind up with a lungful of cigarette smoke" (the kind of line that Shevelove-Gelbart would take for a head-on, straight mockery ride).

Such playwrighting, being to the right of even conservative crit-

ics, is destined for rejection in almost all reviews. It is also likely to
succeed with the sizable far right-wing Broadway audiences. Since
it is innocent of all serious theater concerns in its concentration
upon Broadway-the-salesroom, it can go to the heart of matters
and reach the lowest mass level of ticket buyers. Since it has a television favorite of these buyers as a lure, and their values, humor and
idea of entertainment as a purchase-worth-the-price, it is bound to
satisfy them.

Is it presumptuous, then, to deny its right to exist? *Of course* it is
presumptuous. Theater cannot be "improved" by destruction and
even if we are forced into accepting trash when we follow the thea-
ter-is-theater theory, the theory must be respected. The presentation of far right-wing comedies must be allowed, even if it means
the recognition of imitation theater. The audiences they draw must
be conceded their enjoyment, even if it means their continued depression at low cultural levels. The elimination of right-wing comedies would not encourage an alliance of the wings. In any case, I am
not concerned with what should be done with, about or for these
productions. I merely point out that they exist.

They exist in greater profusion than the far *left*-wing comedies,
which can hardly be described as even existing. Off-off Broadway
humor is generally heavy-handed authority-baiting delivered with
the finesse of a youngster who dashes into his parents' living room,
shouts an obscenity and then flees.

One of the few far left-wing comedies conceived with enough
polish to warrant a price of admission was Kenneth Koch's *George
Washington Crossing the Delaware*. This is a lampoon of American
history, in the style of a grammar school pageant. In seven brief
scenes, it parodies the Washington myth, using the stilted and
superpatriotic dialogue of the typical textbook ("He is a perfect
gentleman, excelling in manners as in speech. His dress is perfect,
his buttoning neat and his shoes of a high polish"). While this is
not dissimilar to W. S. Gilbert, it does move into extremes of exaggeration that typify modern left-wing humor.

For example, Washington will discuss military raids and immediately find himself reciting cheerleader rhymes ("Raids in the
morning and raids at night, raids on our stomachs by candle-
light"). A girl will speak with ultraformality ("Many soldiers re-

turn from wars unhurt, only to engage in some peaceful occupation
in the pursuit of which they are killed by some unforeseeable accident"). Sean O'Casey Irish revolutionaries are kidded ("And me
all the time thinkin' of those that are near and those that are far
away") and Cornwallis is reciting his clichés ("The justness of our
cause," "The future of England"). And all the while Washington is
swallowing his own legend ("I am tired and I need sleep. Good
night, America").

The play, I concede, is a highly limited joke and its attack upon
jingoistic claptrap sometimes becomes heavy-handed in the style of
a college skit, particularly when it describes the chopping of the
cherry tree (Washington's father cries, "What? You chopped down
the tree I slaved for, you little brat?"). But it is frequently very
funny, especially, I think, with a Cornwallis plot to have a disguised Redcoat talk Washington into defecting ("If he is convinced we are right he will join us without hesitation"). This scene
combines the laughing at outrageous legend with broad farce:

WASHINGTON

Halt! Here let us stop and dismount and prepare the boats.

(*Disguised*) FIRST AID TO CORNWALLIS

I come to you from General Haskell, Sir, who is hard-pressed
at Stevens. I mean Stevens, Stevens, Sir, Stevens who is hard-hask
at pretzelled, hart had at Pretzelled, Sir, General Stevens, Sir, hart-
passed at Haxel —

WASHINGTON

Tenwillet, remove this man at once to the medical tent and place
him under armed guard. He seems dangerous.

SECOND AID TO CORNWALLIS

Yes, your worship.

FIRST AID TO CORNWALLIS

The man is a genius! It is impossible to deceive him.

While this kind of humor is not difficult to appreciate, the baffle-
ment with which *George Washington Crossing the Delaware* was
received by the rightist critics indicates the lopsidedness in American comic theater.

It is futile to hope for right-wing Broadway producers to understand such humor in the near future. It is consequently senseless to expect writers like Koch to develop their theater skills to any professional degree. They cannot get the necessary experience and if they continue playwrighting at all they will be produced under only the most amateur of circumstances. What left-wing comedy there is will therefore remain young, inbred and self-conscious, undisciplined by theater needs and undeveloped beyond precosity. And right-wing comedy will continue to ride along the slicked rails of big-time theater and medieval humor.

How far is it from *The Impossible Years* to *George Washington Crossing the Delaware?* Further than from today to tomorrow.

CHAPTER EIGHT

A Word on Plays—I

D RAMA is the nobility of the theater. The musical and comedy theaters have their own identities, their own artistries, but it is in the drama that playwrights have always made their highest contributions to the stage art. This may not always be the case. With the passage of time, the musical, comic and dramatic theaters are merging. Playwrights and directors, as they join forces, are realizing more of the possibilities of the stage. They are growing reluctant to restrict themselves to the formula of the serious play of dialogue, and forms are merging into a free, open concept in which anything, really, can go.

The wing split in American drama is cataclysmic. Broadway, by even the most prejudiced account, is where nearly all the new American plays have been produced and today's Broadway drama is reactionary.

Its right wing is controlled by old-fashioned producers who invest in old-fashioned plays to be judged by old-fashioned critics for old-fashioned audiences. The control is so powerful that established international trends are barely hinted at there, and when they appear they are crushed. For all practical purposes there is no left wing on Broadway. As its comedies remain dominated by Maugham and Pinero, its dramas remain in an Ibsen-Chekhov rut. Occasionally, a modern play will be produced, but it will usually be either misunderstood and condemned by the right-wing critics or mangled beyond recognition by right-wing directors and actors. Because this theater is so violently behind its time, it has been abandoned by the left-wing and middle-of-the-road theater-

goers and exists now as a relic. The handful of right-wing plays that
appear there is hardly worth discussion.

For a country's drama, good or bad, to exist, there must be a
group of *master playwrights* who keep it regularly stocked. These
playwrights need not be artists. They need not be playwrights of
historical consequence. They are ordinarily behind the up-to-the-
minuteness of younger, less busy dramatists. They are right-
wingers, then, but they match the best of the right-wing standards:
professionalism, maturity and practice. These are the criteria for
the "master playwright."

There is no master — no professional, mature, practicing —
playwright in America today. That is the state of our contemporary drama.

It is a long ride downhill from ten years ago, when we had three:
Arthur Miller, Tennessee Williams and William Inge. But although
Miller has long been conceded to be the ranking American playwright, he produced only one play (*After the Fall*) over a span of
nearly ten years (1955-1964) and for a country's major dramatist
to be so inactive is absurd. Such a man cannot be considered a
functioning dramatist and such a country cannot have a thriving
theater.

Both Williams and Inge have fallen apart at the artistic seams,
finally abandoning their natural genres in search of new left-wing
identities. Williams not only lost his grip on style but eventually
allowed his formidable technique to crumble.

This implies no comparison of Miller, Williams and Inge in
terms of either quality or style. As writers they are very different. I
speak only of their categorical relationship to American drama.

I hope that my criteria for the master playwright do not seem
arbitrary or academic. They are, I think, the obvious criteria for
any master of any craft. The professional playwright should have
developed his technique to a level worthy of payment. He must be
a master of his trade — language, structure, development. If he is a
naturalist he must have an ability for creating plots and characters.
If he is a humorist he must have an ability for stage comedy. If he
is a surrealist he must be able to control abstract conversation,
cartoon characters and exaggerated situations. The professional
playwright also must have a full-functioning knowledge of stage

history and needs: he must know what can happen in a theater and what cannot. As an artist (or quasi-artist) he should be able to imagine things as yet untried, but he must know what is practically *possible*. He must be aware of lighting usage, the importance of movement, the value of costume, the shapes of stages and the provisions of scenery. In short, he must have the complete set of theater tools.

Maturity is more intangible. It is most easily defined by itself (I know this is cheating): it is the quality of being grown-up. This does not necessarily mean emotional maturity, since that would disqualify nearly every playwright (as well as critic, I suppose), but a maturity of artistic identity. A dramatist may take a childish attitude toward his object, but both his attitude toward his play and his technique must be adult. His style must be developed. He must use his materials with the confidence, the knowledge, the experience and the care of a grown-up playwright. He must have no weakness for impulse, impulsiveness being the hallmark of the child. And he must have control over his work.

Practice may be the most significant of the three criteria. Without it how is one to become either professional *or* mature? It is also the most difficult to acquire, because a playwright may work in seclusion but he cannot really practice without a production, and that demands a stage and people.

But the practice of which I speak goes a step further. It is the practicing of a playwright who has already received recognition. Once accepted as a mature professional, he must continue to produce: he must build upon what he has already done. He must be a breathing, growing, thriving stage element. He must *exist,* with work coming regularly from the font of a functioning, participating dramatist.

Although there are no such dramatists in American theater, there *is* an American theater. As the badly prepared student will turn in *some* answer on an examination, and that answer will be given *some* grade, today's foundering American drama will have existed in *some* state and that state can be examined.

It must be examined on Broadway. The resident theaters may evolve into stages for new plays, but they haven't yet, and for the present American drama is the drama that has been produced on

Broadway (with the single exception of the American Place Theater, discussed earlier). This is where our drama has always existed and where it exists today if it can be said to exist at all. This is also where every playwright wants to be produced, though for varying reasons.

The most important reason, and it might as well be gotten to at once, is money. The motto of the left wing is that an interest in money is the interest of a philistine. This is typical left-wing childishness. The playwright who is produced in the commercial theater is not, per se, a sellout.

Nor is the artist a sellout who has an interest in income. A sellout is an artist who decides to tailor his work to the commercial marketplace. But a playwright who goes his own way, writing what he chooses, and then has it produced on Broadway, or London's West End, is being honest as well as perfectly logical. He must be permitted the same financial interest as well as any other professional. It is very easy for an outsider to criticize him for seeking maximum income (it is among the privileges of nonparticipation). What has *he* to lose? Moreover, a playwright has a valid reason for being in the main theater arena; it is where he reaches the broadest audience and where he will most likely get his best production and national recognition (well why shouldn't he want *that?*). He will also avoid being mixed up with sloppy management. But most important is the income. The professional is paid for his work and is confident enough, honest enough with himself to work on the highest societal as well as artistic level. He is a major factor in a special sphere of the real world and accepts his role as such. That is the only way to operate if he is to be an adult in every sense of this world. I am not writing this book for nothing and you are not doing your own work for nothing. If either of us did, we would be amateurs in the sense of pay and probably in the sense of output. It is ridiculous to assign another set of standards to the playwright. Of course he should seek Broadway, because it is the big time, like it or not. Just as every artist in every art has always done. And just as every smug, noncreative observer has always criticized.

If the commercial stage seems to be a depressing, even a sterilizing force against true theater, it is not the playwright's obligation to correct it by abandoning it. Abandonment would only murder it as a stage at all. By his very contribution, the serious playwright is helping matters.

Although our playwrights *have* sought Broadway, it responded by murdering American drama, slowly bleeding the postwar health of the master playwrights and those in mid-development while rejecting the left-wingers who should have succeeded them. As a result, its drama is dead. That this is the drama by which modern American theater will be historically judged makes the anticipation of that judgment harrowing.

Right-wing drama on today's Broadway is naturalistic in style and literary in form. It is based on plot and realism. As the stage piece, it relies on the playwright's script and a director's fidelity to it.

Such drama is that of the early Tennessee Williams, Arthur Miller, William Inge and the Ibsenite Thirties playwrights before them (Kingsley, Hellman, Rice, Anderson, Odets, Sherwood, Howard, and so on). With the easy, if somewhat bloody, solution of Depression problems by the Second World War, the idealism of prewar liberals was made obsolete and the adjustment of the American economy to obvious socialistic needs buried it. Miller's masterful *Death of a Salesman* was the last of the anticapitalist plays, signifying the end of that era by being, itself, more involved with the personal tragedies of American capitalism than with its economic problems.

After that, the naturalist playwrights were forced to turn to other reforms. Miller stayed with Thirties problems obliquely, finding material in the McCarthy inquisitions. Williams began a new crusade for message playwrights: sexual reform. After his early paeans to sexual health in *Streetcar* and *The Rose Tattoo,* American playwrights followed his lead. There was a series of Inge plays delighting in animal instincts, modeling their heroes on Williams's Stanley Kowalski. On their heels came dramas pleading for an understanding of homosexuality (*Tea and Sympathy*) and narcotics addiction (*A Hatful of Rain*). All were melodramas, all were stories, all were realistic, all were mechanically geared to get the message across.

Such drama was already doomed, behind the times before it began. European playwrights such as Beckett and Ionesco were already developing the surrealist forms that had been pioneered years earlier by the French. England's John Osborne blasted the very uselessness of reform — and the new generation's disgust for it — in his trail-blazing *Look Back in Anger* (although this play was as right wing in style as it was left in intellectual attitude). On Broadway, there were no more causes and no more playwrights. Just producers, running in circles, seeking a tail that had fallen off.

One must return to the American stage of the Forties and Fifties to identify today's right wing, for the plays that still determine the power-producer's current taste were written then.

Death of a Salesman is subtitled *Certain Private Conversations in Two Acts and a Requiem.* It has all the qualities of theater greatness, building a massive dramatic power on the strength of its particular details while spreading a general relevance around it. The tragedy of Willy Loman is self-powered into the tragedy of the American Way of Life.

What is *Death of a Salesman* about? It is what its title says it is about, and seeks the cause of that death, even a murderer. But is it about a man who based his life on false values and so was foredoomed to tragedy? Is it about a man whose life is beyond his control, set on a fateful course? Is it about the American economic system and its fraudulent goals of material success and popularity? Is it about a way of life so heartless that it can make a man obsolete, just as it does machinery? Or is it about Willy Loman, a salesman?

It is a private and *public* conversation. The granite of this tragedy and the majesty of its grief lie in the presence of all these questions, not in disparate collection but in multiple identity. It is a work of total consistency, controlled by a writer and stage man who knew what he wanted and how to accomplish it. It is written with the combined arts of the literary and the theatrical. The language is disciplined and spare, poetic without being unrealistic. As with all fine drama in the naturalistic mode, it manages to make its characters more eloquent, more articulate, more substantial than real people, while keeping them believable.

Miller had classical tragedy in mind when he wrote the play — he has always been plagued with an intellectualized need to be artistic. Despite the foolhardiness in such self-consciousness, he almost succeeded. But we never believe that Willy was doomed to a fatal course of action by a set of circumstances beyond his control. We never even approach the drama on those terms, nor does it come to us that way. Yet Willy's tragedy is legitimate in the classical sense. It is his environment, his conditioning, his situation, his circumstance, that has doomed him. Miller would like to think that Willy Loman, like the Greek tragic hero, is unable to cope with his condition, but there is no reason for him not to be able to. We have every right to blame his tragedy almost as much upon his own inadequacy as upon the forces that shaped him.

But to put *Death of a Salesman* down (as leftists do) for being "Thirties" and unequal to Greek tragedy is silly. The play stands majestically on its own foundation.

Death of a Salesman was a bitter complaint about the American social-economic system. Miller's next play was written for a more specific purpose, a more specific reference. *The Crucible* is an analogy to the McCarthy witch-hunts of the late Forties and early Fifties. But the playwright was going beyond the strictly message framework of his Thirties predecessors and this play extends the particular lunacy of McCarthy to the eternal human taste for persecution and inquisition.

Miller's retelling of the witchcraft trials in seventeenth-century Salem, Massachusetts, is so well written and so securely reasoned as to represent the first-rate forging of the analytical mind with the theatrical imagination (a combination that Miller presents with nearly every play). Its thrust is twofold, in the brain and in the heart.

John Proctor, its idealistic-realistic hero, is torn between an urge to survive and a revulsion against confessing to a crime he did not commit. His wife Elizabeth is somewhat less understandable to a modern, compromise-oriented sensibility, since she is almost physically unable to lie. Miller's success in creating her is almost as remarkable as the very idea of such pure-bright idealism. Most all of us believe, as one of the play's characters says, that life is God's greatest gift and that to give it up is the greatest of wrongs. Elizabeth Proctor is absolutely moral, and when that absolute morality demands that she die rather than confess falsely to witchcraft, it can be difficult to grasp. Miller makes it believable, even while it is an attitude that can make reason blanch.

Blanching, of course, is exactly what Miller wants his audience to do. He allows no escape — either you are going to bow before the howling mob or you aren't. If the play's Reverend Hale advises, "No principle will justify the giving up of life," what is to be your reply? It is a question that may well frighten any one of us, and one that nobody can answer for another. (It is the same question Robert Bolt asked in *A Man for All Seasons*). Is it true that whatever progress has been made in this world is due to people who died for their truths? Or has it been made by people who lived to make that progress? *The Crucible* applauds the dead, and because it does so with cool thought and hot temper, it is classic.

Miller's *A View from the Bridge* was preceded on a two-play bill by the brief *A Memory of Two Mondays*. He subsequently fleshed out the major work to full length and it is that version of which I write.

A View from the Bridge was again involved with McCarthyism, but in the limited area of Miller's personal experience with it. *The Crucible* had run parallel to McCarthy's effect on the American community, exposing the viciousness and ignorance in mob hysteria. *A View from the Bridge* was analogous to the McCarthy effect on personal trust. In writing it, Miller attempted to combine the contemporary reference of *The Crucible* with the classical structure (or pretension) of *Death of a Salesman*.

McCarthy, of course, had used the bait of personal vindication as a lure for exposing one's friends. So long as "names were named," the accused could be "cleared" of the "charges" of Communist affiliations, association or even sympathy. As *The Crucible* drew a parallel to the weird, inquisitorial idea of confession (even if untrue) as absolution, *A View from the Bridge* asked whether the informer can ever be justified and whether his motives can ever be respectable.

Miller's personal cause was well known. Elia Kazan had been the director of *Death of a Salesman,* and was a personal friend as well as having been a brother-in-attitude during the Thirties. Both, like many others in the intellectual community, had been outraged by prewar American capitalism and Depression conditions. Both, like most people who really cared about any kind of justice, had believed that a drastic change in the American economic system was necessary for the correction of those abysmal conditions. And both had worked for that change.

When they were summoned to the McCarthy star chamber, Kazan sought (and was given) absolution by identifying his affiliates. Miller refused.

It is very difficult to judge Kazan. On the ethical level, it is impossible to excuse or justify his behavior. On the human level, it was very understandable, even while unforgivable. It is very easy to be a hard-nosed idealist about it, especially if you aren't the one it happened to. But there is reason to be disgusted if it happened to you, you resisted and you survived. Miller wrote *A View from the Bridge* in justifiable contempt for Kazan and informers in general (and forgave them in *After the Fall*).

Though the play's tragic hero, the longshoreman Eddie Carbone, reports his niece's wetback lover to the Immigration Department out of jealousy and not self-preservation, it remains the betrayal of a compatriot to authority. Another parallel to the Thirties leftists (in the political sense) is that Eddie and the young man were in conspiracy, trusting each other and being equally astray of the law (the sheltering of an illegal immigrant is as criminal as the illicit immigration itself). Just as were the prewar Communists and Socialists. The play refers to Kazan's disloyalty but, like *The Crucible*, uses the particular as a jumping-off point for the general.

The worst of those other ideas was Miller's pretension to classical Greek tragedy. *A View from the Bridge* is narrated by an attorney-chorus who repeatedly refers to "destiny" (as if repeated reference could make the quality exist). It seeks to imitate the older form in ways far more specific than *Death of a Salesman*. In fact, it goes directly to the incestuous themes that are so familiar in Greek tragedy that it sometimes seems as if Freud created the House of Atreus.

A View from the Bridge is supposed to be about a man in love with his daughter. Reluctant to go this far, Miller made the girl a niece (he was not the first playwright to shy away from such an intention; Schiller evaded a similar situation in *Don Carlos*).

It was but one of many awkward constructions in the play. Unhappy with only jealousy as Carbone's motive for hating the younger man, Miller gave the boy girlish traits, one more unlikely than the other — he sings, he dances, he makes clothes. In doing this, the playwright fell into a trap that handicaps all message playwrights: the spelling out of themes and the ungainly control of characters and situations for point purposes.

It was not a mortal flaw, certainly less serious than the play's obsession with being towering and universal. *A View from the Bridge* is trailed by a shadow that announces, "This is classic, this is forever." Nevertheless, it is a work of great stature with a purity of mood, a handsome essentiality of language and a driving morality. Nor is it rock-tied to its period.

In that respect, Miller rises above his own school of playwrighting and it is why some of his works are becoming American classics. *Death of a Salesman, The Crucible* and *A View from the Bridge* are more than Ibsenite plays of social reform. Just as Miller's earlier *All My Sons* was not. That play, a stock drama existing only for the sake of a temporal argument, had meaning only so long as its subject (wartime profiteering) was current. Its story was contrived to make a point — and how implausible it was that a pilot would be flying an airplane that was built with one of his father's faultily manufactured parts! Such coincidence is indigenous to the Ibsenite play. It can be found in almost any old-time right-wing American drama. Once the problem period is passed, the play loses purpose. It is transient art.

Does that mean that drama should have no relevance to contemporary problems? Certainly not, and *Death of a Salesman* is a perfect example of how a play can be both timely and classic. A play must be a work of art *first*. Its strength must be *its own* and its purpose *itself*. The playwright must have seen a human, rather than an eventual, significance in the situation of his people. He must see the timeless in the transient. If the passing event is but an example of many passing events throughout the course of history, the play will always have meaning. If it is singular, it will become passé.

Too, there is a real place in the theater for a play that *is* transient. There is no great wrong in a theater of only contemporary interest. If the work is only about a temporal problem it may have only temporary value but that value will be there. Robert Anderson's *Tea and Sympathy,* for instance, dealt with homosexuality at a time when America was first admitting the existence of it. The play seems dreadful now and its attitude embarrassingly naïve. Anderson's method of making a point (the obvious he-man is the homosexual and the obvious effeminate is the heterosexual) was much too heavy-handed and his style dragged in the leftover realism of the old-guard right wing. But at the time, *Tea and Sympathy* was an interesting and even an affecting play, and its theme seemed bold. There was value enough in its existence. Today, oddly enough, the extreme *left* wing is emphasizing message plays, although its style is miles away from realism. Weaving together modes of surrealism, vaudeville, music-dance and abstraction, these far leftists are insisting on drama of contemporary relevance. They do not care whether this creates transient art, being, here as in their general philosophy, more concerned with today than tomorrow. Their messages are the usual assortment of left-wing attitudes: anticonformity, antimaterialism, antiimpersonality, antiloneliness.

As for Miller, although working his messages in a theater style light years behind these leftists, he was as handicapped by a need for point references as they. Of course his problems were different. Schooled in naturalism, he was prone to tug at it. *All My Sons* was straight enough melodrama, but *Death of a Salesman* used interchanging time as it had never been used before. It employed hallucination and moved (I think accidentally) toward the surreal. But Miller retreated into straight realism with *The Crucible* and has stayed there ever since. Even the later *After the Fall,* so awkwardly out of character in its search for abstraction ("The action of the play takes place in the mind, thought and memory of Quentin, a contemporary man") never managed the sense it sought. Miller is stuck with his own artistic identity.

He must accept it, and his dreadful *Incident at Vichy* suggests that he *has* accepted it. A playwright cannot continuously pursue the most modern techniques. Having found his own technique, he must then deepen into it. This is the mature artist's greatest responsibility and the fulfillment of that responsibility is the strongest contribution to be made by the right wing, master playwright. My point is that every "good" artist will become right wing as he progresses, and it is there that he makes his greatest contribution. There where he practices as a master.

Miller, however, does not practice. He has written only six full-length plays over a twenty-year period of produceable playwrighting (that is, a period during which *anything* he wrote would have been produced). Today, with his technique and purpose well into the right wing, he is providing no series of masterworks to compensate for the increasing archaism of his style. He can almost be assigned his place in American dramatic history during his own lifetime, and while that place will be ranking, the living placement is disgraceful. It is as much an unhappiness for him as it is for the theater.

Tennessee Williams, too, has probably completed the work that will represent him to long-term American theater.

For eighteen years, Williams was one of America's three master playwrights. From his first major work (*The Glass Menagerie* in 1945) until the play that proved, beyond argument, his complete collapse (*Slapstick Tragedy* in 1966), he created a series of professionally written, artistically secure dramas. Although his development as a serious playwright ended with *Cat on a Hot Tin Roof* in 1955, the commercial works that ensued were close enough to the taste of his period to settle comfortably on the right wing.

Williams was a true artist and a definite left-winger during the early years of his development. While his plays had a point, that point (love) was consistent throughout his central body of work and was not concerned with message so much as with overall attitude. Most important, the plays of Williams could only have been *his* — they all projected his artistic identity. They left behind the naturalism of his contemporaries and edged toward fantasy. They were, as well, the works of a poet — a poet unmatched on the American stage; they were compassionate and arresting, extraordinarily sexual for the time and romantic in a way perhaps closer to times past than to our own. Williams's love for the South and its traditions was as much due to his affinity for its romance as it was to his upbringing there.

Like Miller and Inge, he stayed with his original milieu. Miller's plays reflect his New York City background and Inge's his Midwestern. Williams's early and middle plays, which will certainly be the only ones remembered, are set in his own South, and it is a comment on all these playwrights' limitations that they remained basically unimaginative, at least in this regard (it is a myth that the writer should write exclusively about what he knows).

Williams's first full-length play was *Battle of Angels,* which was taken out of town by the Group Theater and closed in Boston (it was later revised and produced as *Orpheus Descending*). His first New York production was a collaboration with Donald Windham called *You Touched Me,* an adaptation of a D. H. Lawrence story. For our purposes, the starting-off point can be *The Glass Menagerie,* which opened in New York in 1945 and immediately established him.

If it wasn't his first play, it should have been, because it is what first plays (or novels or anything else) usually are — autobiographical stories about young people leaving home to find themselves. It was an especially right first play for Williams because in it, more than in any other work, he showed himself unabashedly sentimental, open and poetic — traits that he unwisely concealed as his career proceeded.

The play begins as the narrator-son steps out to deliver the first of a playful of poetry ("Yes, I have tricks in my pocket, I have things up my sleeve"). The narrator device, an old one, is also an awkward one, intruding on a play's magic. Tom's periodic speeches to the audience interrupt the flowing mood more than once, and what he has to say is usually unnecessary or obvious from the action.

More important, though, over the years *The Glass Menagerie* has grown deeper. Its entwining levels seem to have clarified themselves, perhaps because the play has begun to be period, and it is now easier to sense Williams quietly shifting the sand beneath the soft surface. Amanda is not just a mother hen reluctant to let her chicks go. She is not just a frustrated woman abandoned by her husband to a hopeless present. She is all the good and bad of mother love, bewildered by the escape that each member of this family has found for himself.

For as Amanda has fled into a past that she imagines as lushly belle of the ball, so her daughter Laura has moved into her collection of glass animals and a life of withdrawal. And so the son Tom has fled to the merchant marine. In one way or another, they are all abandoning the people who need them, who love them. Make one thing certain — it isn't loving that Williams talks about so much as it is the obligation to be tender to those who love you — to be there when you are most needed. The flight hurts most because it hurts the person left behind.

Laura is everybody who is left behind. If her lame foot is quietly symbolic of the emotional lameness in all of us, her one chance to be loved is everybody's. And the Gentleman Caller, in his warmth and unavailability, is the worst pain life can inflict. The pain of betrayal by somebody who has really done nothing wrong and so can't be hated — the Prince Charming who is already spoken for.

Williams, then, began his career proper with a play that was legitimately left wing. *The Glass Menagerie* is not built to carry a story line by line, scene by scene. It floats. It has no "message" — it is beyond time and into human emotion. And while its point is love, it isn't concerned with a boy-girl romance, sex or general love need but the *quality* of love that goes past the do-you-love-me and into the human heart. In short, Williams, though no intellectual, had a natural artistic depth.

A Streetcar Named Desire is his most important play and it ranks with *Death of a Salesman* as one of the two American masterpieces of the postwar years. While the Williams does not aim for the philosophically grandiose, it *is* art and its art will endure. For it is an exquisite play — perhaps the most romantic, poetic and sensitive play ever written for the American theater. Though in no way derivative, its kinship to Chekhov is yet to be appreciated.

Streetcar followed *Menagerie* (the foreshortening of play titles is a right-wing tradition to which I am miserable in my addiction) in its concern with the quality of human love, but I do not mean to suggest that it had a literary content as such. There are intellectual points represented in the play, and a conscious interplay of ideas — the pitting of Kowalski's animal life force against Blanche's fragile poetry is the central one. But the play, in true left-wing style, represents the introduction of a new kind of meaning and a new way of stating it into the American theater. *Streetcar* is about *abstract* ideas — ways of living. The closest it ever gets to actually *stating* a point is in saying that "desire is the opposite of death."

That is its guiding point. The breakdown of Blanche DuBois is the breakdown, or death, of a way of life. Beauty and sensitivity are qualities too fragile for their new, hard, healthy but pitiless replacements. The Old South that Blanche and her lost plantation represent had to collapse and Williams does not flinch from that necessity. But he weeps for the betrayal of the lovely and the refusal of the new world to allow Blanche "a cleft in the rock of the world that I could hide in."

The dramatic intensity, the beauty of language and the expertise in construction of this play came as no accident. In writing *Streetcar*, Williams called upon his deepest resources as a master playwright in the dazzle of inspiration. A battery of accessory awarenesses contribute to the play's substance. For example, he uses a sense of painting and color to establish contextual as well as theatrical points. In setting the "Poker Night" scene he writes, "There is a picture of Van Gogh's of a billiard parlor at night. The kitchen now suggests that sort of lurid nocturnal brilliance, the raw colors of childhood's spectrum. Over the yellow linoleum of the kitchen table hangs an electric bulb with a vivid green glass shade. The poker players . . . wear colored shirts, solid blues, a purple, red-and-white check, a light green, and they are men at the peak of their physical manhood, as coarse and direct and powerful as the primary colors. There are vivid slices of watermelon on the table, whiskey bottles and glasses."

Playwrights seldom have fully developed senses of painting, but they will on occasion set a scene with some knowledge of visual values. I have never come across any stage direction that approached this description of Williams's for depth of understanding in matters of composition, color, symbolism, shape, effect and dramatic value (even its *writing* is poetic).

Williams also used an unusual knowledge of and sensitivity to music in constructing *Streetcar*. A blues piano motif is repeatedly employed to represent the easygoing sensuality of New Orleans's French Quarter. It counterplays against the polka that Blanche heard the night her young husband shot himself. Williams also requests the changing of keys from major to minor and suggests specific dramatic usage of music (for example, "Blanche is singing in the bathroom a saccharine popular ballad which is used contrapuntally with Stanley's speech").

But for all such knowledgeable construction, it is the play's central concept — its story, its mood and its lavish characters — that makes it so magnificent a work.

Stanley Kowalski and Blanche DuBois are two of the finest character creations in all the American dramatic literature, perhaps matched only by O'Neill's Hickey in *The Iceman Cometh*. It is almost incredible that a single man could have created two people so entirely opposite and managed a full appreciation of both. Kowalski is extraordinary. He is brutal and stupid, operating almost entirely on animal reflex, but his vitality is the energy of life and his love for Stella is absolute and *real*. He is also enormously funny and serves as a channel for a free outpouring of the Williams sense of humor. Blanche is usually listed prominently in the Williams Collection of Great Female Characters. There is no denying it — the playwright has an enormous feeling for fragile women, strung with webs from more romantic times. His sympathy is always with the lost, the obsolete, the faded, and when they are women it blossoms with a beating sadness. Of all these women, from Amanda of *The Glass Menagerie* through Serafina delle Rose of *The Rose Tattoo* and all the way to the Gnädiges Fräulein in *Slapstick Tragedy,* none is more pitied, none more loved, than Blanche DuBois.

Blanche is the absolute romantic, still believing in purity, honor and gallantry even while her own life has become sordid and soiled. But she *does believe,* and the lies she tells, whether about her past or about her surroundings, are dreams of beauty ("I don't want realism. I want magic! Yes, yes, magic! I try to give that to people. I misrepresent things. I don't tell the truth. I tell what *ought* to be truth." The truth, when finally told, destroys her). She is quick and clever, neurotic and melodramatic, too crystalline, too brittle, too delicate for the new, shoulder-to-shoulder brawling of modern life.

But it would be a mistake to take her for just a symbol of the doomed Old South. While Blanche represents the grand gentility of that way of life (whether it ever existed or not), she is terribly personal and must not be robbed of that personality. Williams writes plays about people and they are his first love.

By mixing such opposites as Blanche and Kowalski, Williams creates an electric situation through character, as opposed to plotting. Given these two characters, and the ways of life they represent, one must be eliminated for the other to exist; pure romance and pure sensuality cannot survive side by side, although they do contain elements of each other (Stanley and Stella, the bloodmated married couple, have a real romance in their animal relationship, while Blanche is almost a nymphomaniac, although only because of her early, traumatic marriage to a homosexual). Blanche devoutly believes that "deliberate cruelty is not forgivable" and Kowalski is congenitally cruel. Blanche lives by the paper moon in the cardboard sky and Kowalski by basics — beer, bowling and bed. Blanche would be religious and Kowalski atheistic, she is the dream and he the earth. In their collision she *must* be destroyed, but all beauty, all poetry, all pity are with her. She — as the play — is written with breathtaking delicacy.

In a way, *The Rose Tattoo* is a continuation of the Stella-Stanley story. The 1951 play is about the end of an animal-love marriage and the widow's frustration until she finds a replacement stud. Although the ecstatic inspiration of *Streetcar* is not there, the play is altogether admirable. Stylistically, it continued the playwright's movement away from the semifantasy of *The Glass Menagerie* and toward the naturalism that would come with *Cat on a Hot Tin Roof*. Its language began the gradual departure from his romantic poetry, although Williams is a natural poet and his dialogue remained lovely, with strong imagery and rhythm, right up to his complete disintegration.

The Rose Tattoo was the last Williams play to trust open hearts, to believe in romance, to risk vulnerability. Perhaps we had already outgrown such values — Williams certainly retained them longer than his time, being an outright romantic. But in all these areas, this play marks the beginning of a distinct turning point in his career.

For *The Rose Tattoo* saw Williams swinging rightward. Although its realism was still pastelled with poetry, it was quite understandable to the Broadway audience. Williams's artistic originality had been accepted by the establishment and his fresh, individual style became part of our theater corpus. Audiences at that time were still young enough to keep a play running a year or two. The

loveliness of the play's writing, the interest of its plot and the validity of its climaxes were now traditional theater virtues and Williams was accepted as artist and master.

But with the freezing of his leftness, the playwright started to
take on time marks. *The Rose Tattoo* is a paean to sex that is
clearly stamped with its period. It is foolishly devoted to an obvious cause and a heaviness of symbol (goats, roses).

There is no quarrel with Williams's rightward movement. As an
artist with a fresh style moving into maturity, he would have to
stop innovating in the process of deepening. This is the natural
order of things. And in the acceptance of him by the theater, that
theater edged slightly leftward. This is how wing interaction is supposed to work and in the middle Fifties there was still some sem-
blance of it. But Williams was the last American playwright to
move properly from left to right.

With *Cat on a Hot Tin Roof* in 1955, he appeared to have found
his artistic identity and to be ready to produce a series of master
plays. He had already begun to influence the theater at large. A
substantial body of work was to be reasonably expected of him.
Cat was not a great play, but it displayed the Williams style, talent
and technique in a highly polished state. It was to be the last of his
art plays until the later failures.

For after this, he became one of the few genuine playwrights to
sell out. Accepting his popular reputation as a Sexy Playwright
even while flinching at this wholesale misunderstanding, he decided
to capitalize upon it. He had already begun to make money — all
his plays (with the exceptions of *Camino Real* and *Summer and
Smoke*) had been sold to the movie studios and *Cat on a Hot Tin
Roof* was a great box office success. Hollywood had realized that
the serious-play treatment it had given *Streetcar* and *Rose Tattoo*
was all wrong, commercially speaking. The Williams cliché was
perfect for splashy, high-budget Elizabeth Taylor movies. Williams
was now eager to profiteer and decided to personally produce
Sweet Bird of Youth, a play that seemed deliberately designed to
fulfill the most vulgar views of his work. I find it impossible to
believe that he took this self-parody seriously: a movie star and a
gigolo; dope, castration, nymphomania and abortion; a little politics thrown in for garnishing. It seemed very *Mad* magazine.

By that time (1959) too, the Actors Studio had moved rightward and its roster included nearly every big Broadway name.
These actors, who had begun as dedicated, serious, genuinely left-
wing people launching a fight against the right wing, had been ridi-
culed five years earlier. Now they were accepted, indeed acclaimed.
Williams worked with the Studio and plays like *Sweet Bird* were
ideal for its specialized brand of "acting" — its leading roles were
played by Studio stalwarts: Geraldine Page as the decaying actress
(after bursting into stardom in *Summer and Smoke,* Miss Page
came to specialize in Williams's fading, chiffon belles, wasting an
enormous — if restricted — stage quality) and Paul Newman as
her Hollywood-obsessed lover-slave. Other Studio people, such as
the very talented Rip Torn, were spread throughout the smaller
roles.

Sadly, though not unexpectedly, *Sweet Bird of Youth* was a critical and financial success, capitalizing on the by now deepening
wing division. With critics and audiences growing ever more conservative, the superslick, supercommercial, supercynical play was
fast becoming the only good dramatic bet on Broadway. And Williams grew fat. His subsequent works (*Period of Adjustment* and
The Night of the Iguana) would continue to be box office successes,
but his art and his heart were dead.

Then, in 1963, he decided to recant. Wiping the post-*Cat* plays
from his mind, he tried to move all the way leftward and join the
surrealists. But it was ten years since he had attempted this
(*Camino Real* still, and naturally, a left-wing favorite). At that
time he had still been a leftist, still was bent on finding himself.
Now he was already formed and such drastic rebirth is a foolish
wish for any master playwright. It is true that some artists have
succeeded in staying perpetually innovative, continuously changing, continuously looking, continuously dipping into leftism (Pi-
casso and Stravinsky are perfect examples). But they are exceptions.

Williams abandoned his previous work, both art and product,
and wrote *The Milk Train Doesn't Stop Here Anymore* — a play
in the surrealist style. It looked like an imitation of a stupid collegiate parody that had had a great New York success the previous
year (Arthur Kopit's *Oh Dad, Poor Dad, Momma's Hung You in*

the Closet and I'm Feelin' So Sad, which, in turn, was a semi-intentional mockery of Williams's *Suddenly Last Summer*). *Milk Train* was an exotic, symbolic drama that implied the then-modish theory of homosexuality that men have been emasculated by dominating mother figures.

Yet it has always been plain that far from hating women, Williams loved them dearly. It wasn't until *Milk Train,* really, that one of his plays mocked its heroine. On the one hand Flora Goforth (so puerile a character name) shared the qualities of Williams's other women, deeply understood, softly floated in dreams of past elegance and a future of tattered solitude. And on the other she was lurid and coarse, almost a mockery of Blanche DuBois (like Blanche, she had loved her young husband and like Blanche, the memory of his early death oppresses her). Equally out of character Williams introduces a young poet (the "Angel of Death"), smugly superior, sexually peculiar and in the favor of God.

The whole business was strange for Williams. Having spent the richest part of his playwrighting life as an artist with no interest in messages, he now had written a thoroughly point-contrived play. It was entirely wrong for him and suggested serious problems. When it was rewritten and reproduced the following season, the problems had grown grotesque, for Williams had added ridiculous elements of Kabuki theater and cast the play with supercamp favorites: Tallulah Bankhead and Tab Hunter.

When a master playwright begins his descent, his artistic maturity turns toward second childhood. Relying on past growth and technique, he continues to turn out works of polish and passing value. Finally, if he goes completely to pieces, the professionalism cracks. This is what happened to Tennessee Williams in 1966, when *The Mutilated* and *The Gnädiges Fräulein* opened under the inclusive title *Slapstick Tragedy.* It had been ready for production a year earlier, but Williams had been unable to get financing.

How strange for a master playwright to be unproduced for lack of investors! Not so strange once the plays were seen. Williams had disintegrated. Left with the skeleton of his poetry, he roamed mistaken streets with a loss of artistic identity, his instincts themselves confused. The two plays were equally boring, equally ludicrous attempts simultaneously to return to his past and to find a future. *The Mutilated* was a neurotic attempt to write a Williams circa 1950 play, while *The Gnädiges Fräulein* was a burlesque, in clown style, of that very kind of play. It was pitiful to watch.

I have implied that Williams's career is over, and while it would be platitudinous sentiment to say *I hope I am wrong,* I honestly am convinced I am right, even as I fear it for Williams's and the theater's sake. Having fallen victim to the right wing's lure of money, celebrity and acceptance, he is a tragic victim of Broadway's wing division.

Less significant a victim, though no less sympathetic, was Williams's friend and protégé, William Inge.

Come Back, Little Sheba, which opened in 1950, was the first Inge play to be produced on Broadway, and although only a moderate critical success with a brief (six-month) run, it established him as a promising American playwright. The play contained all the ingredients of postwar American theater and is typical of the right-wing drama that has since become preserved, even mummified, on Broadway. It is naturalistic, emotional and sentimental. It relies on the melodramatic climaxes that were popular in turn-of-the-century thrillers. It also has a content — a *message.* But the message is no longer political. What replaced the prewar socialistic content of drama was the postwar *psychological* content. American theater, with its sluggish reflex action, was at last being influenced by Chekhov.

I use the term psychological only in the sense that these plays do. It is elementary, pop psychology, and the new causes were equally generalized: the understanding due homosexuality, the need to eliminate sexual prudery, and so on.

Such causes are typical of Inge and they run through all of his work. But if that work is to be considered as drama representative of its period, and artistically judged, they must be ignored. A play will not derive artistic value from its point but from its theatrical validity.

Sheba is a nicely enough written work that has no real value beyond satisfying the transient needs of a transient theater. This is a simple and valuable contribution of the master playwright. But as the first major work of a master, it was appallingly conservative and its message carried the intellectual weight of a presidential Thanksgiving Day address.

Stylistically, Inge calls it "the closest thing to a story play that I have ever written." This is really not true since nearly all of his subsequent works were plotty and realistic. It is a straightforward tale with a straightforward structure. Inge was already capable of establishing interesting characters with individual speech and behavioral patterns, and could separate or harmonize them. The writing itself was very right for the rural Midwestern locale, but so were the stage directions: Marie "wears a sheer dainty negligee and smart, feathery mules on her feet"; furniture is "heavy and rounded looking" and a sofa is called a "davenport"; "no industry whatsoever has been spent in making it one of those white, cheerful rooms that we commonly think kitchens to be."

Such directions are not written by a sophisticate, nor are Inge's plays. His dramatic attitude is open and simple. *Come Back, Little Sheba* is studded with old-fashioned dramatic devices — a whiskey bottle waiting to be grabbed by an ex-alchoholic; a girl studying biology at the play's opening, setting herself up for later sexual developments; a woman perpetually calling for her lost dog. The play ought have been called *Come Back, Little Symbol*.

By the time *Picnic* (later retitled *Summer Brave*) was produced three years later, Inge had developed his craft beyond the need of such obvious dramatic ploys. His dialogical ease, which *Sheba* had already demonstrated, was now professional in every sense. So, too, were his juggling of characters, his interweaving of their stories and his use of them to move a play across a stage. In short, with the writing of *Picnic,* Inge was well on his way to being a master of the Fifties right-wing drama.

Picnic picked up the threads of *Sheba*. The first play had a sexual underpinning that was never explored. The second was about sex itself; a celebration of manliness and womanliness. On this subject, it had its share of slogans: "You're a woman, baby, whether you know it or not"; "Everything he did reminded me that there was a man in the house, and it seemed good."

In writing it, Inge went beyond the rigid story-play restrictions of his genre and began to make full use of stage possibilities. This is exemplified by the famous scene in act two in which lighting, music, movement and the rhythmic quality of dance multiply the dramatic content to achieve a theatrical effect well beyond that of story progress and dialogue. Dealing as he was with sexual excitement, Inge managed to grasp its pulse — its quivering, lush intensity — and spread it thumping over the stage. His technique can be observed in one of the stage directions for the Hal-Madge dance scene: "Some distance apart, snapping their fingers to the rhythm, their bodies respond without touching. Then they dance slowly toward each other and Hal takes her in his arms. The dance has something of the nature of a primitive rite that mates the two young people. The others watch rather solemnly."

Picnic, while having this and several other instances of freer, more theatrical drama, is basically a straight play. On occasion it seems to run away from its author; as in *Sheba,* there are implications that have no connection with the play proper. But by and large, it is one of the best examples of Fifties right-wing drama — just the sort that today's producers still seek.

The writing of *Bus Stop* in 1955 was even more secure. Its three acts were short and tight. Its point (the varieties of love) was consistently hugged. It had interesting and unusual characters and a measure of suspense, a working (if folksy) humor and a good helping of compassion.

Two years later, Inge's concern with love and sex blossomed into a theory worthy of any ladies' discussion group. *The Dark at the Top of the Stairs* was a full-length treatment of Sexual Health and the Meaning of Love. Oddly (or perhaps not so oddly), there were within it some undercover homosexual implications that had been hinted at in *Bus Stop.*

The Dark at the Top of the Stairs was to be his last commercial and critical success for at least ten years, and its release of his most anxious interest in mother-son relationships may prove to have been the cause of his downfall. Interestingly, this play was a revision of his very first, *Further Off from Heaven,* which Margo Jones produced in 1947 at her Dallas Theater. It also is admittedly autobiographical, although Inge transferred its locale from his native Kansas to Oklahoma.

It is about a family with all the symptoms of a case history for a

basic psychology course. Rubin Flood is a harness salesman who is
unhappy in his marriage to Cora, a woman with extremely overpro-
tective inclinations. Rubin is the latest in an Inge string of Kowal-
ski-derived studs. He is restless and his sexual frustrations are relieved by occasional infidelities.

Rubin and Cora have two children: the sixteen-year-old Reenie,
who is well on her way to frigidity thanks to a middle-class education stressing the virtues of being a "nice girl"; and Sonny, moving
toward a homosexuality which the author seems to be either unaware of or afraid to admit. Sonny is Cora's victim, having been
allowed to sleep with her until his tenth year. While Inge "cures"
these problems with the basic psychology methods used by most
Fifties playwrights, he was not to believe the cure himself, and his
next two plays (*A Loss of Roses* and *Natural Affection*) would be
increasingly concerned with the left-wing bugaboo barrelhousing
into Shubert Alley: the castrating mother.

The Dark at the Top of the Stairs is considered by right-wing
critics to be Inge's finest play. It is one of his worst. Although it
probes the same sexual love questions as his earlier works, in seeking precise answers it reveals the author's all-too-uneducated intelligence as well as the coyness of his profundity ("I try to explore
some of man's hidden fear in facing life and to show something of
the hidden fears that motivate us all . . . I felt also that maybe I
was drawing a little on Christian theology to show something of the
uniting effect human suffering can bring into our lives").

As for its introduction of the dominating woman to the Inge
surface, once seen her predecessors become apparent. Lola frustrated and smothered Doc in *Sheba*. The stupid-but-healthy masculinity of Hal Carter in *Picnic* was shot down by a townful of man-
less women. Bo started out by dragging Cherie back to Montana in
Bus Stop but wound up being "sweet" and "gallant." I do not suggest that Inge *intended* these characters to be read that way. I am
sure, in fact, that he thought he was dealing with *real men* at the
time. But in *The Dark at the Top of the Stairs,* his acceptance of
the woman's idea of love was succeeded by a resentment of full-
blown femininity. Put another way, envy of women was replaced
by hatred for them. The play's subcharacters, Lottie and Morris,
have a sexless marriage and Morris is described by Inge as "a big,

defeated-looking man of wrecked virility." Late in the play, Rubin
makes a thoroughly ludicrous speech condemning Cora for her
smothering femininity: "Don't you realize that every time you talk
that way, I just gotta go out and raise more hell, just to prove to
myself I'm a free man? Don't you know that when you talk to a
man like that, you're not givin' him credit for havin' any brains, or
any guts, or a spine . . . or a few other body parts that are pretty
important, too?"

It's that "or a few other body parts that are pretty important,
too" that gets me.

With the elementary nature of this play, and with its rude outline
of psychological symptoms (parental fights, overprotection, etc.)
Inge abandoned his natural talent for sentimental storytelling and
melodrama for a concentration on mother love. *A Loss of Roses,*
produced in 1959, was by far his worst play and his first commercial failure. Its simpleminded description of a boy crippled by a
dependence on his mother made the author appear overly foolish
for the first time.

Inge took the reception very badly, and did not write another
play for four years, his longest interlude between productions. *Natural Affection* opened on Broadway in the late winter of 1963, and
although a powerful drama, it was severely attacked for being
"dirty" (a serious right-wing offense).

Natural Affection is about a passionate love affair and its effect
on the woman's son, a fourteen-year-old whose delinquency Inge
simplistically attributes to the mother's impatience with loving him.
Her inability to provide his due share of love is part of her natural
female destructiveness (according to Inge), also evidenced in her
domination of the lover. The playwright's attempt to balance his
work with sympathy for her, as with Cora in *The Dark at the Top
of the Stairs,* is never convincing.

A subplot is about a neighboring couple with financial success
and marital failure. The husband is obsessed with a somewhat justifiable jealousy of his sexy wife, and spends his spare time watching
stag movies.

With these five thrown together, Inge sets their varying problems
to boiling. There is jealousy between the son and the lover over the
mother. She is torn between her love for the man and her love for

the boy, neither of whom can accept the other. Everywhere the boy looks, love is gone — his mother's and the neighbors'. And that emptiness of love drives him toward a staggering and even monumental tragedy — into a violence of revenge.

But Inge had already left his natural milieu, artistically and geographically. With *Natural Affection,* he abandoned the rural for the urban. He had already absorbed too much elementary psychology for his own good. His reflexive sensitivity to human emotion may have been simple, but it was acceptable when filtered through a personal awareness. When organized to fit rudimentary psychology and pushed in the direction of mother hatred, it ruined him.

By 1966, Inge had lost all confidence in his style and his craft, leaving the both of them (as had Williams before him) to seek a new identity in the surrealism and youth of the left wing. *Where's Daddy?* was an atrocious play that might well have been the work of a beginner. In many ways, it *was* the work of a beginner, for Inge was starting out in a style and attitude completely new and foreign to him. This is the worst mistake a right-wing playwright can make. William Inge was born into naturalism and found a niche there as an American master playwright. That niche was small and his concerns were too minor for a permanent place in this country's drama, but as a playwright of passing importance his was an honorable position. It is a shame he couldn't hold it.

The stories of Miller, Williams and Inge in the twenty postwar years demonstrate the chaotic situation of current American drama. That they were the master playwrights of the time forces history to judge the period by their work. But at least as they were rising and then falling, American drama continued to exist for a while.

During the years of off-Broadway, 1958 through 1963, the left-wing stimulus there had a positive effect on Broadway. So positive that following the successful Circle in the Square production of *The Iceman Cometh,* Eugene O'Neill could finally return from obscurity to proper right-wing recognition with the posthumous Broadway production of his magnificent *Long Day's Journey into Night.* Playwrights like Edward Albee, Jack Richardson and William Hanley could "graduate," the word was, to Broadway.

But it was too late. The story-message play and the intellectual

melodrama had died even as the right-wing producers were intent
on making New York a mausoleum for it. Left-wingers were faced
with a mainstream dammed to them. And the American theater for
new plays moved into its worst years. The only serious play over
several seasons to have a healthy run was Robert Bolt's *A Man for
All Seasons,* an archetypical right-wing play (and British at that).
It is a *good* play, there is no denying it. But it is written according
to an old playwrighting technique and is geared to an old set of
moral standards. I am not suggesting that old techniques are useless or that old moral standards are meaningless. It would be stupid
to reject *any* technique — a play that works is a play that works,
whatever its style (the left wing will dismiss anything but the totally
new and that is part of its chronic immaturity). As far as old moral
standards are concerned, those referred to by Bolt's play remain
heroic and civilized. They are traditional and thus right wing.

The typical Broadway play had become frozen. Archibald Mac-
Leish's *J.B.* with its simpleminded religious philosophy and preci-
osity; throwback courtroom plays (*Witness for the Prosecution, A
Case of Libel* and *The Caine Mutiny Court Martial*); inspirational
plays (*The Miracle Worker*); thrillers (*The Desperate Hours, Dial
M for Murder, Wait Until Dark*); the frankly exploitable (*The
World of Suzie Wong*); the liberalizing (*A Hatful of Rain, Inherit
the Wind*) and the psychology plays (*The Bad Seed, The Rope
Dancers, Toys in the Attic,* and so on). The right wing finally hit
peak control with Frank D. Gilroy's *The Subject Was Roses* in the
spring of 1964. Its winning of both the New York Drama Critics
Circle Award and the Pulitzer Prize proved the absolute domination of American drama by right-wing forces (despite the critical
success of *Roses,* it had a healthy engagement only because of low
operating expenses and ceaseless promotion. The right-wing audience is now too shrunken to keep any average-cost production running).

Now the fact is that Mr. Gilroy's play was very well written and
quite successful at what it tried to be. This *must* be the standard for
measuring any work. In its obvious autobiography and honesty,
and in its clear description of the pains of early manhood, it is
interesting and even moving. But the play could have been written
in 1945. It is absolutely naturalistic; its conversations are written

ronx-Irish speech patterns; its power is dependent
notions and ordinary climaxes; it is designed to
that youth must break away from parents to reach
but that that break cannot be made until the parents are
ed as they are, and neither idealized nor condemned; it uses the
stage strictly as a place to act out stories that have already been
captured on paper. *The Subject Was Roses* would have been just as
effective as a film or a novel — it had no real need for the special
possibilities of a theater's life. I must stress that there was a real
quality to this play and I liked it very much. But it is a representative of the only taste on Broadway — a taste that has become entirely restricted to the right wing.

Apparently, the only master playwright in today's American theater is a pseudomaster: Edward Albee, a left-winger. This is
strange because a master playwright *must* be right wing. Albee is
considered a master because he has had no competition and was
given premature esteem. And with his own producing company
(Barr-Wilder-Albee), his plays were regularly mounted on Broadway. But his control of technique is imperfect and he has yet to find
an artistic understanding of himself. Albee wanders from style to
style, insecurely boastful of a professionalism he has not yet
achieved. He has little control over his own materials and apparently does not even understand his own work. There is a tremendous talent to this playwright — a vibrant sense of the theater and
a great respect for language. But he has yet to move in any direction, too soon catapulted to major status by an overeager critical
community.

Albee's first play was *The Zoo Story,* a one-act, realistic work. In
its two characters, the playwright hoped to pit the complacent, educated, conformative and successful against the jumpy, creative, insecure and individualistic. It is an incomplete play — not even a
play, really, but a dialogue concluded with an old-time, right-wing
theatrical device (the Murder) dressed up by a little O. Henry (instead of murdering the middle-classer, as we have been led to anticipate, the edgy young man tricks the older one into murdering
him). The continuous gibes at cliché targets (respectability, conformity, etc.) become boring and while Albee means to love both
characters, he never really seems to. Still, the play deftly probes the

nature of human relationships and investigates the existentialist dilemma of insider versus outsider. Like the Albee plays to come, it is weak in theory, strong in drama, runs away from its author and has no stylistic relationship to any of his other work except for a self-consciousness in the use of language.

The Sand Box (1960) was the work of a beginner, having nothing in common with *The Zoo Story* but deriving a great deal from both Beckett and Ionesco. Written in the cartoon style, its dialogue is supersimple, the characters are primary-color, hard-edge drawings and the points are primitive-effete. More important is the play's establishment of a pattern that would trail through Albee's ensuing works: a superdominant mother figure, a stupid and subjugated father figure and an alienated, unbelonging son whose hatred for them is matched by the author's admiration and pity for him.

Albee's plays, much more than either Inge's or Williams's, lend weight to the conclusion that while presumably speaking of other things he is constantly alluding to homosexual matters. Some left-wing critics have seen *The Zoo Story* as such a situation (for example, its murder-by-knife as a homosexual act), but I think that relatively farfetched. One needn't go much further than the obvious to find homosexuality in all of his plays, from *The American Dream* to date.

If the right-wing critics and audiences had not missed the homosexuality in *Who's Afraid of Virginia Woolf?* they probably would have condemned it out-of-hand for violation of traditional morality. It would have been a stupid condemnation, but for other reasons the play is one of the most overrated, misunderstood and overanalyzed in modern theater history.

It is also so similar to Strindberg's *The Dance of Death* as to raise questions of plagiarism. *The Dance of Death* is a play in two parts, of which only the first is generally performed. Set on a blasted island off the coast of Norway, it is about a nasty captain and his vicious wife, living in mutual torment and estranged from the community. They sit and rage blackly at each other in a funereal cortège of punishment, insult and humiliation. They also have a child who never appears in the play (at least, not until the second half). *Who's Afraid of Virginia Woolf?* is about a nasty history professor and his vicious wife, living on a symbolic island of their own on the campus of a university. They have a fictitious child created by themselves — a child who is later "murdered" by the husband just as he was "conceived" by their fantasy. This child is one of that string of orphan figures who inhabit, in one form or another, all of Albee's plays. The Strindberg also presents models for other recurrent Albee figures. The powerful mother and dominated father, and Strindberg's hatred of marriage and his contempt for women, are closely duplicated in *Virginia Woolf*.

A great deal of depth has been seen in Albee's play, overcomplicating what is basically simple. *Virginia Woolf* was only an excuse for its playwright to indulge his hatred for women and his taste for brutal invective. The plot structure is amorphous and leads to an artificial climax that never works (the "murder" of the imaginary child). The language, admired as fluid, is often quite mundane. The advertised nastiness is hardly worth the notice — it is in the heavy tradition of the cruel rather than the cutting. As for a point, there is none because Albee was too busy hating mother figures, humiliating father figures and adding general confusion with an underlayer of homosexuality.

The reason that George and Martha cannot have children is because they are really men — homosexuals. How female, after all, *is* Martha, even if one *does* accept the play's direction that she is a woman (Kim Stanley claims that Albee turned her down for the role in a London production because she was too feminine). Even Honey cannot have children. Her pregnancy was a psychosomatic one (in an extraordinary novel by Curzio Malaparte called *The Skin,* a homosexual goes through *nine months* of a psychosomatic pregnancy). Is the running battle between George and Martha — and the *kind* of battle it is — a domestic conflict inherent in heterosexual or homosexual relationships? And isn't the quadruple sexual braiding of George, Martha, Nick and Honey more male-male than male-female in nature? Ingmar Bergman, who directed *Virginia Woolf* in Stockholm, was quoted by the *New York Times* as saying, "I suppose you heard that Albee wanted it staged with four men in those roles?" He added, "I wish I had dared." I wish so too. The play might have made greater sense.

To be fair, if Miss Stanley *was* rejected for being too feminine, it need not mean that Martha is supposed to be either male or lesbian. Albee might just mean for her to be womanly rather than girlish (though Miss Stanley is certainly womanly, if anyone is). And if Albee *did* want four men playing the roles, it might be purely for theatrical effect or the result of a *Genetic* influence (Genet asks for male casting of female roles in both *The Maids* and *The Screens;* however, Genet is quite open in his homosexual reasons for such casting). The homosexuality in *Who's Afraid of Virginia Woolf?* need not be sought in casting alone. It is part of the very fabric of the play.

Yet Albee insists that the play has nothing to do with homosexuality, even though George and Martha (and even Nick and Honey) are about as heterosexual as Mutt and Jeff. If one is to believe him, he is an artist with minimal control over his work. Other aspects of the play seem to indicate this lack of control, for its language is careless and self-indulgent, seriously prolix and poetic in the most artificial of ways. Even when it is good, it is stiffly literary and often unreadable (and Albee allows himself the most unforgivably amateur of inside jokes, at one point paraphrasing the cue line for "So in Love" from *Kiss Me, Kate*. The *Kate* line reads: "Snowdrops! And pansies! And rosemary! My wedding bouquet!" Albee's line for Martha reads: "Pansies! Rosemary! Violence! My wedding bouquet!" This kind of putting his audience on is childish camp. That it is used in a presumably thoughtful play casts real doubt on the playwright's capability for sustained seriousness).

On the other hand, the play must be conceded a great theatricality. While it is writer's theater, it executes excitingly and this is no minor quality. But the excitement is largely dependent upon its cast. With the Broadway first team (Uta Hagen, Arthur Hill) the play was electric, its tension, hatred and sharpness crackling through the theater. The matinee company (Shepperd Strudwick, Kate Reid) was lethargic. Without the tough performers the play became dull and stupid.

For its style, there was no relevance to Albee's previous work. It has been suggested that the play was never meant as naturalist theater, but I take those suggestions as the usual overanalysis. *Virginia Woolf* is obviously realistic, much more so than its Strindberg model (the advanced state of Strindberg's writing is astonishing). Albee's vacillation from the naturalism of *The Zoo Story,* to the

nery of *The Sand Box,* to the social criticism of *The
ie Smith,* back to the Ionesco of *The American
ι* to the naturalism of *Virginia Woolf* shows a play-
onfused about how he wants to write. His subse-
...ι work indicates a continuing uncertainty.

Albee's second Broadway play (1963) was an adaptation of the
Carson McCullers novella *The Ballad of the Sad Café.* In a sense,
this hardly could be called an adaptation, since the original was
almost entirely without dialogue. But Albee was remarkably faithful to the book's spirit and story; the lines he wrote could well have
been written by McCullers.

Again one finds the Albee trio, and his reason for choosing the
novel is obvious: the strong, emasculating woman (Amelia, the
bull dyke); the dominated, humiliated man (Marvin Macy, married
without consummation to Amelia for one week and subsequently
beaten by her in a wrestling match); and their symbolic offspring
the love-cripple (Cousin Lymon, the dwarf who comes to love and
live with Amelia). They are flamboyant characters, yet because of
his eagerness to be loyal to the original, Albee emerged with the
novella's literary soul intact but with a play of little theater value
— a strange product for a playwright whose strongest trait is theatricality.

This stage strength was only momentarily lost and *Tiny Alice*
(1964) is in some ways his most important work to date. The play
is ridiculous, a hodgepodge of philosophical and metaphysical pre-
tensions. It is endlessly talky and lined with homosexuality (again
denied by Albee, although it fairly advertises it). It is about, first
of all, Woman, the archenemy of every Albee play, only now she is
the superdupersuperwoman: God the Mother. It is also about her
murder of the pure (the maternal seduction of virginal Christlike
homosexuals) as personified by Julian, a lay brother of the Catholic Church. Albee makes continuous jokes with "lay brother" (and
church "organs"), comment enough on his wit.

Again there is the Albee trio: Alice, surrogate from the God
Alice, who is the last word in emasculators; the Lawyer, whom she
constantly humiliates; and Julian, their victim, who is so outrightly
homosexual that Albee's denial of this theme in the play is simply
ludicrous.

The proposition of *Tiny Alice* is hardly worth discussion. God Alice, never seen and existing only when people *believe,* is used as a hypothetical Almighty to demonstrate the whimsicality and mind-killing effect of religion. The point is that the reason and purpose of existence may be undefined and perhaps undefinable, but an artificial solution such as God is only illusory. Moreover, a man can be conditioned to accept *any* god figure, given the proper brainwashing. But Albee is not a real intellectual, having neither the patience nor the humility for education, and his discussion of philosophical material is hampered by a weakness of vocabulary, a propensity for exaggeration and an interest in the popular rather than the classical. Nevertheless, for all its stretches of boredom, for all its silliness, for all its drowning in holy water over its head, *Tiny Alice* has a real dramatic power.

Stylistically it is surreal and it seemed at the time the beginning of a personal Albee signature. With neither the derivative surrealism of his early one-acters nor the neo-Strindberg naturalism of *Virginia Woolf,* it struck an honest note for Albee. It was, like all his work, literary, requiring faithful direction (something he always demands and gets from his regular director Alan Schneider), and in some ways this was a pity. There is a dramatic vitality to it — a looming life — that is very suitable for an all-out-theater director.

Schneider's Broadway version was theatrical in many ways, though it fell victim to the long stretches of pseudophilosophical garbage that he was forced to wade through as if in awe of great truths. A more independent director would have demanded revisions and cuts, and while Schneider managed to have the endless final speech trimmed, it was only a start. Still, he drew excellent performances from a classically trained cast in excess respect for Albee's language (although to be fair, American personality actors would have mangled the dense dialogue). John Gielgud built Julian as a fearfully human being, moving through candor, naïveté and sheer goodness into a dreadfully innocent martyrdom (without understanding a word of it, as he later admitted). Irene Worth's Alice was as feminine as possible, considering that at this point Albee was still unable to write a believable female character. John Heffernan's Butler was weird, never letting us know when he was being nasty, when friendly, and this was due to a confusion in Albee's

conception of the character. Schneider followed the play right
down to its absurd crucifixion conclusion.

Compare this with the production of the same play that William
Ball mounted for his American Conservatory Theater. Ball is the
master of director's theater and he treated the play as stage magic,
never pretending to solve its confused intellectual structure (although respecting its purpose). He also made an honest man of the
playwright, recognizing *Alice* as a homosexual play and staging it
that way. He chose a young and beautiful actor for Julian, dressing
him in a white communion (or bridal) suit for his marriage to
Alice, who was fragile here and superdominant there, open here
and covert there, whimsical, crafty, bitchy and frightened (more or
less as Worth played her and as she is in the script). But the Butler
was handled as an outright faggot in tight green pants and twitch-
ing, frugging hips. And the Cardinal, whom the play heavily treats
as representative of a materialistic Catholic Church, was turned
from a hypocrite and onetime homosexual into a black and even
degenerate creature who opens the play wearing sunglasses and sitting on a high throne, his legs dangling high above the floor.

But it was Ball's use of multiple theater orchestration — music,
choreography, color and shape — that grasped the dramatic intensity of the play, even as his production moved away from the playwright's intentions. For example, this is how he staged Julian's
birth-death struggle with the God Alice:

The breathy, thumping beat grows. The fragile, beautiful and
dying martyr climbs the steep central stairs toward the towering
doors at the top. Heavier still the thump until he is white, pure, at
the very peak, and then with a whooshing roar of fright the doors
sweep open, an organ roars and crimson burning curtains come
billowing out, pulsating, blowing, enveloping and releasing him, en-
tangling him in their bloody, living intestines. The red and white
battle screams and tangles and he is thrown tumbling down the
stairs in a headlong, backward, frightful and splattering crash.

There is probably no other director in America who would have
had the wild imagination, the sheer sense of stage and the absolute
shamelessness to pull this kind of stunt. Nor is there one with so
wide a range of experience and knowledge. Who else would have
run an excerpt from Carl Orff's *Carmina Burana* at double-speed,

juxtaposed with gutty rock and roll? Who else would have been capable of continuous dance movement, the actors rolling in patterns, spreading and gathering, moving left, right, up and down stage? The production was extraordinary.

But was it Albee's *Tiny Alice* or Ball's? Albee disavowed it, complaining that Ball had ignored the play entirely. He accused the director of introducing a homosexuality that never existed in the script (extraordinary). He even put Ball down as a faggot, which was pretty funny.

A great part of the ACT production *was* of its director's invention, but the invention was not whimsical. It was rooted in Ball's reaction to the play. There is much to be said about respect for the artist and fidelity to his purpose. Albee *did* write the play. But once written, is a play not the theater's? There is a great deal to be said about the theater as a living stage — as a production — as a composite of inspirations. Is sticking to a script more important than the effectiveness of what is happening on a stage? This is the gist of the current debate over the writer's versus the director's theater. There are points to be made for each side. Insofar as *Alice* is concerned, Ball's approach to it was not necessarily more valid or "better" than Schneider's. It was different, and while I can appreciate Albee's complaint I cannot agree with it. Art if it *is* art (and *Alice* surely is) will always inspire different interpretations, different reactions. In any case, if a playwright expects his work to live (and he hopes, of course, that it will live after him), then it will be subject to all kinds of subsequent treatment about which he will be able to do nothing.

One final point about *Tiny Alice*. The tradition of Broadway as a one-shot theater where plays are useless after an original production is an abominable one. In no other art is the première so paramount. Ball's interest in an already-produced new American play for the repertory of his company is as healthy as it is unusual.

Tiny Alice did not run very long on Broadway, but it *did* raise a great deal of discussion (by everyone including, unfortunately, its author) and was hardly dismissed as a failure. *Malcolm,* produced early in 1966, was a fiasco.

The play was the second of Albee's adaptations, and like *The Ballad of the Sad Café,* the similarity of the adapted work to the playwright's, at least in intellectual terms, made his interest in it understandable. The strange James Purdy novel has as its hero a young man very similar to the Julian of *Tiny Alice*. Pure and implicitly homosexual, he is murdered by a woman (he is literally screwed to death). Malcolm, like Julian and Cousin Lymon and the imaginary child in *Virginia Woolf* and the strange young men in *The American Dream* and *The Sand Box,* is weirdly parentless. Albee himself was an adopted child and his relationship to these central characters is obvious and regular.

Ballad was faithful to the McCullers novella despite Albee's creation of nearly all the dialogue, but the fidelity to Purdy's *Malcolm* drove fidelity right up to and over the wall of absurdity. For it is virtually a *verbatim* duplication of the novel's dialogue. At least three-quarters of this terrible play was written by Purdy, and Albee's disregard of the differing needs of the novel and the theater was reckless. There is no point in discussing the play — it never exists *as* a play — except to note that it finally showed Albee capable of sympathizing with a mother figure, which must be a milestone of sorts.

Whether Albee will continue to alternate original plays with adaptations remains to be seen. If his purpose continues as being a catalytic agent for the transference of admired literary works, virtually unchanged, to the stage, he is doomed to failure as well as a wastage of his own time and talent. The novel is an exciting form, despite the inclination of critics to dig its grave. It is qualitatively different, however, from the drama. If Albee cannot understand this it is a wonder that he *ever* managed to create theater life.

Apparently upset by his inability to succeed critically or financially since *Virginia Woolf,* Albee turned back to that play's style with *A Delicate Balance* (fall of 1966). But by then his free-swinging use of language had been too long spent in a search for profundity and the play was a dictionary with neither definitions nor order — a pile of verbiage accumulated for the sake of a trivial and naïve point: that human beings are too selfish to extend themselves and their sympathies to others.

Thrown in, for no reason other than *Woolf* emulation, were a series of nasty exchanges between a husband and wife. At least they were meant to be nasty. Albee's penchant for invective remained crude, and instead of being biting the cuts were hammer blows ("Agnes — why don't you die?"). Too, he made it clear before the play opened that the confusion with which *Tiny Alice* was received would not be repeated. *A Delicate Balance,* he insisted, would be clear and easily understandable. This was a dreadful thing for him to say. In the first place, an artist should not concern himself with the public's difficulties in understanding his work. His business is only to fulfill his creative imagination — to satisfy himself. Albee's need for approval had become apparent when too many people took him and *Alice* seriously, assuming that there was an obscure but thought-out intellectual scheme to the play. Because of that assumption they did not see the play for the exciting mess it was, but instead felt frustrated. Albee, piqued by their inability to understand his confusion, insisted that the play wasn't about *anything,* but was rather a spooky mystery.

A play's philosophical theme is always there intentionally. Disavowals are usually made because of bad reviews, sagging box offices or confusion. They result from the author's sloppiness or because the critics were baffled. The public is seldom convinced by an author's explanation and the playwright insults himself when he denies his own purposes. If he took himself seriously when he wrote the play he must have the dignity to stand by his work after it is produced. Even after it is rejected. Albee's behavior exemplifies his artistic immaturity.

As for *A Delicate Balance,* it showed the playwright once more in search of a style. At last there was a sympathetic and believable female character, but if that was an encouraging sign, Albee's use of another character for strictly Broadway wisecracks was continuing evidence that his craft still was not developed. And his dialogue remained tangled in overcomplicated sentence structure.

If Albee is ever to develop, he *must* find an artistic identity. He talks of having an *aesthetic,* though if he does the only one apparent in his plays is the little-father, big-mother, orphan-child pattern and the concomitant underlayers of homosexuality. If his denial of these layers is honest, then his writing is uncontrolled and impulsive. Final judgment will have to wait, but for the moment he is still the playwright who should be writing original plays instead of adaptations. He is still the playwright who was prematurely hailed on too slim a body of work. He is still the playwright whose genuine talent and intelligence are marred by preciosity, pretension and an inclination toward immature and effete inside jokes. He is also still the playwright with an exciting sense of bold, extravagant theater. Artistically a child, his premature and fraudulent master-play-wright status may well stop him from becoming the true master he should become. His development remains a question mark.

While Albee regularly receives Broadway productions, the rest of our drama's left-wing playwrights remain separate from the theater proper. Occasionally, one of them manages to find a right-wing producer who usually negates any chance for a worthwhile production by hiring a right-wing director who in turn delivers a right-wing conception with a right-wing cast. The play, of course, is destroyed.

An example was David Rayfiel's *Nathan Weinstein, Mystic, Connecticut* (February 1966). The play had all the markings of up-to-date theater: written in the surrealistic style, it used extrabright cartoon characters in an extrabright cartoon situation, halfway between the realistic and the abstract. Its content was intelligent and substantial, considering a very real problem in American life: the emotional need of the Jewish people to assimilate and the terrible wrongness in the denouncing of their heritage. Its theatrical physique was sophisticated farce, dry and flamboyant, and its sense of humor adult. Like most left-wing plays, it used humor to italicize drama.

Its title character is a Jew who married a rock-solid-American girl from rock-solid-American Mystic, Connecticut, because he felt foreign. After her death he fell in love with Jewishness, partly in overcompensation for his youthful wish to renounce it. Now his children have the same problem. The son is typical of the middle-class Jew trying desperately to be nondescript American (he changed his name to the impossibly implausible "Wang"), and Nathan has disowned him because of it. The daughter is caught between father and brother, eager to be Jewish and eager to forget it. Her half-madness is the result.

Rayfiel mixed wild plot complications into this terribly serious subject and sifted it with very lovely poetry. Most of this managed to escape the director, the cast and perhaps the most backward opening-night audience I have ever encountered.

Nathan Weinstein was also marred by some of the technical uncertainties that one expects of left-wing playwrights, and not everything Rayfiel wrote for the play proved a good fit. If there had been a director up to the script and a cast capable of playing it, this would have been ironed out. And if that director had been a capable and understanding right-winger the result might have been the fruit borne of a left-wing–right-wing coalition. But the director was as rightist as most of Broadway's and the play fell into the chasm. It closed after its third performance, following the release of the right-wing daily critics' perceptions.

Nathan Weinstein, even in its Broadway botching, represented an unusual Broadway wing interaction. The fact that it happened at all demonstrates the possibility of production talent meeting with artistic freshness. When that possibility is realized, as happens less than occasionally, the dream of American theater momentarily materializes.

Such a moment occurred in November of 1963, when the David Merrick Foundation presented *The Resistible Rise of Arturo Ui,* making it the only artistically successful production of a Brecht play in the history of Broadway (a stunning testament in itself to the wing division). Tony Richardson, a director combining left-wing sensibilities with right-wing knowledgeability, staged it with such frightening effectiveness, such cold-blooded ruthlessness, that the essential failure of Brecht's plot idea was eradicated. The production was of staggering intensity, combining supreme theater with devastating political commentary. It was what theater is all about.

Richardson modeled his production on that of the Berliner Ensemble (the company that the East German government created and subsidized for Brecht in 1949). As at the Theater am Schiffbauerdamm in East Berlin, the proscenium was bordered with electric bulbs and the production was designed as a circus of murderous clowns. Richardson also borrowed the staging techniques of Manfred Wekwerth and Peter Palitzsch of the Ensemble for the exaggerated makeup, the broad Thirties gangster clothes, the strut-

ting, crouching, wiggling and sprawling movement. Jule Styne composed a Chicago-ragtime acid-brass score that ripped away in a
racking, spitting bitterness of irony.

For the title role, Richardson hired Christopher Plummer, the
finest actor on the North American continent and certainly among
the best on the English-speaking stage. Plummer had a tough
model to emulate. Ekkehard Schall, playing the role in Berlin, was
giving a dazzling demonstration of the art of acting. It is a virtuoso
part and Schall's performance remains one of the greatest I have
ever seen — a screaming voice that suddenly becomes a gasp; near-
epileptic fits that gurgle; puppetlike, jerky movements; the grasping
at the crotch as a nervous tic. It is a total performance, using the
body, the voice, the mind. Electrifying.

Playing a cartooned Hitler, drawn parallel by Brecht to a cheap
Chicago hoodlum, Plummer was well up to the challenge. He
clumped about in brown and white shoes, growing from a dim-
witted, cowardly, two-bit gangster into a howling, calculating ma-
niac, already a relatively small-time murderer and soon to be the
ultimate criminal. George Tabori faithfully translated Brecht's
mock epic poetry and free and rhymed verse, and Rouben Ter-
Arutunian-designed blown-up charcoal sketches carried a fierce intensity of their own (this was in contrast to the Ensemble's use of
a giant circus tent). The result was shattering.

During its previews, *Arturo Ui* attracted the left-wing audiences
that ordinarily shun the theater. Their reactions were extravagant
and the entire company was prepared for brilliant reviews. It was
deluding itself. The right-wing critics greeted it with their predictable antagonism when confronted by anything different, and the play
was forced to close the first Saturday night.

The artistic success of the bi-winged *Arturo Ui* was an exception
to the rule of leftist plays when they manage to reach Broadway. In
most cases they bear the stigmata of exciting but still-unprepared
playwrights. Jack Richardson, who was accepted with Albee during
off-Broadway's heyday, never managed to reduce his philosophical
verbosity to playing size, again because he received no help from a
right wing that was supposed to provide development. His *Lorenzo*
in early 1963, a play about a seedy band of actors in Renaissance
Italy, was a torrent of florid language drowning a heavily mean-

ingful plot. In Richardson's favor, it must be conceded that the demands of the right wing for box office names led Alfred Drake into the title role, and *Lorenzo* was handicapped by that actor's flamboyant gush, tilted chin, curling fingers and hear-my-music diction. But the play was flawed on its own and despite the matters that the author had on his mind (the ignorant brutality of war and comparisons between reality and illusion), it emerged as a super-abundance of gilt talk and fake grandeur.

Richardson's next play was *Xmas in Las Vegas* (1965) and it had a similar success (a one-week run). He seemed to be having one hell of a time developing a style for himself and this play was only further proof that he was trying too hard and in the wrong direction. Instead of looking for himself *in* himself, he seemed to be looking outside — as if his key was with a school of playwrighting. The school from which *Xmas in Las Vegas* was graduated is the left-wing New School of Saul Bellow's *The Last Analysis* and Jack Gelber's *Square in the Eye* — a school of the surreal, the abstract comedy, where a set of philosophical conclusions is drawn from pop America. It is the search for a deep reflection in a shallow pool.

As the plays of Bellow and Gelber prove, it is not the philosophy but the art that matters (Gelber's play worked and Bellow's didn't because Gelber's was theatrical and Bellow's wasn't). In the case of *Xmas in Las Vegas,* the dramatic art — and the playwright is obviously capable of it — was stifled by a combination of intellectual garbage and a mistaken attempt to write gags.

There is no point in discussing the play's matter. Richardson's annoyance with a supposed American obsession for making-it-without-effort is artificial. But the thoughtless dismissal of the play and the misunderstanding of its style, its subject and its tone of voice by right-wing Broadway was still another example of the left-wing play's problems there. Even when the play is concededly "bad," a situation precluding proper criticism is a dangerous one. That situation applied to *The Last Analysis* too. This was a pretentious play, typical of Bellow in its infatuation with philosophy in the everyday and bumbling Jewish intellectuals in pop America. But like *Nathan Weinstein,* it was abysmally produced. In fact, Sam Levene — a perfectly delightful right-wing performer when

given apt roles such as Nathan Detroit in *Guys and Dolls* — botched
the major roles in both *Weinstein* and *The Last Analysis*. The fact
that a major American novelist wrote his first play — wrote it, logically enough, in a modern genre, just as he writes his novels — and
found it over the heads of Broadway's audiences, performers, directors, producers and critics is enough to describe the situation of
the left-wing playwright in right-wing country.

There were leftists nicely developing off-Broadway for a while,
at least before it followed the Broadway line. After the big years,
when Albee, Richardson, Gelber and William Hanley came out of
the sidestreets, things began to get tougher. The only Big New
Name to emerge was Arthur Kopit, whose *Oh Dad, Etc.*, as it came
to be known, was superdirected by Robbins and looked bright, fast
and slick enough to disguise the adolescent prank it was. Kopit
quickly faded. No-talent will out.

The most impressive new name was Lewis John Carlino. Carlino's first production (1963) was a twin bill called *Cages,* and
the curtain raiser (*Snowangel*) was a silly comparison of the Real
Values of Soul (as possessed by a prostitute) with the False
Values of Intellectuals. But the main play, *Epiphany,* was a fantasy drama of great impact, turning a weakling ornithologist into
a rooster. Only, as the ornithologist was an imitation man, he
became an imitation rooster. And peeling the false coxcomb from
his mask, the tragic man laid eggs. Ignore the female-hating message; it was a running left-wing theme at the time. The drama and
the language were exciting and Carlino seemed ready to go. The
next season, an earlier play of his, *Telemachus Clay,* was produced
off-Broadway and it confirmed what *Epiphany* had suggested. Carlino was formidably talented. He was a natural poet, had a flair for
really exciting theater and was moving with the times. *Telemachus*
was another first play with the typical autobiographical roots, this
time with a touch of the *Odyssey,* but it was thrilling. Though
marred with fuzzy philosophizing and some awkward poetry, the
play made exciting theater. Carlino set his cast on stools, looking
directly at the audience. Each actor played different parts in telling
the story of a young man leaving his home and his girl for Hollywood, disappointment and finally adulthood. The collage scheme
was a limited one and Carlino never used it again, but in the one

try he realized some marvelous effects — there were thoughts and dreams, flashbacks, memories and overheard conversations — an endless number of striking things, especially a childbirth scene fraught with power.

Carlino only produced two one-act plays for off-Broadway after that (*Doubletalk*) — neither of them very good but both demonstrating his native talent. Then he deserted the theater for Hollywood, and the last I heard he had a big farm and a couple of cars. Every once in a while there is a rumor of a new play. Tired of struggling on the left wing, he apparently decided to pick up his Hollywood chips, bolstered by the knowledge that films, these days, were more open to innovation than the theater.

What, then, is to become of original American drama? The modern Broadway stage is so averse to it that even the right-wing play is hardly to be found there, and over the past few seasons there have been practically none. The resident theaters have taken to producing them — both left and right, depending upon the particular orientation. A strongly left-oriented company like Philadelphia's Theater of the Living Arts will produce new far left-wing plays like Rochelle Owens's *Beclch*. A left-inclined group like the Actors Theater of Louisville will try *Nathan Weinstein*. A middle-of-the-road theater like Washington's Arena Stage will produce the relatively conservative new plays of Howard Sackler. And hungrier places will take the $25,000 offers by the National Council on the Arts to produce council-chosen, right-wing plays (the council's point of view is set by its ex-right-wing-Broadway-producer chief Roger Stevens and a board that reflects his taste).

But on the other hand, the experimental theaters, coffee houses and enthusiastic far left-wingers in New York have encouraged a group of young, eager far-left playwrights, such as Lanford Wilson, Jean-Claude van Itallie, Leonard Melfi, Paul Foster, Charles Nolte, Lawrence Osgood and Adrienne Kennedy. If these playwrights — and others like them — are to develop, it will have to be without the right-wing influence that they really should have and through sheer desire and drive. Whether they will continue to have that desire and drive; whether frustration will lead them into conservatism; whether the wings will be brought back to interplay soon enough to avoid catastrophe — this we will have to wait and see.

CHAPTER NINE

A Word on Plays—II

DURING the period of off-Broadway health, European master playwrights were hailed here for their excitement, innovation and art. And well they should have been. The most significant playwrights of our time were being completely ignored by the Broadway theater. Beckett's *Waiting for Godot* had already been accepted in Europe for the modern classic it is, but its 1956 production had failed, in appalling tribute to Broadway's rightism. Ionesco, recognized as a major European artist, was in a different world from the right-wing producers. Genet would have been left wing anywhere, even in his ordinarily left-prone France.

I am not going to presume to discuss these playwrights in a short space. Each demands (and receives) extensive discussion, ranging from doctoral theses to full-blown critical volumes. And I regret their apparent grouping. Genet, Ionesco and Beckett have nothing in common except a general surrealism.

But their introduction to New York (and subsequently national) audiences was part of an internationalization that brought foreign playwrights into our theater to an unprecedented degree. Remember, these playwrights were being presented in American, not imported, productions. Their plays became part of *our* theater and the notion of American theater as the exclusive province of American plays began to disappear (just as chauvinistic senses of theater had begun disappearing abroad).

Waiting for Godot (more properly translated as *While Waiting for Godot*) is one of the most significant plays, written during the twentieth century. Its dramatic style is revolutionizing Western theater. After *Godot,* the theater had passed a landmark by which its subsequent dramas would be measured.

That such a play was completely rejected by Broadway critics and audiences was to be expected, even while being incredible. In its spare, stark use of the stage; in its blend of clown-comedy with basic tragedy; in its management of words themselves as games, rhythms, climaxes; in its use of abstract characters in abstract settings while following traditional systems of story, this play created a new dimension for playwrights. A new way of looking at things.

Beckett's plays are existentialist, but they are thoroughly optimistic. Nor are they terribly complicated. *Waiting for Godot,* despite its right-wing-fomented reputation, is not a puzzling play. One evening during a Hartford Stage Company performance of Genet's *The Balcony,* the man beside me told his companion that he wished *The Balcony* were as uncomplicated as the *Godot* they had recently seen there. You see, if audiences are exposed to intelligent theater they will react intelligently. If they are placed in a situation of right-wing influence, they will react right-wingedly. Great art is seldom difficult to understand. Clarity is part of its greatness (not always but usually). In most cases, if a work of art is not clear, it is not so much the observer's fault as the artist's.

In writing *Godot,* a play about the human need for fulfillment, Beckett was using an idea as a plot. The second act virtually repeats the action of the first as the necessary completion of a cycle — an indication that the waiting is endless and that the acts could continue indefinitely just as does life, and its endless wait for consummation.

In his subsequent plays, Beckett started to eliminate movement and then the physical from his characters — an attitude that began in his early novel *Murphy,* whose leading character was a man who insisted on tying himself to a chair. Beckett's artistic life has been spent in search of a way to leave the body in an attempt to find the mind. *Endgame* has only two characters and one of them remains in a chair with his body completely shrouded. *Krapp's Last Tape* reduces man to the loneliness of his voice and his past. *Play* goes past even this to the pure mind, and although it has three characters, they speak hollowly from burial urns, their situation a mockery of the stage cliché (the romantic triangle).

It would be unwise, though, to conclude that Beckett's plays are undramatic, gloomy or despondent. In fact they are drenched with comedy in the roaring Irish tradition, delighting in literary and physical pranks and a joyousness of life. Beckett, by the very fact of his work, is a participant — a working artist — and to regard him as an absentee human is to misunderstand the man and his art.

The compassion of which Beckett is capable marks him as a poet of great humanity — hardly a philosophical isolationist. *Krapp's Last Tape* is a wise and tender play, even as it deals with as old an idea as the realization, in old age, that nothing has been learned and that youth is never appreciated. Beckett treats this as the terribly sad truth it is. He sets an old man fumbling for bananas through dusty drawers and then rummaging through a lifetime of autobiographical tape recordings. One tape has him say, at thirty-nine, "Perhaps the best years are gone — no, I don't want them back." Now, at sixty-nine, Krapp has only a tape recorder to embrace for the memory of youth's love. Despite a play so masterfully compassionate and poetic; despite Beckett's obvious art, the right wing blithely ignores this magnificent poet whose creative imagination, technical skill, exquisite language and stage sense mark his work as unmistakably classic.

Beckett is an extremist in style, his plays moving further toward abstraction than those of any other playwright. His point of view is devotedly atheistic, well beyond even *considering* the idea of a God. His love for man and for life is radical, especially at its depth, and his management of character, story and language is entirely contrary to ruling styles. Like Genet, his work will probably always remain left wing.

The matter of his small output must be considered, although I am not entirely sure *how* it must be considered. In the relatively trivial matter of whether or not he is a master playwright, how strange that he does not qualify (on the grounds of inconsistent practice). But who cares? The master playwright is necessary to the season-to-season sustenance of a country's theater, but he loses importance in the greater artistic scheme of things. Proust may have written only one major work, but his *Remembrance of Things Past* is a novelistic milestone. The masterpiece by the one-work artist is as significant as the masterpiece by a prolific artist. In the final analysis, the theater is only to be pitied for having so few Beckett plays. We have only four Brahms symphonies. We are grateful that there are four.

Yet, for all his acknowledged greatness, Beckett must be considered a left-wing extremist in the American theater. If it weren't for the good sense of Barr-Wilder-Albee, it is dubious that his post-*Godot* works would have been produced in New York. And even while the plays are presented, no other producers are interested. Even the resident theaters, leftward as their artistic directors incline, keep away from Beckett. Their regular explanation is that they "would love to do it" but the audience-losing risk is too great.

The responsible resident theater director must insist upon producing important plays, even at the risk of losing money while reconditioning his audience's taste. The theater should *lead* popular taste, not follow it. The director does, after all, have a responsibility to the theater. These rationalizations for the omission of important works indicate how possible it would be for noncommercial theaters to fall into exactly the mass-appeal situation of Broadway.

Oddly enough, Jean Genet is in many ways a right-wing playwright. His plays follow traditional story lines: that is, they have "plots"; and they carry very specific messages relating to very specific problems, usually social, sexual or political. On the other hand, he may be the most extreme left-wing playwright in all of major Western theater, for his points of view seem ultimately contrary to those generally accepted. I say "seem" because Genet always bases his perversions on traditional morality, explaining them as reverse-coin idealism. He insists that he believes in ordinary, right-wing "goodness." But despite this, his plays are invariably defenses of his personal way of life; transparent rationales for homosexuality and antisocial behavior — the aesthetic of perversion, evil and ugliness.

Stylistically, he is a surrealist, although he should not be reduced to so simple a description. There is, after all, a Beckett surrealism, a Pinter, an Ionesco and, if one wishes to go all the way back to the origins of surrealism, a Jarry surrealism and that of Kleist before him.

Genet's real talent appears when he follows his emotional and artistic inclinations rather than his intellectual ones. (This is true for most artists.) At such times, he displays a raw ability for stage electricity. Working with ritual and ceremony, with exaggerated formality and bright colors, and always with sex, he conjures up bizarre and magical pictures around basically interesting (if weird) story lines.

He has produced only five works as of this writing and so cannot be considered a master playwright. The first (*Deathwatch* in 1947) was a long one-act play rooted in his prison experiences and his obsession with homosexuality. *The Maids* was written afterward, but produced in France earlier. It indicates the great theatricality, inverted sexuality and hypersensitivity that was to come later. But while it paints a curious, stylized picture of two maids and their mistress as almost papier-mâché, inhuman beings with tangled jealousies and social attitudes, it is transparently a vehicle for Genet's insecurities. As theater it is rather dull, and when observed coldbloodedly, it is rooted in old-time melodrama.

With *The Balcony,* however, Genet channeled his most valuable artistic impulses into a coherent form, making the whorehouse of illusions a place for vivid and exciting theater. The play even contains some serious thinking on matters of rank, identity and social respect, and while it clumsily diverges into an overdetailed plot about a revolution outside the brothel, it generally works. It is Genet's masterpiece and justifies his international reputation. *The Balcony* is properly becoming popular among the American resident theaters.

But to give you an idea of the right-wing influence in New York, Theodore Mann, one of the more adventurous off-Broadway producers and owner of the Circle in the Square, had an empty house in the spring of 1966 and considered bringing in the excellent Hartford Stage Company production. *The Balcony,* after all, had enjoyed a great success when originally produced by Mann. But after seeing Jacques Cartier's production, the producer changed his mind. "It was too sexy," he said (ludicrous, since the play is *about* sex). Cartier had staged the play with an extraordinary understanding of Genet. The "too sexy" production that Mann objected to included a nude-to-the-waist actress robed as an altar boy in the opening Black Mass; and a bloodily realistic self-castration later on. Such staging is necessary for Genet and is in keeping with his lurid theatricality. Mann's refusal to house it is exemplary of right-wing pressures even in a relatively left-wing milieu. (In criticizing this particular Mann incident, I must at the same time point out that he is one of the most art-minded, serious theater producers in New York.)

The Blacks, like *The Balcony,* had a great New York success during the good off-Broadway years, although it is doubtful that anybody understood it, least of all the author. *The Blacks* attempted to understand the black person in a white world, transposing Genet's antagonisms with authority into those of worldwide oppressed Negroes.

But it was obvious that Genet was not as inspired by the social and political situation of Negroes in a white world as he was by the nature of their situation — the oppressed against the oppressors; and by the brilliance of their physical contrast — that is, the colors black against white. Genet always writes personally, and he feels himself an oppressed man in a world of oppressors, a black man in a white world; a world where the ruling morality is evil and so a world where what is supposed to be white, or good, is really black and bad; and consequently a world where the Negroes are wrongly considered evil and the whites are wrongly considered good. *The Blacks* uses the Negro-white complex for Genet's purposes.

Dealing with Kiplingesque colonials in a style already developed by Brecht for the Nazis, *The Blacks* employs masks, extreme makeup and cartoonism in the pursuit of sociological investigation. As with all his plays, the theater devices worked miracles of magic and neverneverland, while making little sense. This was even truer of *The Screens,* which was not even produced in Paris until 1961, five years after it was written.

There were several reasons for this delay. The French are ever touchy about Algerian references and aspersions upon their colonialist history; they were equally concerned about the play's extreme obscenity. The structure of *The Screens* is very complicated, its cast is enormous, it is long and sometimes unwieldy. As produced by the Théâtre de France of Jean-Louis Barrault and Madeleine Renaud at the Odéon theater in Paris, a more valid reason for the production delay would have been its incoherence and sheer boredom. Nor was the fault in the production, which was quite good despite the insurmountable problems.

The problem with *The Screens* is that it has an abundance of Genet's weaknesses and a dearth of his strengths. It is named for a production scheme as well as the point. The only scenery used, except for a series of raised and lowered platforms, is a number of screens of various sizes, rolled on and off stage. These have pictures already on them or drawn by the characters, and those pictures represent the only reality for Genet — the reality of the human mind. This is Philosophy 101, and is typical of the playwright.

As in most of his plays, there is a story — a story that would be practically right wing in its use of character, action and plot development if it were not for the extreme trappings. But after it begins along one line (an Arab trades his good looks and youth for the wealthy bridal bed of the world's ugliest woman), it becomes sidetracked in the playwright's entangled interests in Algeria, colonialism and the old brothel-and-jail business, concluding in an entirely irrelevant meeting of the living and the dead.

As for the obscenity, it seldom seems graceful or even apt, always being superimposed when neither necessary nor natural to the play's flow. Director Roger Blin declined to follow the author's *Maids*-like directions for casting some male actors in female roles; he dropped the seventh of the play's seventeen scenes and severely cut the last one, purposely collecting the most "shocking" speeches into one grand oration and simulated demonstration on the joys of defecation. This drove a number of spectators to vocal protestation and smug departure, probably satisfying them as much as it did Genet, Blin and Barrault.

Ionesco, too, writes message plays in the surreal style, but while Genet deals with sexual, social and political morality, Ionesco is interested in more traditional complaints — the inability of humans to communicate, conformity, materialism, and so on.

His most popular plays are the early one-acters, which were regularly produced off-Broadway and have since become staples for American resident theaters. They are usually performed on a bill with Pinter and produced as a concession to the theater of the absurd, satisfying a company's obligations toward left-wing art and allowing it to proceed, conscience-free, with the season's regular program of Chekhov, Shaw and O'Neill.

These early Ionesco plays include *The Bald Soprano, The Lesson* and *The Chairs. The Bald Soprano* is a precious parody of middle-class married life in England. It is about two couples visiting and chatting aimlessly and brainlessly in platitudes and clichés. Time passes — a lifetime perhaps — with clocks continuously chiming. In their conformity and conditioned behavior, the couples are mechanical dolls. At one point, one of the wives stops stockstill, needing rewinding. The play ends and starts again as the curtain falls, representing life's continuum. It is not first-rate Ionesco but it is extraordinarily original. And remember, it is a first play.

The Lesson treats problems in human communication, adding a superficial (though fascinating) investigation into the nature of language and knowledge. Like *The Bald Soprano,* its situations and characters are comic strip, although it uses the traditional theater devices of terror and murder for melodramatic effects. The play is about a tutor and his pupil. He begins the lesson by testing her knowledge of addition, which is splendid enough, although she can count only to sixteen. She plans to achieve the "total doctorate," which includes "the physical sciences and moral philosophy" (the sum total of human knowledge), and she wants to achieve it in three weeks. Ionesco's comic treatment of human presumption in the face of civilization's accumulated knowledge is an excellent combination of perception and comment within a theatrical context. The lesson then turns to linguistics, Ionesco's prime interest at the time (1951). The play is already well into a mockery of our most elementary accomplishments, describing them as monumental successes. When it finally gets down to what everything has been about — the fundamental incompatibility of humans and logic — the play turns to horror with the guileless comedy that masked it neatly from the start. It is very clever and very funny.

Most of Ionesco's other works have not been seen in the United States. His *The New Tenant* (1953) was once produced off-Broadway, but while it was typical of the playwright's striking style, it was not clever enough to compensate for his platitudinous points (besides, the play was extremely reminiscent of the Dylan Thomas story

Adventures in the Skin Trade). *Victims of Duty* was the major half of that twin bill at the Writers Stage in the spring of 1964. While the production was impeccable, the work showed Ionesco in so fanciful a mood that every new idea seemed to give birth to another that would in turn provide further inspirations. The play was like a toy glider that sweeps and loops in breezy accident. Intended to comically explore the hopeless quest for self, *Victims of Duty* constantly finds itself diverted into academic theater games.

Although Ionesco's *Rhinoceros* was produced on Broadway, it did not represent any genuine acceptance of him or signify a genuine left-wing influence there (its anticonformity message was more or less right wing anyway). Except for a visit by Barrault's Théâtre de France in 1964 (when they did *The Pedestrian of the Air*), none of his post-1958 plays has been presented in New York. It must be conceded that the majority of these were full-length works demanding right-wing technical resources beyond the limited possibilities of off-Broadway. But since the later one-acters were not produced either, it can be reasonably concluded that no more Ionesco will be forthcoming from the progressively right-tending off-Broadway producers.

Harold Pinter is perhaps the playwright most benefited by the beginning internationalization of American theater. (Although Osborne is regularly produced in New York, the productions are by *English* companies — they are *imports;* Pinter, thanks to the growth of internationalization, has become as active a playwright, in theaters across the country, as any American.) It may be because Pinter hit his stride just as internationalization was developing, and it may be because his second full-length play *The Caretaker* was the result of a personal artistic stipend (not unlike patronage) granted by the right-wing American producer Roger Stevens. This provided *The Caretaker* with a Broadway showcase, and although the play was reviewed with confusion, it did well enough and even won the right-wing Drama Circle Award. Since this was just before the death of off-Broadway, when there were still bi-wing traces in evidence, Pinter was able to have most of his plays produced there, where they were acceptable to most critics and met with success.

What is remarkable about this playwright is that he manages so marvelously to combine basic right-wing theater values (mystery, suspense, comedy) with a left-wing sense of strangeness and unreality. Pinter himself calls his works "basically 'well-made plays.' " The surrealist has a broad range of exaggerations from which to choose. He may go as far as Genet into fantasy. He may work with the Ionesco cartoon or the Beckett simplicity. Pinter stays much closer to the facade of reality, and the special tone of his work is achieved by his presentation of the impossible in the guise of the actual.

His work has been the object of endless discussion. Some critics have pronounced him indecipherable, assuming that there must be a terribly complex philosophical point to his plays. Others have classified him as an "absurdist." *Whatever* his points, *however* original, they are subservient to his drama; it is the *theater* of Pinter that makes him the most important contemporary playwright for the English-speaking stage.

The Pinter play that ultimately clarified him for me was his first full-length work, *The Birthday Party,* which I saw in 1966 in a Theater Group production at the University of California at Los Angeles.

The Birthday Party is about the terror of being insecure in a world of confident people. Such a point seems to me terribly striking. It is so fundamental, so general, so applicable to man in today's society, that it would appear incredible for no playwright ever to have dealt with it before.

The Birthday Party is also an excellent example of the playwright whose final artistic identity is apparent in even his early works. The Pinter style is rooted in basic melodrama: the hearing of dark, echoed, fearful footsteps on a lonely night. But in old-fashioned melodrama, those footsteps are imaginery and the fright unwarranted. Pinter makes the footsteps real: there *is* somebody following you and there *is* cause for fright. Our worst, weirdest fears are confirmed as the illogical occurs.

The Birthday Party applies this scheme to a person with all the usual irrationalities of the human mind, but a person for whom those irrationalities have become exaggerated to the point of psychosis. The play brutally watches his imagined fears grow increasingly tangible until they are full-throated hallucinations, entirely realized. By this time the man is psychotic and we never know whether we are seeing what he is *imagining* or what is really happening. In short, we learn what it is like to be psychotic, since for the psychotic person, the hallucination is absolutely real.

Yet, the basis of poor Stanley Weber's imagined fears is part of all our lives. He is unsettled by the superficially confident and envious of their security. Insulating himself from the demands of this fear, he finds it threatening his cocoon. Pinky-ringed slickers come to "get him." They besiege him with the glib and shallow collection of clichés, slogans and sentiments that get most people by on the surface of day-to-day existence. It is such sureness that the unconfident person despises, craves and desperately fears.

Pinter's earlier *The Room,* a one-act play, also dwells in areas where the neurotic materializes, although it is not as subjective as *The Birthday Party* and the later plays were to become. Still, I would call it a perfect one-act play. Set in the shabby apartment of a working-class couple, it moves into threat as the playwright plants a suspicion in the basement ("Who lives down there?"), only to abandon it for meaningless chatter. Soon he is back with another clue and before long a landlord arrives to talk in circular riddles. Then a gum-chewing couple mention that "a man" in the basement told them that the couple's rooms would soon be vacant. The menace grows.

While the place is swathed in mysterious tension, the small talk wanders in calculated paths. Pinter's greatest asset is his mastery of an easygoing dialogue that steps all over itself in human confusion. The foolish, the repetitious, the obvious, the vacant, while unspoken fears lurk in the commas and silent question marks. Then the fear materializes — the neurotic becomes actual — and action comes tumbling over action until *bang!* the play is over.

A Slight Ache (1959) developed the neurosis realizations that *The Birthday Party* explored. It is about a paranoid "theological and philosophical essayist" who begins the play as a small-time sadist trapping a wasp in marmalade and then murdering it with boiled water. The man then moves from an obsession to an involvement with a mysterious and silent beggar who has been selling matches at the garden gate. His suspicion of plots and secret designs finally leads him to invite the man in, grow from gruff to obsequious, and finally be intimidated and destroyed by him.

Again, Pinter is dealing in panic. It is a purely imaginary fear that something dreadful is about to happen: a why-is-that-man-staring-at-me fear; a somebody-is-following-me fear. The slight ache of a slight madness realizes all fears.

The Caretaker (1960) continued Pinter's concern with mental aberrations, and one of its major characters was a man neutralized by electric shock therapy. But the play deals with the responsibilities of one human being for another, and asks whether such responsibilities are reasonable. Perhaps they are only foisted upon men by thoughtless moral slogans leading only to mutual dependence, mutual resentment.

The Caretaker also presents a good example of Pinter's interest in the imaginary person — that is, the person we *think* we are talking to, but who is really only a reflection of our own emotions. Aston, the brother who is kind toward people but expects them to take advantage of him (that is *his* neurosis), sees Davies, the derelict, as hostile, presumptuous and ungrateful. Mick, the brother who is cold-blooded and nasty, needs to step on people — to prove them inferior to him — and *he* sees Davies as sniveling and cowardly. So, that is the way Pinter has written Davies in his scenes with them. When we watch Davies in conversation with Aston, he behaves as *Aston* sees him and when we watch him in conversation with Mick, he behaves as *Mick* sees him. In fact, whenever we see Davies alone, he is a nonentity, which is what he *really* is. This is not unlike Weber's vision of Goldberg as "Goldberg the Threat" in *The Birthday Party.*

It is also related to Pinter's recurrent reference to behavior-as-a-pose. Is Goldberg really poised, or is he going through the *motions* of poise? Do the husband and wife of *The Lover* really behave as "lovers" do or are they just *acting* that way?

Pinter does not use subjects as such. He does not "investigate" a question and provide an "answer." He merely probes an area, posing leftish questions, his main concerns being the theater itself and the tricking, beguiling, confusing and alarming of an audience, interspersed with real and good humor. He works more deeply in the basics of theater than any other master playwright today.

With *The Collection* (1961) he returned to the one-act form, further exploring his interest in abstract human questions. This play is an exercise in the relationship and conflict between emotion and language: how we describe what we see — what we believe we have seen — is not always the same as what really happened (the idea is very Pirandello). More often, it is what we would like to have seen, what we would like to believe.

Pinter did not write *The Collection* "about" this. Rather, his play demonstrates it. A man fears that his wife has been unfaithful. He says she told him so, but that is not so certain. The lover he suspects is a homosexual who may be ambisexual. The play clicks back and forth from the homosexual and his male lover to the husband and wife. It switches partners, switches again, with different stories being told, never letting us know what the truth really is. What the truth was really makes no difference. All that matters is what these people believe, and they believe what they *need* to believe. It is pure Pinter, existing as idea and as theater piece. It is still another perfect one-act play. I should point out, too, that this work demonstrates a left-wing method of making a point. The playwright never creates a mouthpiece. The points are made obliquely, through implication. Metaphorically rather than explicitly.

The Lover (1963) continued into areas of human imagination as distorted by neurosis. A couple, ostensibly highly civilized, seem to have a wonderfully casual attitude toward infidelity (although from the very start casual civilization is quietly satirized). While the husband is busy with high finance, the wife entertains a lover. And the husband accepts her dalliance with the same relaxed interest as she treats his having a mistress.

Then Pinter begins asking questions: Has the lover ever arrived? Blackout, and the husband returns. Has the lover ever been there? Blackout. Does the husband really visit a mistress? Blackout. Is there any jealousy? Blackout. Is the wife's coyness pretense?

At last we are told. The *husband* is the lover and the *wife* is the mistress. That is, the couple *pretends* to be lover and mistress during the afternoons. He leaves for the office in his banker's grays, returning in midafternoon in suede jacket and ascot. And, as lovers do, they play bongo drums, become superpassionate and make mad love under the table.

But do *real* lovers love this way? Or is this just *another* pretense? No, real lovers don't act this way. What we realize, suddenly, after Pinter has sneakily built us up to highwire tension and real terror, is that the husband is mad and that his wife, to keep him and satisfy his psychoses, is playing at this bizarre humoring of him. And all of this is set with masterful writing that juggles cliché with mimicry and parodied parody, spinning horror and wit inside out and coming up with heady fright.

Such writing is most effectively handled in *The Homecoming*, a brilliant play that Pinter wrote for the Royal Shakespeare Company and which subsequently opened on Broadway early in 1967. The ideas implicit in this play are deep and complex, having as their general reference the relationships between people. This is as it has been in every Pinter play. In *The Homecoming*, the characters are members of a family pretending as most (all?) families do that fathers are paternal, mothers maternal, sons fraternal and filial. At some point, each of them spouts the picture-magazine clichés of family life. But in fact they are frauds — their relationships are violent and hateful. Yet, they are bound to each other, as all family members are.

The commonplace situation that begins this play is the classic one of a son bringing his wife home to "meet the family." But we are in a Pinter family, one step away from reality. As is his style, the playwright sets surrealistic situations in normal trappings. And once creating a bizarre premise, he proceeds to let everything follow a natural, logical course. In other words, the plays exist in their own dimension, proceeding normally *within* that dimension.

In *The Homecoming*, the father, a cruel, stupid and coarse man, greets his daughter-in-law by saying, "I've never had a whore under this roof before" (adding, for a typical Pinter joke, "ever since your mother died," which is meaningful itself since the mother had not been the All-Britain Mother's Day Mom she is made out to be, but an unfaithful and perhaps unpleasant woman). The sons are equally violent — the youngest is a boxer, the middle a pimp who enjoys beating women, the eldest a professor of philosophy who has attempted to escape his family and become the model of a civilized man. His brutality is controlled but it is there. Their violence is a disguise for the masculinity they lack and they all are finally subjugated by a woman (the wife) who has the ultimate power over all men — the power to grant or withhold sexual gratification. The father and the two brothers intend to make her their whore but instead she becomes their ruler.

All these intellectual threads give the play a profoundly stimulating texture and they are carefully woven into the verbal fabric. In the use of the English language and in the understanding of informal dialogue, word sounds, conversation rhythms, exact meanings and real poetry, Pinter is peerless. His humor is wonderful — ironic and dry, verging on the nonsense and entirely within modern modes. ("What you've got to do is learn how to defend yourself, and you've got to learn how to attack. That's your only trouble as a boxer. You don't know how to defend yourself and you don't know how to attack.")

When *The Homecoming* opened in New York, it created much confusion about its "meaning." This was somewhat due to the predictable right-wing bewilderment when faced with left-wing theater. Subsequent and extensive newspaper discussions were also the producer's partly conscious and partly lucky scheme for publicity (a scheme that worked — although opening to right-wing critical rejection, *The Homecoming* managed to reach New York's alienated left-wing audiences through word-of-mouth and they left their movie lines and off-off-Broadway theaters to keep the play going for a healthy run).

Pinter proceeded to exasperate New York's right-wingers by refusing to "explain" his play. This was wise behavior on several grounds. In the first place, a playwright should *never* explain his own play — it is the play that exists and art must represent itself. Second, the varieties of meaning in any work of art emerge as the result of the work's *artistic effectiveness* and not necessarily because the artist consciously "inserted" them. Do you really think that Shakespeare could have gotten *Hamlet* written if he had concentrated on the infinite levels of meaning that have since been seen in it? It takes so much work to write a play — and so much of it is done on an emotional, carried-away wave — that complicated

meaning-injection is impossible. Also, the playwright who concen-
trates on intellectualization is prone to artificiality and preconstruc-
tion.

But just because the playwright did not have *your* meaning in
mind does not mean that you are "wrong." If the play substantiates
your analysis, the analysis is valid. Right-wingers habitually insist
on being "correct" — on having their interpretations verified by
the playwright. It is a habit that should be corrected.

The leftism of Pinter is rooted in his antagonism to the moral
and intellectual traditions of contemporary England, as well as in
his unique style. His rightward movement into polish, artistic maturity and poise is representative of the healthy wing interaction in
England. His acceptance by American theater is the best example
of the internationalization that is presently occurring in Western
theater.

As with the musicals and comedies, drama has its extremists. On
the right wing there aren't many examples because right-wing extremism is prompted by the prospect of big money returns and
Broadway drama is no place for profit. Occasionally there will be a
play produced strictly to appeal to Jewish audiences, Negro audiences, and so on. But these are imitations of theater.

If you want examples, and I'm not terribly interested in this,
"plays" like *The World of Suzie Wong* or *The Sweet Bird of Youth*
or *J.B.* or an all-star *School for Scandal* or *Hamlet* are deep into
the right wing. Also, a drama like John Whiting's *The Devils* although not because it was *written* to appeal to ticket buyers so
much as because it was *produced* to. Advertised as a great event,
it held down two big-name stars (Jason Robards and Anne Ban-
croft). It was promoted as guaranteed culture. Whiting's wishfully
Elizabethan style was seriously right wing and his dialogue ranged
from the thickly melodramatic ("There's been fornication! Lust!
She's been had!") to the pompous ("All things, no matter how
incomprehensible, are a matter of love"). As for his central thesis
("The assertion of self in man is the ascendancy of the devil"), it
was self-seriousness at its most embarrassing. But far right-wing
drama, at least these days, is as much the producers' doing as it is
the playwrights', being a group effort aimed in the direction of the
nearest bank.

Extremist left-wing theater developed during the best years of off-Broadway, went on to café theaters (or "off-off Broadway") and then spread to dozens of studios, lofts, store fronts, anywhere. These theaters, enthusiastically amateur, became homes for the young, sometimes recklessly avant-garde playwrights and directors, as well as the untalented pure and the Bronx bohemians. For all the silliness in many of the productions, they are generally serious, and represent the feelings, the attitudes, the essential sobriety of today's young. The total alienation with which they regard mainstream, right-wing theaters is the most severe product of the wing division. Certainly, left-wing extremists will always be antagonized with an establishment, but the distance between New York's most innovative theater people and the professional conservatives of Broadway is immeasurable.

The leaders of today's far left wing in New York are the Judson Poets Theater, the Living Theater (whether in exile or not), the La Mama Experimental Theater Club, Theater Genesis and Café Cino.

Judson presents weekend performances of wild, camp musicals, obscure plays by such writers as Gertrude Stein and far-left original dramas by playwrights like Rochelle Owens, María Irene Fornés and Rosalyn Drexler. Its popularity is enormous, especially for splashy camp musicals like *Gorilla Queen.* This was a very Thirties movies, pop art and fag work by Ronald Tavel. Drawing upon "King Kong," the traditional camp favorite, its title character was Queen Kong, a transvestite giant gorilla. Surrounding him-her were characters of various, dubious sexual identities, the humor intended in precisely that confusion. The chorus of queer apes was called the Glitz Ianos (I admit some of the business *was* funny, especially a line about "deus ex Mattachine"). Other of Mr. Tavel's people were Clyde Batty and Karma Miranda, all influenced by Andy Warhol's queer, camp, but startlingly original imagination. The structure was impossible, the obsessive and defensive supersex so broad and repetitious, the music and staging so sloppy that staying beyond one act was unthinkable. It was typical of Judson and Judson is typical of far-left extremism and amateurism. But one important point must be made: The Judson Poets Theater does turnaway business. It appeals not merely to campers but to hippies, would-be hippies, and, finally, the growing mass of young people who are hippie-influenced. Though these young people are very strange — and consequently frightening — to older generations, and though their preoccupation with drugs, hallucinogens, rockout music, pure sensation and withdrawal seems alien, our world *has* to become theirs. Soon they will be dominating all of America and if we ignore or reject them we will have no influence at all on their development. They will remain leftist and estranged. In any case, *our* theater is hopelessly backward to them and as long as it remains so they will flock to Judson and other far-left places. If things continue as they are, these people will never return.

Judith Malina and Julian Beck began the Living Theater conventionally enough with a production of Christopher Marlowe's *Doctor Faustus* at the off-Broadway Cherry Lane Theater. It grew slowly during the Fifties, moving uptown to 100th Street and finally settling into its own theater on 14th Street. There it had its greatest commercial success with Jack Gelber's *The Connection,* a far left-wing play in ultramodern modes, dealing with narcotics addiction. It continued in repertory with increasingly unusual plays (such as Brecht's *In the Jungle of Cities* and *A Man's a Man* and William Carlos Williams's *Many Loves*).

This period culminated with the production of Kenneth H. Brown's extremely left-wing *The Brig,* a strange combination of photographic reality with the pure stage. The play was a fact-for-fact duplication of life in a Marine Corps prison, seeing in those facts both choreography and musical rhythms. It meant to reveal, through that relentless beat of military inhumanity, the unbelievable machinery that men devise to destroy themselves. And while it did not quite work (its repetition bored rather than built power), it was the beginning of a new attitude by the Living Theater — the attitude of company-created production.

But in October of 1963, the Bureau of Internal Revenue charged the company with nonpayment of admissions taxes and locked the theater. Malina, Beck and the company chose to sit-in for three days and were arrested for "impeding federal officers in the performance of their duties." They were sentenced to thirty- and sixty-day prison terms respectively and soon left for Europe.

There they became gypsies, roaming the countryside and performing the Brown play (later joined by Genet's *The Maids*). Interrupted only by the departures of Beck and Malina to serve their sentences, the company performed under near-starvation conditions in London, Paris, Antwerp, Basel and Berlin.

Then they created *Mysteries — and Smaller Pieces* for the American Students and Artists Center in Paris. This was not a "play." It had no script and virtually no dialogue. It was created by the company as a series of eight, nine, ten scenes, and was based on the writings of the French theater theorist Antonin Artaud. Artaud's intention was to reach an audience through shock. To elicit a plain, physical, agonizing, almost hysterical gut reaction. It was his "theater of cruelty" which became the basic text for the leaders of the pure-stage, director's-theater, absolute-theater, total-theater (or whatever you wish to call it) movement.

When I spoke with Beck and Malina in Berlin late in 1966, they described *Mysteries* as "a series of theatrical events which explore all of the physical senses, simultaneously tracing both the physical defects and physical glories in man's present estate." Their work, then, has a "content" — a literary meaning — and since they are pacifist-anarchists of the it's-a-groove intellectual school, it is bound to be very *protest-movement*. But the value lies in its sheer theatricality.

The final scene has twenty-five people dying of the plague, the deaths taking as long as each actor finds necessary. Then six of them rise to bury the others. This has come after such things as ten minutes of blackout during which there are sensations: female voices, constellations of light and odors of incense (all the senses are being attacked).

Now committed to the creation of its own works, the company decided to do its own version of Mary Shelley's *Frankenstein* in September of 1965. This was "a spectacle, like *Götterdämmerung*," according to Beck, "based on the attempts by man to improve his own state — attempts that backfired just as Dr. Frankestein's did, and which resulted only in the creation of destructive monsters." It draws an apt analogy to modern science.

While *Frankenstein* has some conventional dialogue, and even lines from the original Shelley, it is a free-form work. Over three hours long, it uses overlapping languages (as in simultaneous translations) and continued Artaudian effects, as well as various ideas suggested by Beck, Malina or members of the company. There is, as in *Mysteries,* the use of ceremony, ritual, incantation. There is also the gore — electrocutions, garrottings, gas chambers.

The monster himself is a part of it — an eighteen-foot amorphous shape played by a group of actors. And later in the play the action occurs within his head — a giant scenic head. The dialogue is limited and much of the sound is just sound — on tape and in partly extemporized chanting by the actors. This music continues throughout the production in "mystical chord," as Beck describes it.

In productions such as *Mysteries* and *Frankenstein,* the Living Theater intends to entirely eliminate the playwright and the director from the theater (going beyond director's theater into theater's theater, if there can be such a thing and I don't think there can; without control there can be no artistic coherence).

It is ironic that Beck, Malina and the Living Theater are working out of an American intellectual-theatrical framework for the benefit of a superpowerful right wing that has alienated them. However simplistic their ideas and however muddled their thinking, they have delved more deeply into the idea of pure theater than anybody working in their own country. Beck and Malina realize that they must eventually return or die of artistic sterility in an alien environment. They are basically and irrevocably American and they know it. So long as they are away from their natural home they will be refugees and fugitives. They finally scheduled a return to New York for the fall of 1967.

The Becks' artistic and intellectual commitment has in a sense caused their own exile, since by giving in to right-wing pressures (both theatrical and political) they could well have continued to function in New York. But they are extreme left-wingers in all things and the artist who creates in wild unconventionality will not turn around and conform in nonartistic matters. Theirs is a probably insoluble problem, but one thing is clear: they belong in America. It is terribly like our country to reject its most original (and so

most valuable) artists. The Living Theater, though abroad, remains one of the most significant, if not *the* most significant, American theater development at present.

Another major left-wing extremist theater is Ellen Stewart's La
Mama Experimental Theater Club. Not a company like the Living
Theater, it is a *place,* made available to adventurous young playwrights for work-in-progress staging of their dramas. They are free
to try anything. Miss Stewart's only stipulation is that they be far
left wing. La Mama is operated on less than a shoe string, charging
only a one-dollar admission fee and not paying any of its personnel.

Even with Equity actors and professional directors, La Mama
produced semi-amateur work. This was largely because of the unfinished talent of its playwrights, but that was exactly what this theater was designed for. In any case, it is in the nature of the left
wing — and especially the far left wing — to be unprofessional.
The nightly packed houses that La Mama drew was proof enough
of the willingness of left-wing audiences to put up with production
crudities for the sake of modern theater.

Though not everything at La Mama was crudely produced. For
instance Rochelle Owens's *Futz,* as presented and revived there, is
an ambitious, original and regularly thrilling play, though most of
its excitement comes from the broad opportunity it gives for creative and musical direction. There was nothing at all sloppy about
its production, though God knows it was far left wing in substance,
values and style. Its story, weaving through flashes ahead and back
and developing through anecdote and implication rather than
straightforward plotting, was built around a farmer who was in love,
truly in love, with his pig. And its point was that his rejection and
ultimate murder are what awaits any kind of purity or individuality
in a vicious, Victorian, hypocritical, immorally moral America.
The story elements were kept quite simple, with broad strokes for
ancillary characters and great, swirling slashes of theater things.
And it was marvelously directed by Tom O'Horgan (a La Mama
regular).

A number of talented young playwrights either worked or started
at La Mama, among them Lanford Wilson, whose *This Is the Rill
Speaking* used sound patterns, movement, intertwining time and

song to paint a picture of a hillbilly town, its people and its rhythm. A sugar-free *Our Town,* it found loved life in a dramatic collage of back porches, cars — everywhere. Moreover, it was an early example of a movement away from the intelligibility of dialogue. This sounds silly, but if you listen carefully there is an overlap to daily conversation that turns meaningful words into the beat and music of existence itself. Wilson grasped the feel and rhythm of human conversation. But while the technique was exciting, it was also unresolved. Yet that's all right; that's exactly what La Mama and the far left wing are for — the new, the ambitious, the still-being-born and experimental. And a year after *Rill,* Wilson had developed the style for viable, full-length drama — *The Rimers of Eldritch.*

Also working through La Mama was a Living Theater offshoot, Joseph Chaikin's Open Theater, and out of its activities came a marvelous off-Broadway production of Jean-Claude van Itallie's *America Hurrah.* This was an unusual instance of a play being born in the far left wing and then receiving enough right-wing influence to be refined and polished. By the time it had a public première it was being done as well, probably, as it ever could be. It remained left wing in ideology and conception, but its production was completely professional (superior to many right-wing productions, in fact, in sureness and ensemble playing). Such occurrences as this encourage one to look for *some* kind of wing interaction in the future, or at least to *demand* it.

America Hurrah was a program of one-act plays. The first was directed by Mr. Chaikin in a style closely related to that of the Living Theater. Originally called *Pavanne,* it was retitled *Interview* for the off-Broadway production, probably for fear that the right-wing audiences would need a thread of understandable plot in order to accept it. The new title was misleading, for although the play begins with a brutally surrealistic depiction of modern, frigid job interviews, it moves into a variety of areas where today's Americans find themselves groping for friendship, for love, for *help,* always to be rejected by an aloofness, a withdrawal, a cultural iciness and impersonality.

Mr. van Itallie wrote this, and Chaikin directed it, with an ultramodern, fugal sense of sound, movement, shape, color, visual sense, choreography and musical overlap. These elements built a theater excitement upon a basis of intellectual detachment and compassion, emerging as a stunning *production.* The other plays in *America Hurrah,* while not as flamboyant in their construction, were no less impressive. *TV* still used the juggling of dialogue and visual imagery, but it also showed van Itallie capable of writing perfectly realistic conversation when he needs it. The final one-acter was a wildly funny juxtaposition of the futuristic motels that are laying a Formica veneer on this country with the kinds of people who patronize them. Encasing his actors in gigantic papier-mâché dolls, van Itallie sends an American dream husband (toothpaste grin in a sweater-ad face) and wife (platinum blonde with a cantilevered bosom) into a chromium motel room. There, the hair-curlered manageress recites the bought-from-a-catalogue attractions of the house for the duration of the play while the customers proceed to cover the walls with hilariously obscene drawings and graffiti before destroying it entirely. As in the other plays, van Itallie seized upon a terrible reality and processed it for new theater purposes.

Another far-left Open Theater production that came out of La Mama was Megan Terry's *Viet Rock,* which displayed the all-production method as applied to a full-length play. Like the one-acters in *America Hurrah, Viet Rock* moved completely away from plot. In more or less revue form, it presented the extreme left-wing attitude toward the official American line on the war in Vietnam. In some ways it was silly, too ardently pacifist and completely uninterested in recognizing or coping with the complexities of that war. Moreover, the murder of the innocent is as unforgivable when the Viet Cong commit it as it is when the Americans do, and *Viet Rock* refused to concede this.

The Open Theater's far-left devices were there — music and choreography and mixed sound and rolling, miasmic structure (very much like the new musical theater). And it was generally exciting theater.

In any case, there is no point in being encouraged by the occasional far left-wing examples of exciting, modern theater that are tempered by moderate influences and emerge as fulfilled works. More frequently, far-left works are ingroup, confused and silly. The most flamboyant of these are the happenings, which range

from living room affairs to massive mixed media presentations em-
ploying complex electronic equipment. Whether or not happenings
are theater is not even a question, though it is perpetually asked by
right-wingers. The definition of theater must be maximally loose.
What is important is that the happenings are being *tried*. What's
more, where theater people are receptive they are having their
effect. (Peter Brook, the Royal Shakespeare Company director of
Marat/Sade and a leader in the production theater movement, admits a powerful influence from the happenings. But then, that is
England, where reactions to left-wing stimuli are possible.)

The stupidity of the far left could not have been better demonstrated than in the only one of its plays to open on Broadway:
Terrence McNally's *And Things That Go Bump in the Night.*

The play ran through a hodgepodge of styles from Beckett to
science fiction, horror movies, ritual theater and vaudeville. Its
point was a collegiate melange of clichés — a defense of humanism and faith by displaying the false face, the false values and the
false God of cynicism and nihilism (a paraphrase of McNally; do
not attribute the fraternity house sound to me). Between the imitation poetry and the sadism, the ambisex and the end-of-the-world,
the very young playwright gathered all the trademarks of the far
left wing and settled them into a disaster.

The problem of amateur far left-wingers, estranged left-wingers,
conservative right-wingers and reactionary far right-wingers remains with us. With nearly everybody in the theater as well as the
audiences so severely divided between the young and the aged, the
modern and the archaic, the mature and the childish, the drama is
suffering from the wing division to a more consequential degree
than any other part of our theater. It is still the kind of theater that
we must depend upon for serious art and surely will always be, no
matter how far theater modes integrate. And so it is the most important. How can we claim any kind of American theater when our
most professional, most advertised, most international dramatic
stage — the Broadway stage — is dominated by the forces of age
and backwardness? Will you stoop to its theater for the sake of the
professionalism there? Will you put up with off-off Broadway's
childishness for the sake of modernity? Why should only an un-
acceptable set of alternatives exist?

So long as the choice is necessary — so long as serious playwrights cannot develop and experienced playwrights go to artistic pieces — our drama will remain schizoid, its two halves incomplete. So long as the division continues, the American theater tradition of no tradition will calcify.

CHAPTER TEN

The Race Against Time

THERE are, then, two broad categories of legitimate American theater: New York's fully grown but largely moronic and crippled Broadway, with its offspring off-Broadway and in summer and winter stock, road companies and music tents. And the resident companies, which can include the true repertory systems, grandiose cultural-center operations and summer festivals. If New York is so destructively dominated by reactionary forces and if the young resident theaters are already so affected by divisive influences, what can we expect of the *future* of the American theater? If there is to be one.

The Broadway stage must be revitalized. As the core of the right wing's thrust, the working ground for the master playwright, the competition level for the superprofessional and the representative of mass-America taste, Broadway is necessary to the American theater for its stabilizing value and its dedication to the new, full-scale work. It is where the varieties of our theater should coalesce — where all branches should flow into the mainstream. Although it has been (and should always be) criticized by the left wing for its commercial nature, it is precisely in that commercial nature that its value lies.

The destruction of Broadway in the name of art would be the destruction of a theater medium. It would solve nothing. It would be as wasteful, as negative, as any destruction. It would merely eliminate a kind of theater, and the United States is in no position to sustain such a loss.

There *must* be a popular theater — a theater that reflects public taste — just as there must be an art theater that *educates* public taste. Art has never thrived in a protected climate; such a climate is sterile. The left-wingers who demand such protection are in a position to determine neither the direction of development nor the kind of theater that "should" be existing. Nobody is in such a position. This is benevolent aristocracy and Plato notwithstanding it is doomed to prejudice and the cramp of cultural dictatorship. The theater, like any other art, must be left free to develop. If commercial exigencies hamper the development of Broadway theater, private tastes will limit that of the protected, "pure" theater.

The artist must deal only with himself, in communication with the world. If he chooses to write on the television level, that must be his privilege. And if there are audiences who respond to such tripe, that is *their* privilege. As a matter of fact, I wish there were more garbage for the mass audiences who would love it (the worse the better). There is no danger in *any* play's existence, whether it is the far-right drivel of some Broadway comedy or the far-left drivel of a freakish avant-gardist. The only protection the theater requires is protection from protection.

But while today's Broadway rejects *anything* leftist, is that its nature? Can the wound heal? Can the division be resolved? Is the theater big enough to straddle it? Or is it absurd to expect the theater art to thrive, or even exist, in a commercial situation?

Although the Broadway producer is a businessman, his product is an art form. He is very like the book publisher or gallery owner. He is interested in profit, but he is also aware of artistic values, and like the powerhouse publisher or art dealer he assumes a responsibility for culture. While refusing to apologize for his commercial output, he uses it to pay for the artistic. Too, his experience with hardcore commercial products gives him a clarity of judgment which the strictly art-oriented lack. As a result, the producer who knows what musicals are ready will also know what plays are in working shape. He is not about to be carried away by amateur enthusiasm.

His professional demands are stricter than those of the nonprofit producer, because he is more aware of giving value for money than the "pure" artist. In many ways, artistic criteria are more lax, technically speaking, than business standards.

Businessmen — competition-bred people — require practice at

the highest levels. The only theater place possible for such practice is a commercial one, because the highest pressures for excellence are there. This sounds as if it is good for the theater to exist in a sales situation and in a sense it *is* good. The theater person on Broadway, London's West End or in any commercial theater must eventually account to the box office and so to the theatergoing public. He must be worth his pay. If he is trying to be funny, he had better be. If a new device is being attempted, it has to work.

The view of Broadway as an anachronism and a desecration of the *idea* of theater is a minority, left-wing notion. It is not a detached view. Serious theater people are well aware of the ridiculous situation on Broadway, but to the world and to history, the theater of America is the theater of Richard Rodgers and George Abbott. So long as that fact is unrecognized, there can be no truthful picture of the American stage.

Accepting that as we must, we are forced to see that a wish for Broadway's destruction is, in effect, a wish for the destruction of American theater *as it is*. Left-wingers gleefully pursue that wish, seeing only progress after the holocaust. Accept the premise and see where it leads you. It leads you past the arms of the bi-wing theater and out to off-off Broadway, extremism and the happenings, the underground. Can that be a country's theater? Not so long as it is primitive.

With no commercial stage, a country's theater would be without the stimulus to produce the marvelous. It would be without the drive for public excitement. Nor would the noncommercial theaters be free of the pressure to satisfy the public. Even a subsidized theater needs audiences, and empty houses will always discourage subsidizers. The commercial theater provides a variety of theater that the noncommercial could never possibly allow. After all, how many subsidized theaters could there *be* in a single city?

Finally, the noncommercial theater will necessarily be an institution and institutionalization is a dreadful theater fate. It is not unavoidable (as the National Theater of Great Britain is proving), but it is likely. Nor can the noncommercial theater's propensity for protecting official theater and moral values be ignored.

On the other hand, subsidized resident theaters would present professional versions of the great literature, period and contemporary art plays and new works of quality. They would condition the American public to higher artistic standards. They would provide art, magic and entertainment. But would they satisfy the insatiable public need for novelty? The public, like a child, is ever restless. Its attention must be coaxed and held. The commercial theater, so dependent upon the public's excited business, will fight for that attention. The noncommercial theater can never match its drive.

Obviously, there is *no* perfect theater system. The commercial theater provides and omits and so does the noncommercial. The most desirable theater is the most theater. The more styles the better. The more individual playwrights with individual styles, the better. The more techniques, the more systems the more *theater,* the better. Commercial theater serves its purposes, noncommercial theater *its.* And the far right, the far left, *theirs.* The problem is how to encourage the prolificacy of productions and how soon it will be before a resumed wing interaction will combine values and draw back young, intellectual, diverse audiences. Once those audiences return, our theater will be able to proceed once more.

The health *can* be regained. For proof we need look only to the English stage, which turned in the mid-Fifties from a right-wing-dominated miasma not unlike today's Broadway to a thriving bi-winged garden.

England's theater grew so alive that some of its excitement bled through to Broadway. With the right-wing domination of New York theater, producers could find no American plays to satisfy their tastes. Unable to understand the leftists, they turned to importing plays. This made simple sense. Producers could not only view the finished work in London but could observe its box office appeal in a veritable Procter and Gamble test market. Thus, able to minimize risks, they stepped up their interest in the West End. And because the more exciting dramas on that West End were the products of a healthy wing interaction the plays they brought back were seldom either left or right wing but ranged healthily between them (*Chips with Everything, Entertaining Mr. Sloane, Semi-Detached, Inadmissible Evidence, How's the World Treating You?,* and so on).

This trend grew alongside an unexpected resident theater fad for native plays. It is ironic that there should be such a fad, since the left wing had been traditionally contemptuous of American drama, putting it down as "Broadway" and "commercial." In part, the fad was nurtured by foundations, which began giving duplicate grants to playwrights and companies for as yet unwritten works. But the scheduling of new and old American plays has primarily been the result of a resident theater weariness with the classics, an eagerness to please audiences with the contemporary and a propensity for follow-the-leader behavior.

Chauvinism is unjustifiable in any area, but in the theater — or in any art — it is unforgivable. The only proper motive for choosing a play is its inherent value. Whether or not the playwright is American is irrelevant. Nevertheless, Washington's Arena Stage is completing a new theater to be entirely devoted to American plays. The Theater of the Living Arts in Philadelphia gave over its entire 1966-1967 season to American plays. And almost every resident theater in the country began scheduling new American plays or revivals of old American comedies like *Room Service*.

There is a very obvious need for the production of new-style American plays. Broadway ignores them, and the resident theaters are perfectly justified in doing them. It is only when these theaters abandon their responsibilities to the theater literature as a whole that this tendency becomes dangerous. In any case, the lines of communication between American playwrights and the resident theaters are very tangled. Many of the writers are barely aware of the resident theaters. Their agents are either similarly uninformed or are more interested in the big royalty possibilities of Broadway. The Theater Communications Group will circulate among its members any play that one of its resident theaters produces, but it has only a sketchy program for reading and circulating unproduced scripts. As a result, the theaters around the country choose their new plays from those submitted directly to them and from the few plays they hear about through friends.

As for older American plays, what is there for these companies to produce? Since the American theater has grown up on Broadway, all the works that comprise our literature have been written for commercial production. This includes the better dramas of O'Neill, Williams and Miller. But it is largely made up of trash. Because the more sophisticated artistic directors are disinclined toward *all* American dramas, they choose American comedies. The irony, of course, is that there has been no kind of theater more consistently shallow than American comedy.

Still, these directors deceived themselves into seeing them as some kind of folk art. The plays of George S. Kaufman became weirdly modish, although they were merely the commercial theater of their time. Abysmally dated, they suddenly were revived as nostalgia. Various directing techniques were laid upon them. *Once in a Lifetime* was burlesqued off-Broadway. APA camped *You Can't Take It with You.* Tyrone Guthrie gussied up *Dinner at Eight* in a far right-wing Broadway production that attempted to pass off a number of minor names as "all stars." Barr-Albee-Wilder used some Rockefeller money for *The Butter and Egg Man,* and if *their* approach — the wonderful Burt Shevelove technique of straight-face put-on — didn't work, then nothing could. It didn't. Nothing can.

The foundations that encourage the production of new and old American plays will assume an ever-increasing role in the development of American theater. The extent of their power has already been discussed and the promotion of new American plays and the revival of old ones is but one direction in which it is used. The possibility of a wing interaction is to a great degree dependent upon the intelligence of these foundations.

It is one matter for an outsider to assess the direction of the theater. It is quite another to set about *determining* it. Because the foundations have such enormous funds at their disposal, they are quite capable of affecting that direction. Moreover, there is no check upon them. If Ford decides to promote, say, happenings, and pours a couple of million dollars into creator and production grants, you will soon be walking into your local resident theater to find yourself on a massive television screen while computer-controlled lights blink madly, melted butter drips slowly from the ceiling and a tape of Lyndon Johnson singing "Let the Good Times Roll" is played backwards.

Too, the new interloping force of foundations could well prove a deterrent to the very playwrights who receive grants. I wonder what effect five or ten thousand dollars has on a writer who had previously been driven by sheer enthusiasm? Creation is a solitary act and once a large organization becomes involved with the individual artist, his impulses may well change. Why shouldn't he grab the money and go off to Greece?

Now I am hardly about to say that the foundations are not needed. The theater just cannot thrive under commercial auspices alone. The conditioning of the vast American public to serious theater is going to involve a long educational process. The resident theaters will never be self-supporting. All of this demands subsidization. Yet it is entirely possible that the foundations will do more harm than good by interfering with natural artistic directions; by supporting favored people and favored theaters; by superimposing theories upon the necessarily individualistic growth of theaters; by providing an artificial security for resident theaters and creative people. It will take a real self-discipline for the foundations to provide help without demanding corollary concessions. It is natural for them to desire some control over what they are assisting (a simple quid pro quo). And they certainly cannot exist as free-for-all money troughs. But their attitude must be essentially laissez-faire if they are not to upset the fragile nature of the theater's art.

Now if all this wing business is true, if all the foregoing accurately describes the situation of American theater today; if our theater really is sharply split between the forces that press for retention of old forms, old values, old styles and those that reach out for change; and if the conservatives have far more control of our theater than they should — if all this is true, *then* what?

There is nothing we can "do" about it. The theater is not a tangible, malleable *thing* that can be shaped or led. It is a vague, spreading assortment of individual creations, the composite of many people, many ideas, many phenomena. Nor can it be "corrected" (the foundations notwithstanding), and it is all the more fortunate for that.

For any correction would be the idealizing of the theater from the limited perspective of a particular interest. And the one thing the theater does not need is limitation. A healthy theater depends on ultimate diversity, not a set of attitudes, not a particular ideal, and certainly not a condemnation of "the commercial" and encouragement of "art."

Are we then supposed to sit back and watch it all go to hell? To divide and collapse? It might be striking to say, *the theater is incapable of collapse — it is too fine an art, too central a part of man's nature.* That is striking but untrue. At least, it is nothing to depend upon. There is nothing specific to be done about it — a program to follow, a legislation to enact, a course of action that "we" or "the theater" must pursue.

But there *is* an ideal to hope for and a development that can be reasonably anticipated.

A healthy theater depends on endless variety. There is no single style that is to be desired, no set of attitudes or purposes to be encouraged. Surrealism will pass, moving rightward. The director's theater and the theater of production will inevitably influence the mainstream into budging slightly leftward. Because of that influence, writers will take stage matters more specifically into account. The playwright will always be the basic creator, but he will have to accept the fact that a play is more than lines to be read. All of these innovating factors will join and become part of the right wing. Because of the lethargic reaction threshold of today's theater, this will take much longer than it should, but the reaction will take place. Then more styles will arise as the postwar generations assume their mature roles. Other playwrights, other directors, other new kinds of theater artists will conceive still other ideas and practice them. They will add to the store of theater methods and purposes. Hopefully, all of these, together with the stage literature and the inventions of the theater's past, will continue to be vital.

As far as new plays are concerned, naturalism is dead. That fact will have to be faced by the right-wing producers, directors, actors and audiences. As the current, retarded generation of realistic playwrights phases out, few straight story plays will be written. It is doubtful that any but the right-wing-dominated resident theaters will ever again produce a new play written in the realistic style. This hardly means the end of stories. The tale is fundamental to literature and the good one will always make an interesting play. Just as it would be very sad if we were never again to see a mystery, a melodrama, a thriller, a courtroom drama, so would it be depressing to live in a future without realistic plays. Hopefully, they will be written, but they can never again be a reigning drama mode. But there are other ways of using realism — collage techniques, open-time methods, interplay. These are new, exciting techniques. In surrealism, and whatever succeeds surrealism, the story will obviously still be used, but in different styles. Broadway producers will see ever fewer conventional plays that are well enough written for production. And right-wing audiences will become ever more sparse as there is less presented for them.

With this burial, some of the master realists — Ibsen in particular — will lose their literary status because of artlessness. Others will enter or stay in the literature because of classic value, just as there are Greek, Elizabethan, Restoration, Classical, Romantic and Expressionist plays that have. The great plays of Chekhov will certainly remain in the classic literature, as will the amazing postnaturalist plays of Strindberg. Even Shaw will have his place, although, ironically, it will not be his pet plays of political and social reform that will be timeless, or the fatly philosophical ones like *Man and Superman,* but the comedies, which are simply natural in their appeal. Only art will endure, ever.

In America, the possibility of developing a true, national theater tradition will just be starting. With the country beginning to find a maturity and with theaters finally opening up to seriousness, the basis will be laid for an American theater personality. With growing internationalization, our audiences will be exposed to a broad range of dramatic invention, and with a young, educated, questioning country moving into adulthood, there is every reason to anticipate theatrical excitement. Meanwhile, the flamboyant, sensation-oriented psychedelic phenomenon will consume the artistic inclinations of our youth. What interest could they possibly have in our archaic theater — or even the films — when the rocking, electrified music and the staggering, electronic-environment discothèques offer so much more excitement and newness? That generation will have to be won back and the winning will require an assimilation of *its* tastes.

But that is in the very distant future. In the meanwhile, we can expect increasing relevance to political matters. It is ironic that the far left wing in today's theater is pressing for the same stage motives as did the Thirties activists who so bore them. These days, in the resident companies, the graduate schools and off-off Broadway, the cry is for message theater. On the one hand they scoff at Thirties socialism, while on the other they pursue the same liberal aims that those Socialists would have pursued had they been here today. These left-wingers despise the message theater of Miller and Odets, yet, ironically, they follow the same path (although in contemporary stage language). Such is the nature of the left wing.

Like those Thirties plays, today's message dramas will date. How long will it be before Vietnam is an old story, replaced by some later madness? And like those message plays, today's message dramas will die because of their betrayal of theater art. Art must go beyond the immediate and into the timeless; otherwise it is doomed to transience. Transient theater (like *Waiting for Lefty* or *Viet Rock*) will keep the theater going from day to day, from year to year. In the long run it will be insignificant.

Should the theater creator even be *concerned* with whether his work will be transient? Talking about their communal scheme of creation, Julian Beck and Judith Malina once told me that not only were they unconcerned about becoming dated but that they were not even worried about the impossibility of committing their amorphous works to paper. They were uninterested in whether years later some producer could resurrect their work; in fact they were positively antagonistic toward him. That producer, they said, should be concerning himself with works of *his* time, and should not bother with what was done before.

The Becks' point seems idealistic, but a theater that has no literature can never develop. Without a literature, art cannot grow, because there is no level on which to build the next one. The Becks would never have devised their creative system, for example, without the productions of Brecht and the writings of Antonin Artaud. Now they have a similar obligation toward the future.

So long as any play concerns itself with transitory problems, it will be of passing interest only. The Becks would say that Vietnam, or The Bomb (their caps), is more important to them, *right now,* than broad, universal matters. That is their privilege. Yet if they invoke that privilege their work is doomed to be forgotten.

Now does that matter? So what if a play has a built-in obsolescence? Is it, therefore, inherently less valuable than one that deals with "universal" matters? It isn't less "valuable," because there is

no constant against which to measure "value." Nor is it even less
artistic. It just *will not endure*.

I think, however, that the main point is this: the person *in* the
theater has no business being consciously involved with his role in
the history or development of art. His only interest should be in
creation; in the fufillment of his private vision. For him, transience
or classicism should be of no concern. Only from the point of view
of the critic and of history are these matters important and they
are of the *greatest* importance, for they represent the very development of art.

But it is senseless to even *talk* about matters of future or historical art in reference to American theater today. Broadway *remains*
our theater and the wing division is going to continue there for
many years.

What must be awaited is a new generation of producers, directors and actors to staff a theater capable of ultimate variety —
artistic, intellectual and moral variety. Some of these must be right-
wingers, for Broadway has to remain the bastion of professionalism, but they will have to be far more receptive to the new and the
different. Otherwise they will be incapable of attracting the left-
wing audiences that make diverse theater possible.

This cannot be achieved by the elimination of today's Broadway.
The writers and mounters of the abysmal Broadway dramas and
comedies may be monumentally backward, but they are the only
professionals we have. While waiting for their successors, we must
cherish them as the working, producing people they are. A theater
present must be retained while a theater future is built. Without a
present there can *be* no future.

Certainly, the various concerns with ticket prices, theater parties, curtain times and producing costs are real enough, though they
are minor. A thriving theater would overcome them. Nobody really
stays away from the theater because of the price of a ticket — the
prices are no higher now than thirty years ago if dollar value is
taken into account. The audiences don't come because the theater
is dull while movies are exciting, and the whole *idea* of attending
has become a complicated, pre-planned affair instead of the regular, natural, informal thing it should be. Theater parties may pres-

ent homogeneous audiences who attend for social reasons, but they are *there* (the fact is that without them, whatever theater we *do* have would probably collapse out of sheer financial chaos). As for the inaccessibility of Broadway for the suburbanites, that problem lies in the massive power of the right wing. The suburbanites have been conditioned to accept only Broadway as major league theater. What winter stock theaters have sprung up in their communities are avowedly imitation Broadway and only reinforce this attitude. It is absurd for the giant population skirting New York City to depend upon Manhattan for its theater. These communities are bursting ripe for professional companies offering a different *kind* of theater, and there is little doubt that first-class resident theaters in Nassau, Suffolk and Westchester counties would do well once their audiences were reconditioned.

As for Broadway itself, there is no reason to expect it to turn about and become artistic. No reason and no need. Broadway is the popular theater, will remain so and provides its greatest value as such. It is important for that commercial theater to be strong. It is a reflection of mass taste and a standard for technical expertise. It provides a very real kind of theater.

But its dramas will have to become more versatile, the comedies will have to develop the modern sense of humor, the musicals will have to dig more deeply into the modes so well begun instead of hanging back so insistently with the *Broadway show*. Musicals must be recognized as the valuable theater they are. The Music Theater of Lincoln Center must change from a commercial, all-star operetta enterprise to a repertory musical theater that revives the best of our musicals, including the experiments and the failures. This will depend upon a wholesale education program for the Center's trustees, who still think of the theater as Broadway. So long as they demand splashy, scenery-littered productions, repertory is impossible. If they allowed designers to employ the imaginative techniques used for ballet repertory, reasonable budgets could be followed for a seven- or eight-production repertory each season. Lincoln Center must stop considering the musicals as commercial, nonart theater that can be used for profit-making. The Music Theater is the Center's only unsubsidized component and that will have to be changed.

As for dramatic repertory, New York City's companies must represent this country's resident theaters as the most accomplished — they must be the leaders. New York needs several companies: one (theoretically, Lincoln Center's) for contemporary noncommercial plays, forgotten classics and modern art. And another (perhaps APA) for the dramatic literature. They must lead the way for a national development of true, classically trained actors and inventive yet tradition-steeped directors.

As for the resident theaters that are now developing across the country, they must continue their process of training actors and providing real theater for the rest of this country. They will have to move away from series productions and toward true rotating repertory if they are to be able to present works of special interest as well as train actors thoroughly.

The directors of these theaters must keep away from management problems. Too many of them become so involved in their company's business that they lose track of the artistic drives that originally brought them there. It is natural that they would begin their companies by directing nearly every production personally and then become producers, but the present abandonment of directing by so many of these young men is very bad. It was *their* drive, *their* vision that established these companies, and that drive, that vision must not be forsaken. It would be a good idea for them to guest-direct with other companies. Exchanging productions for short runs would also be beneficial.

The problems in subsidization will continue. Resident theaters will always need money, and while that money is presently flowing there is going to be a need for more of it. The foundations cannot supply it all and it is not good, anyhow, for these God-complexed private forces to have so great a power over the American theater. An obvious source of financial help would be the major corporations, but the present tax privileges for cultural contributions are much too limited to inspire their accounting-oriented interest. Resident theaters receive practically no help from private industry.

The federal government could do important things for resident theaters by encouraging corporate contributions, making available immeasurable monies while minimizing political interference and centralized power. As for governmental subsidization on the federal, state and municipal levels, it is a measure of our country's philistinism that so much time has passed without official recognition of culture as a national asset. Pressures for benefits to various constituencies are already making the National Council on the Humanities and the Arts a politician's feed bin rather than an artistic boon. No doubt they will continue as various governmental subsidies for the arts begin in the United States. But government participation is going to have to be necessary, such nonsense notwithstanding. The National Council's urge to join resident theaters to educational systems and to control artistic decisions will have to be curbed.

The cities that are throwing up lavish theaters for resident companies must not be allowed to build hollow mausoleums. The whole business of intercity cultural competition is a silly one, but it *is* producing splendid theaters across the country and must be taken advantage of. Official art is perhaps an unavoidable handmaiden of such official theaters and these companies will probably be at the mercy of boards of trustees. But some organized method must be devised to begin these theaters solidly or else they will be built for nothing.

One of the more obvious solutions is to ally them with local universities. The work of universities already exists and they are the intellectual centers of their communities. They are far from ideal, since their drama departments are not staffed with professional theater people and are prone to be academic-ridden. But at least they are serious and that is something.

Yale's Graduate School of Drama was typical of the classroom-ridden state of American university drama departments. Though maintaining a reputation as one of this country's most important drama schools, it had grown old, tired and very right wing. Its concept of American theater was not only Broadway but the Broadway of thirty years ago. In a sudden about-face, Robert Brustein was hired as dean.

Mr. Brustein had been the left-wing critic for the *New Republic* and a member of Columbia University's drama department. Antagonistic toward Broadway and devoted to overlooked classic playwrights, forgotten works by major playwrights, experimental forms and plays with antiestablishment themes, he restocked the Yale faculty with leftists. Joseph Papp was hired to teach directing — a bewildering appointment since his work had long since grown perfunctory; Arnold Weinstein (*Dynamite Tonite*) to teach playwrighting. Kenneth H. Brown (*The Brig*) was given a residency in playwrighting. Brustein announced that Yale would become a practical training place for professional theater people and that the resident theaters — *not Broadway* — would be the theater for which they would be trained. Emphasis would be on classic technique and modern innovations applied to theater as an art rather than as a commercial enterprise.

Brustein's aversion to Broadway, while unrealistic and typically leftist, could not change the fact that if his students were well trained they would do that much better in the commercial theater. Admittedly, his general attitude was excessively subjective. His taste for leftist instructors resulted, in several cases, in the hiring of people who had minimal experience. His eagerness to create a professional theater at Yale omitted students from many activities. His flat rejection of musical theater represented a frightfully restricted theater vision. But his general attitude was refreshing and exciting in a field that had grown sterile, impractical and theoretical. Brustein set out to rattle the Shakespeare–Thornton Wilder syllabus of American drama schools.

Yale thus becomes the first left-wing drama school. Its influence is bound to affect the classroom, blackboard orientation of the others. Frankly, I am more prone to trust the less flamboyant but deeper techniques of Carnegie Tech, where there is careful, disciplined, thorough training. But in any case, the Brustein leftism was desperately needed to revitalize Yale and perhaps its publicity will help the drama schools across the country grow toward the freshness and practicality necessary for them to work with resident theaters in their communities. But to help them, a crash program must be instituted to fertilize drama departments. There is going to have to be some place to inspire and teach the directors, actors and subsidiary creative people who will work in the new theaters. The foundations have been awarding grants for training programs only to find that there are no teachers to staff them. Drama schools will have to train drama teachers and the best place to find them is among the working professionals. America must utilize the resi-

dent theaters already established to filter the experience and technique down to those just beginning. But the training of teachers is a
difficult problem (not just in the theater but for education in general). No answer has yet been found. It will have to be.

As for the extremists, the theater needs them too. The far right
wing practices an ultraprofessionalism that sets a brilliant standard. It also provides general audiences with a readily accessible
theater experience. The far left provides an outlet for the most imaginative, most daring, as well as most cockeyed theater youngsters. It provides *the value of the bohemian*. Some parts of today's
far left wing are properly extravagant and I am thinking especially
of the happenings, whether they occur in living rooms or in giant
armories. Their involvement with electronic devices, mass audience
influences and fashionable but crackpot theorizing is healthy and
alive. But too often, today's far left wing is not far enough *out*.
Experimental theaters are working with methods that are too close
to the left and even the right wing. They should be trying the *wild*.

Certainly, the future does not lie in the far left wing. It never
does. But it does lie in the far left wing's *vitality*. As long as there
are hectic skirmishes around the perimeter of the established theater, that theater will be fluid. It will be aware of agitation and will
react to it. Will live. Unlike today's listless, stagnant, sluggish, inert
dramatic repository.

The possibility of that future, though, depends upon the time it is
going to take for a resumption of wing interaction. With each passing season, the leftists grow more pessimistic, more frustrated,
more estranged from enduring lines of theater development. The
rightists grow more entrenched and their habits more deeply en-
grained. They become ever more conservative in theater taste,
theater style, theater point. The chasm between the wings grows
wider and deeper. And the centermost shreds of our theater become less likely to reweave.

For the break to knit, the most positive events will have to
occur. Younger-minded playwrights will *have* to keep writing
plays, production or no, grant or no, encouragement or no. Producers will *have* to reorient their thinking along modern lines, appealing not to the old-timers but to the mentality and sensibility of
today. Accomplished playwrights will *have* to write regularly for

the stage and reject movie money despite their frustrations — they *must* become masters. (Movie money will come from drama sales anyhow, as Albee has proven, and Pinter says he does not intend to ever write for the screen again.) Broadway will *have* to forget its murderous old-line directors and begin to hire adventurous, already-proved resident theater people (without interfering with their regular work), correcting its misconception that these men are amateurs. Actors will *have* to keep working in resident theaters and discard their foolish dreams of Shubert Alley marquee billing — those dreams are pure Cohan. Critics will *have* to assert their most positive power and cope directly with the plays from their wing opposition — they will *have* to learn what the other side is doing and find out what is happening in today's theater world. The foundations and the National Council on the Arts will *have* to learn to keep their hands out of theater affairs and contribute money as delicately as possible. Boards of trustees with resident theaters and cultural centers will *have* to stop meddling with artistic policy and really trust their directors, just as they promised they would. The internationalization of theater will *have* to continue, spreading one country's innovations and creations through the others. America will *have* to murder the première myth and realize that a previously performed play is not equivalent to a used car. Resident theaters will *have* to forget "education" and do the great, the artful, *now*. Distinctions between American and foreign plays will *have* to be eliminated — art is no place for chauvinism. Directors will *have* to become ever more creative and attitudinized. And, beyond all of this, the active, free-flowing, fresh audiences will *have* to be recaptured by the theater. This is at once the most important and the most difficult of all these necessities, since the audiences will not come unless there is an excitement and yet there can be only so much production without support.

But only if these things happen *soon enough* can a wing fusion be effected and the final split avoided. If the pace is too sluggish, the whole structure of American theater may collapse of its own dead weight, each half atrophying and disintegrating because a left-right integration failed to happen soon enough.

Yet there the future lies, waiting as if to see whether our theater is going to move into it or collapse in its face. The future lies in life.

And there is life ahead. It can be sensed. The age of the musical art theater is already well upon us. New theater forms spurt here and there. Today's sense of humor, so absent from the theater, is roaring everywhere else. This country is growing brighter and intellectualism has left the library to move into the current of American life.

This new American intellectualism — this new artistic adventure — this new health is waiting to move into the theater just as it is moving into all other phases of modern life. In the face of the gaping wing division, a great new straddling spirit is in the air, ready to bring to theaters across the country the fantastic and mysterious, the enchanting and provocative, the real artistic brilliance of which only the live theater is capable.

I have no intention of winding this up on a phoney thrill. There *is* a sense of an oncoming theater excitement, but it is only a *sense*. What matters — the only thing that exists — is what *is*. Not what might be, could be or even seems to be coming. And what exists, what has been existing, is a mighty division between the slow and the fast, the old and the young, the mummified and the radical, the traditional and the adventurous. The polarization of these elements has produced a vacuum in the center, depriving each of the other's influence and leading the theater not vitally between them — as it should be — but into one wilderness or the other.

If those influences do not soon rejoin, our theater will not stand the strain.

Index